Slavery
and
Rebellion
in the
Roman World

CISALPINA

Mutina

ETRURIA

UMBRIA

PICENUM

CORSICA

Reate

SAMNIUM

ROME

Ostia

LATIUM

APULIA

Mt. Gerganus

C   Minturnae

Capua

Sinuessa   Nola

Cumae   Pompeii

Nuceria

SARDINIA

Metapontum

LUCANIA

CALABRIA

Brundisium

Thurii

Cosentia

Petelia

BRUTTIUM

Messana

Rhegium

Lilybaeum

Mt. Etna

Aquigentum

Syracuse

25 0   50   100 Km

MAP I. Italy and Sicily

Slavery
and
Rebellion
in the
Roman World,

140 B.C.–70 B.C.

KEITH R. BRADLEY

INDIANA UNIVERSITY PRESS
Bloomington and Indianapolis

B. T. BATSFORD LTD
London

This edition first published in the United States by
Indiana University Press
Tenth and Morton Streets, Bloomington, Indiana
and in Great Britain by
B. T. Batsford Ltd
4 Fitzhardinge Street, London W1H 0AH

Manufactured in the United States of America

Library of Congress Cataloging-in-Publication Data

Bradley, K. R.
Slavery and rebellion in the Roman world, 140 B.C.–70 B.C. / by
Keith R. Bradley.
p.   cm.
Bibliography: p.
Includes index.
ISBN 0-253-31259-0
1. Slavery—Rome—Insurrections, etc.   2. Rome—History—Servile
Wars, 135–71 B.C.   I. Title.
HT1191.B73   1989
937'.05—dc19   88-45757
                                                                CIP

1 2 3 4 5   93 92 91 90 89

ISBN 0 7134 6561 X (B. T. Batsford Ltd)

For Diane Elizabeth

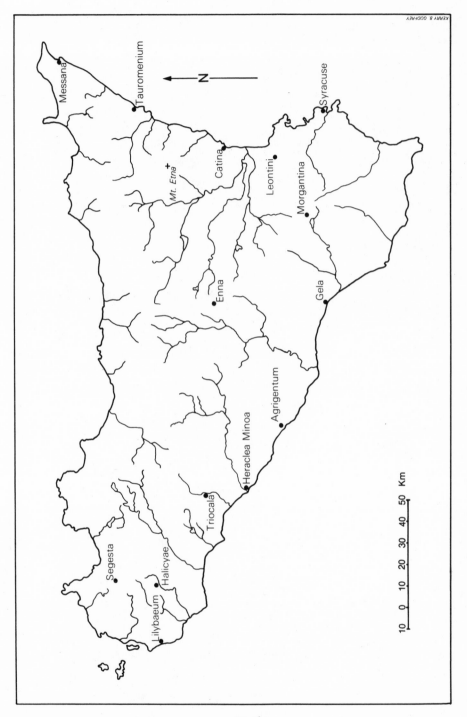

MAP 2. Sicily

Contents

Preface

My purpose in this book is to offer a concise and coherent account of three important episodes in the history of slavery at Rome, the occasions on which between 140 B.C. and 70 B.C. slaves rebelled against their masters on a grand scale. These events have been discussed previously by many scholars. But rather surprisingly, no modern book in the English-speaking world has been devoted to them. The reason is to be found perhaps in the intractable nature of the sources on which knowledge of the rebellions depends, the paucity of contemporary evidence on Roman slavery at large, and the virtual despair to which the historian is driven when attempting to make sense of what is available. However, the present undertaking has seemed worthwhile, first in view of the perpetual fascination the subject appears to hold, especially among students, and secondly because of the great renewal of historical interest in slavery generally that has been characteristic of the recent age. There is a need, I believe, for a straightforward narrative of the slave rebellions, set within their immediate context, that at the same time is related to the wider background of modern slavery studies. It is my hope that this work will form something of a contribution to the history of Roman social relations in particular and to the history of slavery in broader compass and that it will be considered useful to students and more advanced readers alike.

For various kinds of support during the composition of the book my debts are substantial, and it is a pleasure at this point to be able to acknowledge them. Given the abundance of earlier scholarly writings pertinent to the book's subject and the need nevertheless to maintain a sense of proportion in my apparatus, I have found it impossible to signal every helpful item of secondary bibliography. At the end of the book, therefore, I list only those works actually cited in the notes, not everything consulted in the book's preparation. I trust, however, that my indebtedness to others' writings will be sufficiently clear. The award by the Social Sciences and Humanities Research Council of Canada of a Leave Fellowship for six months in 1986 and of a Research Time Stipend for twelve months in 1987–88 created periods of much-welcomed free time to devote to the project, while successive grants from the Faculty Research and Travel Fund of the University of Victoria provided access to materials locally unavailable. This assistance is appropriately recognized. To two expert Roman historians, John F. Drinkwater and Erich S. Gruen, I am deeply grateful for the critical readings they gave my manuscript; and I hope that they will observe the improvements for which they are responsible without being unduly upset by the fact that in some places I have tenaciously clung to my own convictions despite their counsels of restraint. I dare not claim to have fully convinced them in my views, but I remain thankful for their interest and advice. To my colleague Samuel E. Scully I am obliged for a meticulous critique of my presentation, as too for certain forms of practical help made in his capacity as Dean of Humanities at the University of Victoria. I should like to pay tribute also to the encouragement received from the late M. I. Finley when working on a recent paper, parts of which are now incorporated here. And as in the past special thanks are due to A. Nancy Nasser for her invaluable services at the typewriter.

Above all, however, I wish to thank Diane Boyle Bradley for creating a domestic haven of peaceful relief from the stresses of writing this book and for her refreshing ability to restore all matters academic to a proper and sane perspective. In again dedicating my book to her, I can only make a hopelessly inadequate gesture of repayment for all I owe to her.

Prologue

In the seventy years between 140 B.C. and 70 B.C. Rome was confronted by three major insurrections of slaves, each of which involved substantial numbers of dissidents. Two of the insurrections occurred in Sicily, the island which in the aftermath of its first war against Carthage had become Rome's first overseas province. The third, most memorable of all due to the leadership of the gladiator Spartacus, took place in Italy and at one point posed a potential threat to the city of Rome itself. This series of events was unique in Rome's history, for slave uprisings on such a dramatic scale had never been known beforehand and similar episodes were never to recur despite the long endurance of slavery in the Roman world. Moreover, the events were also exceptional in the history of slavery on a longer view, for it was not until the rebellion led by Toussaint L'Ouverture in the French colony of St. Domingue at the turn of the nineteenth century that slaves anywhere again rose against their masters in comparable degree.

In the past the Roman slave wars, as they are conventionally called, have been variously interpreted by historians. Some have detected forms of primitive communism in the rebels' actions, and Spartacus in particular has been portrayed as a champion of the oppressed in Roman society— a revolutionary hero of the historical class struggle. Others, pointing to the participation in the uprisings of people who were not slaves, have denied that the rebellions were slave rebellions at all and have argued in favor of more broadly based forms of opposition to Roman authority. Indeed, since the three uprisings took place within a relatively short period of time, some commentators have been tempted to posit connections between them and to envisage at this stage of Rome's history a widespread surge against established power on the part of the exploited. Still others have shared a popular view of the Sicilian rebellions, believing that rebel slaves set out to found their own servile states, systems that were based on prevalent models of Hellenistic monarchy with which the slaves had been familiar in their countries of origin and that were, presumably, to be maintained indefinitely at Rome's expense. It has been thought, on the one hand, that rebel slaves had as their goal a radical, even utopian, transformation of society, and it has been asserted, on the other, that the slave wars were of no historical importance at all.[1]

It hardly seems necessary to point out that historical judgments fashioned to serve historians' own ideological imperatives have to be regarded with some skepticism as the distortions they are, even if it is acknowledged that no historian can altogether escape the confines of his own cultural environment. Views dependent upon theories of class struggle therefore must be deemed inherently inappropriate. And while it is certainly true that there is evidence of nonservile participation in the slave wars, there is no sound reason for rejecting their designation as slave movements in essence. Although, admittedly, the sources are all subject to limitations, being relatively late and unconcerned with the servile perspective of events for its own sake, it would be absurd to imagine that ancient authors did not know the difference between a rebellion primarily of slaves and a rebellion of other groups of dissidents. In fact, the source tradition overwhelmingly presents the three episodes as slave rebellions, and some respect consequently for the integrity of the writers who comprise the tradition is required. Thus to regard the rebellions as forms of opposition to the power and rule of Rome, as being somehow similar to the Social War, the war Rome fought against its allies in Italy from 91 B.C. to 87 B.C., is fundamentally to misconceive the nature of the events and to misunderstand slavery. For while chattel slavery was only one of a number of types of involuntary labor identifiable in antiquity, between which the lines of demarcation were often blurred, and while many slaves doubtless accommodated themselves to their condition and even at times benefited from it, it remains undeniable nonetheless that their rightlessness and total subjection to the authority and will of their masters made slaves an element in society utterly distinct from any other, no matter what the degree of differentiation among them. The slave wars were therefore not the outcome of resistance to a particular political dispensation but to the reality of slavery and the material conditions it imposed. Moreover, it has to be said that a dismissive attitude toward the slave wars is symptomatic of an approach to history that may fail to appreciate the importance of any group in Roman society other than the elite, in this case always a very small minority, and to realize that those who had recourse to the logistically and psychologically demanding extreme of violent protest took actions of considerable importance, and danger, to themselves that might fully merit historical inquiry.[2]

But it is not the object of this book to try to refute all previous interpretations of the slave wars point by point or to argue the superiority of any one earlier theory about them over all others. Instead, the purpose of the study is to present as impartially as is feasible an analytical description of the events themselves, to the extent that they can be recovered, and to place those events in a sequence of contexts allowing their genesis and nature gradually to unfold. Thus the immediate context of each rebellion is examined in the early portions of chapters 3, 4, and 5, and a more discursive historical context, a survey of slavery in the Roman heartland in the second century B.C., is presented in chapter 2. To begin, however, a less orthodox context is sketched in chapter 1, where an outline of modes of resistance to slavery in the modern slave societies of the New World is offered. This unconventional point of departure has been chosen in the belief that since the institution of slavery has not limited itself historically to any one place or time, understanding of any one of its manifestations might benefit from comparison with any other. In fact, because Roman slavery forms part of an historical continuum that has extended well into the modern era, it would be excessively myopic and parochial to pretend that the various phases of the continuum have no points of overlap that might be profitably observed; and for present purposes especially, when the surviving primary evidence has so many inherent shortcomings, the resistance to slavery represented by the Roman slave wars might well become more comprehensible than it has been in the past once juxtaposed with the better documented resistance activities of slaves elsewhere. Indeed, without at all minimizing the particularities of the Roman historical situation, it might well be legitimate to expect that Roman slavery provoked modes of resistance analogous to those in other slave societies and that the latter might serve an illuminating function.

By evoking a plurality of contexts, therefore, the present work aims to show the relationship of the Roman slave wars to other more common forms of resistance to slavery and to suggest that the wars were essentially aberrant extensions of those other forms. Once this is understood, the search for grandiose objectives beneath the rebellions can be seen to be basically misguided. All modes of servile resistance were predicated on slaves' desires to ameliorate the burdens of oppression they bore and to palliate the subjection to which their condition bound them. The extremes to which the pursuit of these wishes could drive slaves—in this case with tragic issue—mirror above all the extremes of brutality and degradation their masters imposed upon them. For presupposing exceptional provocation, revolt was an extreme form of resistance. Equally, however, it was at best only a beginning, an act, or sequence of acts, that if successful required further measures for sustaining the fragile independence quickly obtained and for replacing slaves' relationships with their masters with new social forms and identities. It becomes necessary above all, then, to delineate the conditions of provocation and to identify the practical means by which resistance was maintained.[3]

Slavery
and
Rebellion
in the
Roman World

[I]

Slave Resistance in the New World

Resistance to slavery was a constant, uninterrupted feature of the history of the slaveowning societies of the New World. Whether in the United States, Latin America, or the Caribbean, the exploitation of black slaves by their white masters produced among the oppressed not simply passive resignation to the virtual permanence and hopelessness of their condition, but active opposition to it as well. Indeed, the several forms of resistance—which ranged from Africans' refusals to cooperate docilely with their captors at the time of enslavement and transportation to the Americas, through desertion and day-to-day petty sabotage of their owners' crops and property once situated in their new environments, to suicide and armed revolt against bondage and the cruelty that sustained it—have been said to have formed part of the very process of accommodation to slavery. Moreover, resistance did not diminish as first generations of African slaves were replaced or complemented by the appearance of Creoles, men and women born into slavery in the New World, for well into the nineteenth century the struggle against oppression was vigorously kept up whereever slavery existed.

The purpose of this chapter is to illustrate briefly some aspects of this continuum of resistance activities through extensive quotation from the modern historical record. The emphasis will fall on the endemic character of slave resistance; and the importance of maintaining sensitivity to the servile point of view when reconstructing the history of slavery, whether ancient or modern, will be underlined. But there is one important point to be made at once. Because the slave societies of the New World are closer in time to the current age, the efforts of black slaves to acquire freedom and the severity of the conditions that prompted those efforts can have a greater immediacy and vividness than is the case for antiquity. Scarcely a page of Greek and Latin literature can be read without the appearance of a reference to slavery, and it is a commonplace to say that the Romans (and the Greeks) took the existence of slavery for granted. The familiarity of the institution, however, has tended to breed in the modern student of antiquity if not contempt for, then at least indifference to the harsh realities of slavery. In Roman legal procedure, for instance, it was common for slaves' evidence in criminal cases to be taken under torture, and the law of the Imperial age was explicit on how this was to be done. The essential lack of humanity in the formal situation, however, can easily be lost upon those used to the basic facts. By way of contrast, the execution of eighty-eight slaves following the detection of a conspiracy in Antigua in 1736, when "5 slaves were broken on the wheel, 6 gibbeted alive, and 77 burned," strikes the modern reader as barbaric and shocking in a way that Roman torture of slaves does not, given its remoteness in time. The modern material is to be seen therefore as a way of stating that factors of chronology should not blind moderns to the equally cruel and brutal conditions in which the majority of slaves in Roman society lived their lives, and that these circumstances must be understood to form the prelude to resistance against slavery as much in the Roman world as in the New World.[1]

The many studies of New World slavery published in the last generation have led to a clear picture of the prevalence of desertion, or flight, as a specific type of servile resistance that at once deprived slaveowners of their property and impeded the maintenance of law and order. In particular, analysis of newspaper advertisements describing and offering rewards for runaway slaves has revealed the frequency of flight in eighteenth-century Virginia, but the phenomenon was by no means confined by time or space: similar advertisements and complementary complaints about runaways were common in the nineteenth-century American South, while in Cuba and elsewhere in the same period desertion by slaves was a problem of epidemic proportions. In Brazil, for example, the issue of *O Diario do Rio de Janeiro* for September 17, 1821, alone contained at least eleven notices of fugitive slaves, of which the following, coupled with a comparable illustration from the *Virginia Gazette* of November 21, 1745, is a typical example:

> On Saturday the 7th of this month disappeared a black named Pedro, of the Caçange nation, who has been working out on his own, with the following features: youthful, short, full-bodied, and with an ulcer which is still small on his forehead. He was dressed in large gingham trousers and an English shirt, also of gingham. He does not speak Portuguese very well except a few words, and these very badly, and he has been in this city for fourteen months. Anyone who has news of him is asked to come to Rua do Catete just past house No. 6. He will get a good reward.

> RUN AWAY about the First Day of *June* last from the Subscriber, living on *Chickahominy* River, *James City* County. A Negroe Man, short and well-set, aged between 30 and 40 Years, but looks younger, having no Beard, is

smooth fac'd, and has some Scars on his Temples, being the Marks of his Country; talks pretty good *English*; is a cunning, subtile Fellow, and pretends to be a Doctor. It is likely, as he has a great Acquaintance, he may have procur'd a false Pass. Whoever brings him to me at my House aforesaid, shall have two Pistoles Reward, beside what the Law allows.[2]

Slaves resorted to flight for various reasons. In many cases departure from a plantation or urban household may not have been intended as anything more than a temporary truancy when a slave wished to visit a spouse or some other family member situated nearby, to escape a hard regimen of work, or to gain revenge against a master for punishment recently received (*petit marronage*). But the desire for complete removal from the harsh conditions of slavery also prompted slaves to flee, and at times a record of an individual's view of the attempt to liberate himself fully from bondage becomes available. In 1827, for example, a certain Anthony Chase, the slave of a Baltimore woman, wrote to the man to whom he had been hired out and from whom he had absconded to explain his actions:

I know that you will be astonished and surprised when you becom acquainted with the unexpected course that I am now about to take, a step that I never had the most distant idea of takeing, but what can a man do who has his hands bound and his feet fettered [?] He will certainly try to get them loosened in any way that he may think the most adviseable. I hope sir that you will not think that I had any fault to find of you or your family[.] No sir I have none and I could of hired with you all the days of my life if my conditions could of been in any way bettered which I intreated with my mistress to do but it was all in vain[.] She would not consent to anything that would melorate my condition in any shape or measure[.] So I shall go to sea in the first vesel that may offer an opportunity and as soon as I can acumulate a sum of money suficient I will remit it to my mistress to prove to her and to [the] world that I dont mean to be dishonest but wish to pay her every cent that I think my servaces is worth . . . I dont suppose that I shall ever be forgiven for this act but I hope to find forgiveness in that world that is to com.[3]

To escape by ship to another territory or homeland and thereby to extricate himself permanently from the authority of his owner was perhaps the best prospect of success a potential fugitive might imagine. But if the motivating power of freedom to impel the attempt at complete removal from slavery is comprehensible, only a few slaves had the combination of initiative, financial resources, and web of contacts needed to realize the ideal and to find a place where safety and liberty might be indefinitely enjoyed. A peculiar by-product of flight as a mode of resistance, therefore, was the formation of what modern historians of slavery term "maroon societies," that is, communities of fugitives and slaves in revolt organized in hideouts on a paramilitary basis as a way of creating an alternative life to the one previously spent in slavery (grand marronage).

Communities of this kind, often semipermanent but with a capacity for mobility stemming from the guerrilla aspect, came into existence throughout the New World, especially in the period up to the turn of the nineteenth century; and although their several histories show significant variations, they nevertheless shared certain common features. The fugitives who formed them were frequently first-generation slaves, and men more often than women, individuals who found the process of acculturation to a new environment, both physical and psychological, difficult. The victimization of slavery led them to abscond, either singly or in small bands, and to create societies separate from, but in parasitic relationship to the plantation societies left behind. That is to say, maroon communities, although they might become viable economic entities in their own right, often depended upon neighboring plantations for the appropriation of essential commodities, including weapons; and they continued to expand at the expense of the plantations by serving as focal points of attraction to those still in slavery and by functioning also as vehicles for furthering subversion and rebelliousness. With open frontiers to exploit and penetrate, maroons usually established their communities in remote geographical locations that were difficult of access, sites chosen to permit concealment from authority forces intending to recapture them and conducive to guerrilla methods of warfare, the only practicable means of fighting available. In some cases the communities endured for long periods of time: the lifespan of Palmares ("Palm Groves") in Brazil, for example, covered most of the seventeenth century and indeed the maroons of Surinam have survived into the contemporary world. In other cases the communities became so locally powerful that their inhabitants were able to extort formal recognition of their strength from established society, as was the case in 1739 with the Jamaican maroons led by the notorious Cudjoe. But more typically the lifespan of the maroon community was relatively brief, and formal recognition of its autonomy less common than de facto independence. The real keys to success were careful organization and rigid discipline, for the achievement of both of which strong leadership was a prerequisite. Above all, however, the community's most salient feature was that it was a society continuously at war, as successive groups of fugitives found refuge with predecessors and continued their armed struggles for freedom against the forces of slavery.[4]

Maroon communities have been regarded as prime instruments of slave resistance in colonial Brazil, where the most spectacular creation, just mentioned, was the agglomeration of settlements collectively known as Palmares in the northeast of the country. Palmares began its life in the early years of the seventeenth century and withstood a succession of attempts to reduce it before it finally succumbed to Portuguese military pressure in 1695. Its long survival, however, makes Palmares an exceptional case, and perhaps more typical of the Brazilian *mocambos* or *quilombos* was the rebel community near Salvador da Bahia known as Buraco do Tatú ("Armadillo's Hole"). In 1763 this settlement too was destroyed by the Portuguese, but its features are relatively well known, not least because of a letter sent to Lisbon reporting the success of the provisional government of Bahia against the maroons. The following is an extract:

> Most Illustrious and Excellent Sir: The entirely reasonable complaints which came repeatedly to the attention of the government from the residents of the farms and plantations in the forests up to two leagues distance around this city, the frequent damage done to them by the slaves living in those forests, emerging from them to commit robberies and damage on the plantations, attacking the homes of the inhabitants of those places, stealing their cattle and other stock; appearing on the roads to strip travelers of their clothing and money, mainly black men and women who come to the city daily with produce grown in their gardens, returning on the same or following day with the profits from those sales; carrying off to the *quilombo* by force the black women who were most attractive to them; and, finally, entering the city streets at night to supply them with gunpowder, shot, and the other kinds of equipment needed for their defense; having contacts with the city blacks and those of the countryside, and even with some whites who feared they would be murdered in their isolated homes, or that their crops would be destroyed—all these reasons moved the government to seek precise information about the existence of such a "*quilombo*" and the true extent of its strength.
>
> Having acquired authentic information, the government fully verified the existence of the *quilombo* called Buraco do Tatú, that it was established twenty years ago, and that it was made up of a large body of blacks, and that it would be dangerous to approach it because of its location and the existence of an abundance of covered pits filled with many sharpened stakes, a plan of which is being sent to Your Excellency so that you may have some impression of the layout of the *quilombo*.

The letter goes on to describe how the slave community was overcome and its members brought to trial and justice. But the section quoted, together with the survival of the plan it mentions, has permitted reconstruction of the *quilombo*'s main features. Thus, in its jungle location the village formed "a rectilinear pattern of six rows of houses divided by a large central street," and access was rendered very difficult in view of a complex arrangement of defenses. Protection of the rear was made possible by "a swampy dike about the height of a man," and of the three remaining sides "by a maze of sharpened spikes driven into the ground and covered to prevent detection." In addition, there were "twenty-one pits filled with sharp stakes and disguised by brush and grass. Leading into the *mocambo* was a false road especially well protected by the spikes and camouflaged traps." A sentry therefore had to place planks over these obstacles to allow entry to and exit from the village. As the official letter shows, the Buraco do Tatú depended upon a predatory economy and assistance from outside collaborators, while its political organization was headed by two chieftains; one was specifically a war leader, and each had a consort styled a queen. The village was not designed to supply a base for "a total war of liberation against the slave-owning segments of the population," but only to offer permanent refuge for the fugitives who had extricated themselves from slavery.[5]

One year before the destruction of the Buraco do Tatú, the Saramaka maroons ended a century of warfare against the Dutch by concluding a peace treaty that gave formal acknowledgement to the society they had created in the rain forests of Surinam. During the period of resistance the maroons had survived by conducting systematic raids on nearby plantations to acquire arms, tools, and finished products, and by drawing on immediately accessible resources to help sustain themselves, "making barkcloth and palm salt, using bush candles and palm butter." The predatory aspect of Saramaka economic life is as clear as in the case of the Buraco do Tatú, and so too the guerrilla-style tactics the maroons employed in warfare against their Dutch overlords. Carel Otto Creutz, the leader of an expedition against the maroons in 1749, recorded how he found his enemies all "positioned behind trees so that they could not be seen. However," he continued, "we went on shooting at them and they fled, screaming, and we could find nothing [left behind] but a little blood." Similarly, the journal of E. G. Hentschel, the commanding officer of a further expedition in 1755, contains several items describing Saramaka responses to the colonial military presence:

> The runaways are constantly swarming around us, yelling out to us that we shall never get to the top of the mountain at the fourth village.

> Today the runaways have been roving about around us, making a great deal of noise. . . . The runaways surround us on all sides. The soldiers must all keep watch even during the day . . . which weakens them very much. . . . [That] there are thousands of runaways . . . does not seem unlikely judging from the amount of screaming and yelling we hear around us every day.

> The runaways . . . roam constantly round about us and make it very unpleasant for us to gather food. . . . The runaways have set fire to many of their villages.[6]

But what is especially interesting about the history of the Saramaka maroon wars is that contemporary Dutch accounts of the expeditions of

1749 and 1755 can be compared with present day oral traditions to give some sense of the original maroon view of events, which is rather different in perspective from the official colonial version. Creutz reported a battle of November 5, 1749, as follows:

> We marched forward, and were awaited by the runaways on the hilltop, who with a terrifying shouting made it clear to us that they intended to prevent our getting to the top; but we made a charge up the mountain, in a little rush, sending a hail of bullets and hailshot before us, and finally arrived in the village, without their daring to do anything further.

The modern Saramaka record, however, diverges in detail, tone, and nuance:

> Bákakúun [the village name]! That's where they rained down those stones upon the whites. They couldn't get up the hill. . . . The whites' guns were useless there. They killed the whites like nothing. The big ditch. In order to get up the hill, you had to walk in it. They rolled the tree stumps down there . . . all the way down to the bottom. So many were killed!
>
> They were living on the mountain top. And they dug a giant trench running from the very bottom up to the top. It was the only way to get in or out of the village. They cut big logs, just the width of the trench, and many men together rolled them to the top. When the whites came up the path, they did not know that things would come pouring down the trench to kill them. They came up and up until they were close. They could see the blacks. Then they [the Saramakas] released the logs. Well, there was no way to run fast enough to avoid them! They were mashed to a pulp. No way to escape alive.

Similar disagreements or difficulties occur in accounts of the career of Kwasimukamba, an ex-slave of the tribe of the Djuka and an intriguing character, who collaborated with the Dutch and was involved in the campaign of 1755. According to Saramaka oral tradition, Kwasi "led several expeditions" against the maroons "in the area of the plantations" and "a peace-making expedition far upriver." He "later came to Saramaka on his own, where he lived for some time as a spy who feigned amity." Then he "escaped back to the coast, where he gathered an expedition against them, and ultimately had his ear cut off in punishment by the Saramakas, in the wake of a great battle . . . after which he fled to the city." Yet in the Dutch version of what took place Kwasi did not join the Saramakas voluntarily but "was taken" to their territory; and he "became a central issue in the negotiations between the whites and Saramakas that came in the wake of a battle . . . after which he returned to the city." Both sides, it should be noted, claimed to be victorious in this battle. The truth about how Kwasi joined the maroons is unknowable, but the Saramaka record of what happened after the battle (and by extension the Saramaka record as a whole) is confirmed by independent evidence. According to Hentschel, Kwasi was wanted very much by the Saramakas after the fighting, but nothing more than this is stated in his record. There is no confirmation of the Saramakas' claim of having taken revenge on Kwasi by removing his ear. A late eighteenth-century engraving of Kwasi, however, shows the renegade wearing a bonnet with a flap pulled down over the right side of his head: the ear had indeed been severed.[7]

As a corrective against the bias of officialdom, the history of the Saramakas makes plain how valuable the servile perception of resistance activities can be. But it is worth emphasizing also that the factors which conditioned flight in Surinam were essentially the same as those which led to the formation of *quilombos* in Brazil such as the Buraco do Tatú: a plantation economy with a high ratio of slaves to free persons and a constant element of African as well as Creole slaves; a concern on the part of the planters to make their estates as financially successful as possible and a corresponding lack of interest in the slaves' material welfare; extreme brutality and cruelty in slave treatment and the availability of terrain suitable for the creation of villages that could be concealed from and defended against colonial forces. Additionally, the local effects of international crises could provide periodic opportunities for successful escape. Above all, however, the potential of marronage for developing into sustained servile opposition against the slaveocracy is visible in the case of the maroons of Surinam, and against a background of comparable conditions a similar pattern emerges from the record of marronage in colonial Jamaica, where fugitives again built communities based on African memories both as alternatives to plantation life and as incentives to resistance for those still in slavery.[8]

Sporadic maroon activity is on record in Jamaica from the age of Spanish rule before 1660. But by the early eighteenth century two principal constituencies of maroons had emerged, the Windward and Leeward, each group comprising at least two subsettlements. The Leeward maroons became particularly memorable due to the leadership supplied by Cudjoe, the most celebrated of all maroon figures, who headed what has been called an "autocratic polity cemented by kinship in the style of the Asante, rather than the Amerindian-style confederacy . . . developed by the Windward Maroons," where leadership was far less rigid and formalized. But by 1730 "many of the differences between Windward and Leeward Maroons had been eliminated by their adaptation to a common environment, by the exigencies of a mutual struggle for survival, and by recruitment from a common pool of disaffected slaves." The efforts of the plantocracy to eliminate the maroons led, as in Surinam, to periods of real warfare, the eventual outcome of which was the signing of treaties in 1739 under which the British recognized the autonomy of the maroons in return for a cessation of hostilities and the maroons' future assistance in quelling new incidents of slave revolt or escape. The maroon communities thus survived in relative quiescence, though later in the century it was still possible for violent resistance to flare up again from them.[9]

As elsewhere in the New World, geography played a vital role in the success of the Jamaican maroon communities:

> The Windward Maroons formed settlements in the Blue Mountains, which are the highest in Jamaica, with peaks reaching 6,000 to 7,000 feet, and in the intersecting John Crow Mountains. The Leeward Maroons settled initially near the mountainous center of the island, but later retreated into the west-central part, around an unusual limestone formation called the Cockpit Country, which offered refuge and defense. This wilderness consists of a succession of sinkholes whose sides rise up to form low but steep hills; jagged rocks are interspersed with dense vegetation; surface water is scarce.

But if such country was ideally suited for providing hiding places, by the mid 1720s, when the First Maroon War in Jamaica began and the rebels themselves numbered in the thousands, the need for decisive leadership was paramount, not just for the promotion of social and economic order in the various settlements that made up the two main forces but even more so for the organization of military resistance against the plantocracy. Cudjoe was remembered as a ruthless and brutal character, whose selfishness at times injured his own followers and whose suspicion of all whites was finally eroded by the establishment's offers of peace. But his military organization was impressive, as the contemporary description of James Knight makes clear:

> [He] occasionally appointed as many as were necessary, of the Ablest under him as Captains and divided the rest into Companies, and gave each Captain, such a Number as he thought was proportionable to the merit he was possess'd of. . . . The chief Employment of these Captains was to Exercise their respective men in the Use of the Lance, and small arms after the manner of the Negroes on the Coast of Guinea, To Conduct the bold and active in Robbing the Planta. of Slaves, Arms, Ammunition etc. Hunting wild hogs, and to direct the rest with the Women in Planting Provisions—and Managing Domestic affairs.

Cudjoe styled himself "captain," and among "the Ablest" who also bore that title were Accompong and Johnny, subordinate leaders who, under Cudjoe's supreme command, were responsible for directing the village components of the Leeward complex. Of the less formidable Windward maroon leaders, Cuffee was a strict disciplinarian who set himself off from his supporters in the manner of his dress: he wore a silver-decorated hat and carried a small sword. He too was a "captain" and, like Cudjoe, was remembered for his skill and shrewdness. He headed the principal Windward center of Nanny Town. But the town itself was named after a different kind of influential leader, the chief *obeah* woman among the Windward maroons, Nanny, around whom a true mythology developed. The planters feared the combination of religious and inspirational leadership she provided in strengthening servile resistance and fostering high morale among the rebels. But the "captains" themselves lacked a religious sanction to their authority. The Jamaican maroons' capacity to fight British regular troops on their own terms, however, in the same style adopted by the maroons of Surinam and elsewhere, reinforced the psychological advantage afforded by religious stimuli, as the early eighteenth-century account of R. C. Dallas shows:

> [The maroons] disposed of themselves on the ledges of the rocks on both sides [of a canyon] . . . through which men can pass only in a single file. . . . [They] lay covered by the underwood, and behind rocks and the roots of trees, waiting in silent ambush for their pursuers, of whose approach they had always information from their out-scouts. [The troops] after a long march, oppressed by fatigue and thirst, advance towards the mouth of the defile. . . . A favorable opportunity is taken [by the Maroons] when the enemy is within a few paces to fire upon them from one side. If the party surprised return the fire on the spot where they see the smoke of the discharge . . . they receive a volley in another direction. Stopped by this, and undecided which party to pursue, they are staggered by the discharge of a third volley from the entrance of the defile. In the meantime, the concealed Maroons, fresh, and thoroughly acquainted with their ground, vanish almost unseen before their enemies have reloaded. The troops, after losing more men, are under the necessity of retreating; and return to their posts, frequently without shoes to their feet, lame, and for some time unfit for service.[10]

The use of military titles by the Jamaican maroon leaders and the traces of monarchical features in the Buraco do Tatú form parts of a much wider pattern of behavior characteristic of maroon societies at large. Before 1700 or so, when maroon leaders tended to be men who had been born in Africa, systems of monarchy based on African notions of kingship were the customary means by which a rudimentary political organization was effected. The long survival of Palmares, for example, meant that the monarchy of King Ganga Zumba assumed truly dynastic form; and if Palmares is an extreme case, many other instances of short-lived kingdoms are on record. After 1700, however, European influences tended to make themselves felt on maroon leaders, who, like Cudjoe and his subordinates, increasingly called themselves captains, colonels, or governors rather than kings. Perhaps the most bizarre development in this respect was the appearance of Indian leaders of resistance in Brazil of the late sixteenth and early seventeenth centuries who, under the impact of Portuguese Catholicism, styled themselves popes. It is certain, therefore, that maroon leaders commonly resorted to the trappings of authority with which at any one time they were most familiar in order to buttress their individual positions and to strengthen the viability of their societies as communities at war. Equally, however, it is clear that these affectations were not grounded on programmatic ideals for establishing new states *per se*, in any formal, comprehensive, or European sense, but were only vehicles for maintaining resistance. The acquisition and maintenance of freedom were the driving impulses behind Cudjoe's activities, and, ironically, when Jamaican maroon autonomy was eventually guaranteed by treaty, diminution of maroon independence in Jamaica was the corollary, as establishment forces sought to enforce the provisions of the agreements as strictly as possible."

As long as slaves had the option of deserting and the capacity to build their own refugee communities, the pressures that built up within the plantation regime could be lowered and even dissipated. In turn, the creation of maroon communities could provide a basis for sustained servile rebellion against the ruling class. Yet not all slave insurrections in the New World depended on the existence of maroons as a prior condition of revolt. Indeed, revolts on individual plantations could and did precede flight and the formation of maroon societies. For Jamaica in particular the record of slave rebellions is so rich that a typology of revolt has been proposed in which maroon activities form only one dimension of analysis. According to such a schema, the revolts as a whole were either (i) small-scale, spontaneous events in which slaves seized a convenient opportunity to exact vengeance against their owners or simply to escape the hardships of slavery; or (ii) planned events, encompassing in reality or design all slaves, or a large heterogeneous group of slaves across the island, who sought to overthrow their masters and to rule Jamaica for themselves; or (iii) events that arose from marronage. The third category requires no comment at this point, and the first can be set aside as self-explanatory. But as an illustration of the second category the episode known as Tacky's Rebellion of April–September 1760 can be noted, an event that was organized in great secrecy among the Coromantee slaves throughout Jamaica. More than a thousand dissidents were involved in the uprising, and despite its brief duration the rebels caused much damage and terror. But the crisis was averted by the plantocracy's vicious suppression of the rebels; and their leader, Tacky himself, was soon dead. On the contemporary evidence of Edward Long, the slaves had aimed at "the entire extirpation of the white inhabitants; the enslaving of all such Negroes as might refuse to join them; and the partition of the island into small principalities in the African mode; to be distributed among their leaders and head men." If these primary aims were not realized, however, the slaves seemingly had an alternative plan. Their choice for the outbreak of revolt had been St. Mary's Parish, an area that contained large numbers of Coromantee slaves and relatively few whites. But according to the same source, the region was also close to "extensive deep woods" suitable for concealing groups of fugitives in the event that the revolt backfired. In other words, "the rebel strategy was marronage on an unprecedented scale."[12]

From this single episode the possible overlap between artificially imposed categories of analysis—valuable as those categories might be—becomes evident. But an alternative tripartite schema for the rebellions in Jamaica would still include Tacky's Rebellion in a category of movements led by Africans that aimed to eliminate the whites completely and to replace the European plantocracy with Akan-style autocracy. Maroon revolts, and revolts often sparked by forms of evangelical Christianity and led by Creoles seeking a free, self-directed, peasant-style existence, would remain distinct from those of the kind represented by the events of 1760. Slave autocracy, however, was never achieved in Jamaica, a sign of the sheer difficulties involved in trying to supplant any ruling establishment with adequate resources of control and retaliation. But to judge from Tacky's Rebellion, the slaves' intentions in any case were not to reproduce the European system in monolithic terms, so much as to create their own much looser version of a multifaceted autocratic community.[13]

The history of slave rebellions in Jamaica and elsewhere in the New World is the history of violence breeding counterviolence from establishment forces. It is not altogether surprising, therefore, that only in St. Domingue at the end of the eighteenth century were slaves able to convert rebellion into revolution and to create a new state fully independent from European domination. To give one particularly graphic summary:

> The slaves, in an uneasy and inconsistent alliance with a large minority of propertied mulattoes, defeated the Spanish, inflicted a defeat of unprecedented proportions on the British, and then made their country the graveyard of Napoleon's magnificent army as well as of his imperial ambitions in the New World. In the end, the Americas had their first black national state.

Yet the extent to which the Haitian Revolution—which was inextricably bound up, for its genesis and development, with the wider context and events of the French Revolution—served to alter the nature of later slave revolts in other areas of the New World is a matter of debate. On the one hand, it has been proposed that before St. Domingue, slave revolts were essentially "restorationist" in character, as rebels attempted to extricate themselves from slavery first and then subsequently to create an autonomous existence based on African patterns and ideals. After St. Domingue, by contrast, slaves aimed through rebellion to destroy and to transform existing society and then to participate fully and equally in a new system founded on the democratic ideals of the Age of Revolution. On this view, the effect of the events in St. Domingue was a revolution of black consciousness and a contribution to the progressive "democratization of the modern world." On the other hand, such posited wider ramifications of the Haitian Revolution have been denied, at least as far as the British Caribbean is concerned, and the whole notion of progressive revolt has been rejected. Rather, slaves' reasons for revolt continued to be "internal, intrinsic and traditional," their ideology being "freedom to make, or to recreate, a life of their own in the circumstances in which they found themselves," even as revolts tended to be led in the later era by elite Creole slaves.[14]

Certainly in Brazil the Tailors' Revolt of 1798, a movement involving free whites as well as blacks of various descriptions, shows signs of inspiration from the atmosphere engendered by the French Revolution, though it has been thought that in some regions the putative transition from "restorationist" rebellion to slave "revolution" may have begun to manifest itself before the climactic events in St. Domingue. In Antigua in 1736, for instance, a very extensive and well-prepared plot incorporating Coromantee and Creole slaves was discovered at the last minute by the white authorities: led by a slave king named Court, the rebels had organized a conspiracy "whereby all the White Inhabitants . . . were to be murdered, & a new form of Government . . . Established, by the Slaves, among themselves, and they intirely to possess the Island." Among the factors that produced such aims were Antigua's compact size and the cessation of marronage as a viable strategy of resistance in the eighteenth century. But because the conspiracy did not come to fruition, the manner in which the rebels might have sustained their regime after revolt was obviously never made clear. Similarly in the United States, the conspiracies led by Gabriel Prosser in Virginia in 1800 and Denmark Vesey in South Carolina in 1822 represented attempts to overthrow the prevailing slave system and to establish black states. Prosser intended to spare whites sympathetic to his cause and to seek assistance from both poor whites and Indians. Vesey, himself a freedman in 1822, planned to gain aid for his new state from the Caribbean and Africa. The revolts each incorporated about seven thousand adherents, by far the largest numbers recorded in American slave conspiracies and rebellions, but neither came close to achieving its goals. To conceive the idea of a slave state was far different from harnessing the resources to complete its realization.[15]

Moreover, the Tailors' Revolt has been regarded as exceptional, and otherwise in Brazil "the great series of slave rebellions of the early nineteenth century seem in the main to be ethnic revolts, organized around African affiliations or religion and combining a rejection of slavery and of white society with deep and persistent motives related not to France or Haiti but traditional African polities and religious divisions." Furthermore, a caveat has to be issued against viewing the revolution in St. Domingue itself in overly simplistic terms as a monolithic uprising of all black slaves against their white masters. The events of the 1790s in St. Domingue were infinitely complicated, and it is a mistake to believe that the motivations of the rebels all stemmed, in uniform manner, from the pursuit of an abstract ideal of freedom. For some, immediate improvements in material conditions were equally important; for others, the securing of revenge against cruel masters. Just as the slave population itself comprised a variety of differing sectors, so the aims of the dissidents diverged. Further still, unanimity of participation was as absent as unanimity of purpose, so that "despite what has been written about the 'revolution of half a million slaves,' Saint Domingue was never to experience anything like a general insurrection."[16]

To adopt a fixed position in this debate is, fortunately, unnecessary for present purposes. All the same, the controversy serves to underline an important and relevant conceptual distinction that must be made between revolution and rebellion. The establishment of a completely new state such as Haiti, whether or not in the event for the benefit of a greater number of the community's inhabitants, meant on any judgment the creation of real change, the substitution, predicated on theoretical or intellectual assumptions, of one all-embracing form of government and social organization for another. The mounting of rebellion by slaves, however, meant no more than protesting in a violent manner the inequities and injustices of slaveowning regimes. Those rebels who suffered and reacted to oppression and victimization caused by the existing social structure may well have sought personal deliverance through rebellion, but their actions in the main had nothing of the revolutionary about them, for there is little evidence to suggest that slaves generally sought to effect radical transformations of established social and political orders. Apart from the case of St. Domingue, it must be emphasized, the possibility of progression from rebellion to revolution was never successfully realized in the history of New World slave societies.

Nonetheless, rebellion remained a constant feature of New World slavery, and, the various types of rebellion which have been distinguished by modern historians aside, the conditions under which it was likely to occur have been stated unequivocally and generically:

> In systems of slavery where the following conditions prevail, there will be a high tendency, increasing with the conjunction of such conditions, towards slave revolts:
> (1) Where the slave population greatly outnumbers that of the master class.
> (2) Where the ratio of local to foreign-born slaves is low.

(3) Where the imported slaves, or a significant section of them, are of common ethnic origin.

(4) Where geographical conditions favor guerrilla warfare.

(5) Where there is a high incidence of absentee ownership.

(6) Where the economy is dominated by large-scale, monopolistic enterprise.

(7) Where there is a weak cultural cohesiveness, reinforced by a high [male: female] sex ratio among the ruling population.

On another view, not dissimilar but differently nuanced, revolt and rebellion are to be expected in situations where:

(1) the master-slave relationship had developed in the context of absenteeism and depersonalization as well as greater cultural estrangement of whites and blacks; (2) economic distress and famine occurred; (3) slaveholding units approached the average size of one hundred to two hundred slaves, as in the sugar colonies, rather than twenty or so, as in the Old South; (4) the ruling class frequently split either in warfare between slaveholding countries or in bitter struggles within a particular slaveholding country; (5) blacks heavily outnumbered whites; (6) African-born slaves outnumbered those born into American slavery (creoles); (7) the social structure of the slaveholding regime permitted the emergence of an autonomous black leadership; and (8) the geographical, social, and political environment provided terrain and opportunity for the formation of colonies of runaway slaves strong enough to threaten the plantation regime.[17]

These factors clearly resemble those that at times prompted the emergence of maroon societies, a fact not surprising in view of the connections that have been noted between marronage and rebellion, regardless of whether rebellion preceded or followed the formation of fugitive communities. But what now requires attention is the question of whether typologies of this sort can in any way be useful for analysis of servile behavior in slave systems other than those of the New World and, beyond that, of the extent to which marronage may offer a suitable focus for explicating rebellious servile activities elsewhere. Indeed, with account duly taken of the cleavage that must be interposed between rebellion and revolution, the latter aspect of the question is particularly sharp in the light of the suggestion that "all sustained slave revolts must acquire a Maroon dimension, since the only way in which a slave population can compensate for the inevitably superior military might of their masters is to resort to guerrilla warfare, with all its implications of flight, strategic retreat to secret hideouts, and ambush." Specifically, of course, the issue at hand is whether the rebellious activities of slaves in the Roman world can be usefully interpreted through knowledge derived from modern slave societies.[18]

A cautiously encouraging response to the question seems to come from a description of a much earlier episode in the history of slavery than those considered so far, the Zanj rebellion of 869, which severely affected the Abassid Empire in what is now southern Iraq. The Zanj were black slaves who had been forcibly transported from East Africa in order to provide the labor force needed for projects of land reclamation and new cultivation. Their owners were for the most part absentee masters residing in the city of Basra who were content to leave to subordinates the regulation of their slaves and the wretched conditions in which they worked. But at a moment when the Abassid Empire was wracked by internal political dissension and the powers of the Baghdad caliphate were in jeopardy, "the Zanj rose in what was to become the greatest slave revolt from the Roman servile wars of the second and first centuries B.C. to the black revolution of the 1790's that destroyed . . . Saint Domingue." Although the principal leader of the rebellion was not himself a slave, and while the episode is not clear in all its details, there is no doubt that unrest among the Zanj was great enough to assume the form of violent resistance or, most importantly, that the rebels organized themselves in the style of modern maroons: "the blacks produced their own military leaders who displayed tactical skill," ambushing the armies of the empire, sinking the boats carrying troops sent against them, killing their prisoners, or else enslaving them. Moreover, after an unsuccessful assault on Basra itself, "the Zanj established what may have been the first 'maroon' communities in recorded history—that is protected, self-sufficient communities of fugitive slaves," and the rebels maintained their resistance from these bases until 883, when they were finally destroyed by superior Arab power. Until that date, however, in villages "geared to limited goals of plunder and survival," the slaves remained free, "using tactics similar to those of the later maroons of Surinam, Jamaica, and Palmares."[19]

There seems to be every justification, therefore, to go back to an earlier point along the continuum of slave history in order to see how the record of slave rebellions in the Roman world can be elucidated through reference to the framework of knowledge that has been sketched here. Caution is obviously necessary; the easy temptation of assigning the Roman slave rebellions to categories of analysis that may be totally anachronistic or otherwise irrelevant should certainly be avoided; and the limitations of comparative history must be observed. Moreover, account has to be taken of the fact that the slave systems of the New World were different from that of Rome in several important respects, despite the continuity in the history of slavery that can be traced from one age to another. The former were introduced by European immigrants into economically undeveloped regions characterized by expansionary frontiers and absences of local supplies of labor. (The enslavement of indigenous populations quickly proved unremunerative.) In addition, their economies were always closely tied to those of the immigrants' original countries. Roman slavery, in contrast, grew up alongside other forms of dependent labor, never fully supplanting them, and its potential was naturally limited both by the boundaries of the Roman heartland and the long traditions of urban settlement and agricultural development within them. These disparities in the economic sphere, however, are less important than the similarities of manner in which the slave regimes of the New World and of Rome were organized and administered, or than the similar kinds of social relations between masters and slaves they engendered. Thus, at the very least, the record of slave resistance in the New World suggests ways by which an examination of the Roman situation might be informed, and the "Maroon dimension" in particular, with all that it implies about "restoration" and "revolution," can well be taken as a guiding principle of investigation. The object, it must be stressed, is not to try to prove a direct equation between the Roman rebellions and later episodes of servile behavior; it is only to suggest that the ancient events, once set out in detail, can be seen to carry something of a maroon character. In turn, these correspondences, to be pursued after the ancient events have been narrated in their own historical context, may be taken to point up the nonrevolutionary nature of the Roman slave movements. It is in this that the chief pertinence of the modern material lies.[20]

[II]

Slavery and Slave Resistance
at Rome

By 140 B.C. Rome's control over all Italy was, as yet, incomplete. But its dominance of the peninsula was virtually unassailable—or so it could be thought. The Social War was of course to offer a brief, though intense, period of Italian opposition to Roman power, but Rome finally emerged from the episode the stronger leader of a more united Italy. Overseas simultaneously the core of an empire that was ultimately to encircle the Mediterranean had already been established. In the West, provincial commands existed in Sicily, Sardinia and Corsica, Spain, and North Africa, where, in the wake of the savage destruction of the Punic city of Carthage in 146 B.C., direct rule had been imposed most recently. In the East, moreover, the province of Macedonia represented only a token of Rome's involvement in the affairs of the Hellenistic world, for the two principal kingdoms, those of the Ptolemies in Egypt and the Seleucids in Syria, not to mention lesser dynasties such as the Attalids of Pergamum, were by this time subject to less overt but nonetheless effective forms of manipulation. As for mainland Greece, the razing of Corinth, also in 146 B.C., had physically signaled the beginning of a long era of subjection to Roman authority that its inhabitants were to experience. Through the next century and a half more provinces were to be brought into being as Roman military might spread itself further over a West that lay beneath Rome's own level of material civilization and an East whose energies became increasingly dissipated through the shortsighted and futile ambitions of its own rulers. Yet already by the middle of the second century Rome had transformed the political map of the Mediterranean world, and in the eyes of the contemporary Greek historian Polybius, Rome's achievement even then was breathtaking.[1]

Incipient world rule, therefore, was the chief product of Roman military expansion in the middle Republic (264 B.C.–146 B.C.). But for the men and their families who comprised Rome's political elite, a further consequence was a rise in personal wealth on an enormous scale, wealth that in due course intensified individualism and political competitiveness and led further to an increase in social ostentation among the members of the upper classes. By 140 B.C., indeed, a process of fundamental change in Italy was well under way. The financial rewards of successful overseas warfare were used by the elite to acquire land in Italy that became available when the peasant farmers Rome required to man its armies could no longer independently maintain their holdings and sold out, through choice or compulsion, to those with excess capital at their disposal; and in turn the peasants were replaced by the vast numbers of slaves thrown onto the market in the age of territorial expansion. Or rather it might be said that, in a less traditional but perhaps more accurate formulation, the elite gradually came to stock with slaves large holdings of land built up in consequence of the steady decline, but not total disappearance, of the peasantry in order to accommodate the shortage of labor the erosion of the peasantry caused. But whether at the expense of expropriated peasants or alongside those who remained or both, the slave population engaged in agriculture increased substantially, its numbers fueled by the continuously successful wars of the period. For it was a longstanding convention of ancient warfare, and one maintained by Rome, that war captives automatically fell into slavery. The decline of the Italian peasantry and the growth of slave labor in both arable and pastoral farming thus compounded each other, with incessant warfare acting as the essential fulcrum of change. At the same time, slaves were used as domestics in the urban households of the elite in similarly increasing numbers, providing their masters with entourages and retinues that heightened more and more the latter's social profile.[2]

The three slave insurrections that occurred between 140 B.C. and 70 B.C. were therefore the direct outcome of the formation of Rome's empire and the concomitant transformation of the Italian economy. By the middle of the second century B.C. Rome in fact was a genuine slave society, though such a description does not have to depend solely on the quantitative criterion of the servile proportion of the total population. Some historians believe that for the label of slave society to be properly applied to any historical community a minimal proportion—say, 20 percent or more—of the overall population has to be of servile status; so that on this reasoning Rome will have been a slave society only after or toward the end of the third century, since by *circa* 225 B.C. the slave proportion of the total population of Italy can be estimated at approximately one-third. But long before that date Rome had made what might be termed institutional responses to a servile presence, in its legal and religious life, for instance, and from this qualitative point of view Rome can justifiably be called a slave society much earlier. Slavery at Rome had, in reality, always been integrally connected with Roman warfare, and for the period of the Italian wars details are on record of large-scale enslavements of defeated enemies that are reasonably reliable. So by the time (264 B.C.)

Rome was drawn into extra-Italian conflicts it already had considerable experience of managing and accommodating a slave population through internal institutional mechanisms, and there are indications that in the early third century Roman attitudes toward slaves were beginning to harden, perhaps as a result of their growing visibility in society at large.[3]

By 140 B.C., however, the complexity of Roman slavery was undeniably greater than in any previous era, and the various facets of that complexity need to be exposed at this point before the large-scale rebellions that belong to the subsequent age can be properly understood. The object of the discussion that follows therefore is first to show the diversity of the Roman slave population, the stress falling on sources of recruitment and the variety of work-roles slaves filled; and secondly to illustrate the ways in which slaves resisted their servitude, the emphasis falling on flight and sporadic revolt. A contrast will become evident between a constant current of opposition to slavery on a piecemeal basis and the absence of resistance to slavery on the grand scale, a contrast to be explained by the essential lack of cohesion in the slave body as a whole that accompanied its heterogeneity. In turn, the aspects of Roman slavery given detailed attention will prepare the ground for judging the great movements of the period after 140 B.C. not as carefully orchestrated attempts by slave leaders to raise vast numbers of slaves in the hope of effecting radical changes in the prevailing social structure or system, but instead as abnormal extensions of more common and predictable modes of coping with subjection.

To begin, it has to be emphasized that, through the second century and beyond, the Roman slave population was maintained by diverse means of supply, the result of which was the formation of a very heterogeneous slave body in which no sense of common identity or community of purpose is perceptible.

Warfare continued of course to be a vital mechanism for the creation of new slaves, its enduring importance made plain by a classic legal statement from the Imperial age:

> Slaves (servi) are so called because commanders generally sell the people they capture and thereby save (servare) them instead of killing them. The word for property in slaves (mancipia) is derived from the fact that they are captured from the enemy by force of arms (manu capiantur).

Indeed, from the middle of the third century to the close of the Republic, Rome was involved in continuous expansionist warfare, and the surviving narratives of historians such as Polybius and Livy frequently give details of the numbers of captives taken and enslaved by victorious Roman commanders. The numbers recorded regularly run to the thousands and tens of thousands. There is no doubt, consequently, that for the period from the first war against Carthage to the eve of the first slave war in Sicily, the scale on which Rome enslaved prisoners of war was colossal, the process encompassing practically all areas of the Mediterranean in which the presence of the Roman military machine made itself felt. But the figures give far from a complete record of mass enslavements, for the narrative historians often fail to specify totals of captives in their accounts of military events, which means that the full number of slaves acquired from expansionist warfare in the middle Republic is strictly unknowable. The existing record, however, is rich enough as a whole to make comprehensible, even if not properly speaking credible, the claim of Scipio Aemilianus that the Roman *plebs* in the late second century consisted chiefly of former slaves he had himself once brought to the city as captives. The story vividly points up the fact that as a result of warfare the Roman heartland was constantly receiving supplies of slaves for whom the experience of slavery was a new, and suddenly imposed, reality. It is not the case that all defeated enemies were brought back as slaves to Rome and Italy; some quite clearly were ransomed by family members or friends, others were retained as slaves in local areas. But although precise figures continue to be elusive, it is inescapably true that in the second century the existing slave population was often strengthened by new arrivals of first-generation slaves, many, perhaps most, being mature adults. In Cicero's matter-of-fact formulation, "Many Carthaginians were slaves at Rome, many Macedonians after the capture of King Perseus."[4]

The means by which such people were transported from the sites of enslavement to the Roman heartland varied. A Roman commander had the option of taking or sending captives to Rome himself if he wished: so in 133 B.C. Scipio Aemilianus kept fifty slaves from Numantia in Spain for display in his triumph. The commander might distribute captives among his troops, as Caesar was to do after the battle of Alesia in Gaul in 52 B.C., when each of his men received a single prisoner; presumably in such circumstances soldiers took their property back to Italy with them on discharge from the military. Alternatively, however, prisoners were simply sold off in the theaters of warfare in which they had been captured, and it was the particular responsibility of the quaestor, if one were available, to effect the sale. Thus the siege of Corbio in Spain in 184 B.C. was immediately followed by a sale of prisoners; in 177 B.C. the more than five thousand captives taken from two Istrian towns were auctioned off; and the one hundred and fifty thousand Epirotes enslaved in 167 B.C. were likewise sold at once. The procedure could assume a prosaic character: after the fall of Pindenissum in Cilicia, the complaisant Cicero informed his correspondent Atticus on December 19, 51 B.C., that "the Saturnalia was certainly a merry time, for men as well as officers. I gave them the whole of the plunder excepting the captives, who are being sold off to-

day. . . . As I write there is about HS120,000 on the stand." The purchasers
of those who were not ransomed were slave dealers, middlemen who
bought up the captives and redistributed them through the main com-
mercial centers of the Mediterranean such as Delos. They followed in the
wake of Rome's armies, whose commanders had to see to it that "a crowd
of peddlers and merchants came along, equipped with ready cash and
means of transport," and although detailed information is lacking, the
convention is nevertheless sufficiently perceptible.[5]

Commerce in slaves, however, did not depend solely on supplies generated by warfare. In the second century especially, piracy and kidnapping
contributed to Delos's ability, according to Strabo, to dispose of tens of
thousands of slaves in a single day, its volume of traffic being specifically
geared toward Roman demand. In addition, local leaders in some parts of
the Mediterranean world seem to have been willing to connive at the
enslavement of their own people in return for material goods, and in this
respect connections between the slave trade and the broader political
history of Rome are becoming increasingly clear. From an examination
of the distribution in Gaul of Italian wine jars, for example, it has been
argued that, in the late second and first centuries, Gallic slaves were
regularly exchanged for Italian wine, to the possible number of fifteen
thousand each year, until Augustus's reorganization of Gaul brought such
activity to an end. Similarly, large hoards of late Republican coins discovered in the lower Danube basin have been explained as cash payments
for batches of slaves bought in that region in the 60s, 40s, and 30s of the
first century and transported to Italy by dealers. Doubtless the volume
of the slave trade fluctuated over time, but it was well organized and
stable enough to permit further convoys of first-generation slaves from
many geographical centers to enter the Roman heartland. It remains true
that little is heard of individual slave dealers. The reason is that they
were men of low social esteem and so hardly worth the attention of upper-
class men of letters, though Cicero was not unaware of the profits to be
made from the slave trade. Also, some may have disguised or concealed
their activities by trading in commodities other than human merchandise,
and still others by dealing through their own slaves. But occasionally the
identity of a slave dealer is revealed, as when Cicero permits a glimpse
of a certain Lucius Publicius bringing slaves to Italy from Gaul for sale
in 83 B.C.; and at any moment in the second century the sight of a figure,
such as the later freedman A. Kapreilius Timotheus, leading a small train
of chained slaves for subsequent disposal must have been common
throughout the Mediterranean.[6]

Against this backdrop, the circumstances surrounding enslavement
can, at a safely speculative level, only be regarded as unenviable. The use
of shackles was probably common. Many who spoke only a local language
of origin must have been unable to understand the language spoken by

their new masters. Forced migration over vast distances can be assumed to have been accompanied by a high incidence of disease, malnutrition, and mortality. Physical deracination was surely followed by psychological or emotional deracination, with many of the newly enslaved suffering separation from family members. The sudden deprivation of freedom and personal autonomy was thus intensified by factors of a severely harrowing kind, which the all-pervasiveness of slavery in the ancient world can have done little to alleviate in individual cases. It is understandable therefore that mass suicide could be viewed as an alternative preferable to living in slavery when Roman power exerted itself over a local community.[7]

The varying geographical origins of the first-generation slaves supplied to the Roman heartland by warfare and trade already suggest the futility of seeking a common servile mentality in the slave population as a whole. Any such anticipation is further cut short by the fact that in the second century the slave population was reproducing to a significant degree, which means that slaves who grew up in slavery encountered a radically divergent set of experiences from those for whom slavery was a sudden imposition. True, it is often said that slavebreeding under the Republic was of no more than minimal importance and that the absolute numbers of home-born slaves (vernae) were very small: on this view, the servile population was overwhelmingly male, because women were little needed for agricultural work and children were even less employable; when new stocks of men were required, supplies from warfare were so abundant that reliance on servile natural reproduction was unnecessary. However, although Rome was continually at war in the middle Republic and although one of its war aims may have been the acquisition of new slaves (a highly controversial issue), it still remains the case that no military campaign at the outset could be regarded as an automatic guarantee of slave captives. Further accretions of slaves might certainly be anticipated, but Rome did not always exploit its military victories by imposing permanent enslavement on its defeated enemies. It makes little sense therefore to believe that slaveowners depended overwhelmingly on a single source of supply that was of incalculable and spasmodic efficiency at best. Admittedly, references to slave offspring in legal sources and inscriptions referring to vernae are much more common for the late Republic and early Empire than for the second century and so seem to lend support to the hypothesis that in the earlier period warfare was the primary means of supply, with breeding of only marginal significance. But the case is unsound: the number of texts in the great Roman law codes which derive from the Republican era is generally very small, and no fair comparison can consequently be made between Republican and Imperial material. Thus texts which reflect any servile reproduction at all under the Republic ought in actuality to carry a disproportionate amount of weight. The same is true of inscriptions commemorating vernae, and it should be acknowledged that narrative historians writing of expansionist warfare are likely to have overemphasized enslavement in that context at the expense of natural reproduction, a topic of no concern to them. The fact is that a significant presence of female slaves can be established for the second century, and once this is done natural reproduction can safely and logically be accepted as an important means of maintaining slave numbers.[8]

First, it should be noted that there are indications of a significant female slave presence at Rome well before the second century. As early as the time of the Twelve Tables, manumission of women as well as of men was considered important enough to be given legal recognition. In the religious festival of the Matralia, the extreme antiquity of which is indisputable and which may have achieved its mature form *circa* 400 B.C., when a new temple to the goddess Mater Matuta was built in the Forum Boarium, slave women were expressly banned from participation except for the one slave girl who was ritually beaten in and then expelled from the temple by the free female participants. Further, the institution of another set of rites known as the "Slave Women's Festival" (*feriae ancillarum*), which are traditionally ascribed to the immediate aftermath of the Gallic invasions of the early fourth century, makes little sense unless *ancillae* were available for participation. It must be acknowledged, therefore, that there was a long history of female enslavement at Rome. Secondly, the extant record of mass enslavements dependent on Republican warfare shows clearly that female captives—and children—were enslaved, not just men, and it is unrealistic to believe that none of these slave women reproduced once settled in their new conditions of servitude. The record for Rome's Italian wars is for the most part unspecific on the gender of captives, but for the subsequent overseas campaigns there is no doubt: female slaves were to be expected as a consequence of warfare, so Livy makes plain, and Polybius's account of the fate of Anticyra in Phocis in 210 B.C. could be taken to signify that Rome's enslavement of women and children had become habitual. In 146 B.C. L. Mummius is reputed to have sold Corinthian women and children into slavery, while according to Orosius the destruction of Carthage in the same year was followed by the enslavement of thirty thousand men and twenty-five thousand women. Sallust records that after the siege of Capsa during the Jugurthine war, C. Marius actually killed the male captives but sold into slavery the rest of the population; and women and children were included in T. Didius's sale of all the inhabitants of Colenda in Spain in 97 B.C. Even within Italy itself Rome had shown no hesitation over enslaving men, women, and children when the city of Capua was punished in 210 B.C.[9]

It is a tenable statement therefore that "the women and children of the enemy, and non-combatants generally, were normally enslaved, not butchered" by victorious Roman generals, and sometimes, because of exceptional circumstances, individual enslaved women appear in the literary record. In 210 B.C. Scipio Africanus set free a woman, brought to him by his troops, who turned out to be betrothed to a prominent Spanish leader. Also spared was another chieftain's daughter who had been captured with her two brothers in 179 B.C. after Ti. Sempronius Gracchus's siege of Alce in Spain. And Chiomara, the wife of a Gallic chieftain captured during Cn. Manlius Vulso's campaigns in Asia in 189 B.C., is said by Plutarch to have been taken together with other women. Obviously enough, the high status of these individuals brought them a historical distinction that most failed to achieve. Given the convention of female enslavement, consequently, the information that Cato charged his male slaves a fee for admission to the female slave quarters and that his wife Licinia nursed the offspring of their slave women becomes perfectly credible, pointing to an interest in servile reproductivity in the early second century that can hardly have been unique to one household. The context here is probably urban, that is, a context in which slave women will have been used as domestics, but female slaves are just as likely to have been present in the rural sector as well, even though this is often denied. It is said that Cato's silence on *ancillae* in his agricultural handbook, the bailiff's wife (*vilica*) apart, when compared with the increasingly more suggestive references to female slaves in the later agricultural treatises of Varro and Columella, provides evidence that in Cato's day slaveowners preferred to purchase slaves rather than to breed them. But there is an obvious objection: in view of the blatant discrepancies of scale and sophistication visible in the works of the three authors, no sense of historical progression can be justifiably founded on what is omitted by one and included by another. Columella devotes a whole book to beekeeping, but Cato has nothing on that topic; it does not follow that beekeeping developed in Italy only after the composition of Cato's *De Agricultura*.[10]

In any case, Cato is not altogether silent on slave women or children. Admittedly, he refers to male slaves being shackled and suggests that the men's sleeping quarters were spartanly furnished cells in the *villa rustica*, not perhaps ideal for procreation. Yet he also envisions the *villa urbana* as a comfortable residential unit for the owner, and one therefore that would require domestics, including women. Further, the *vilica* is specifically cautioned against visiting or receiving visits from neighboring or other women, and the latter could easily be assumed to be female domestics. More tellingly, in describing the uses of cabbage as an antidote for colic, Cato says that the treatment is the same for a man, woman, or child; and in recommending a cabbage cure for sores, he maintains that when the remedy is given to a boy or girl barley meal is to be added to it. The prescriptions continue: babies bathed in the urine of a habitual cabbage eater will never be weakly, and a woman's private parts will never become diseased if warmed with this same urine; Cato even tells how this is to be done. Finally, in prescribing medicine for dyspepsia and strangury, he observes that it should be administered to a child according to age. The point is of course that, since these references occur in a practical work on estate management, Cato, and his peers who composed his audience, fully expected women and children, including infants, to be present on the kinds of estate he wrote about, and servile reproduction is therefore not to be doubted. A later passage in Columella suggests that women could in fact be expected to work in the fields, apart that is from whatever domestic jobs they performed, and that expectation cannot have been peculiar to the middle of the first century A.D.[11]

Altogether, then, there is no sound basis for rejecting as anachronistic, as is sometimes done, the crucial statement of Appian on the middle Republic: "At the same time the ownership of slaves brought the rich great gain from the multitude of their progeny, who increased because they were exempt from military service"; for natural reproduction by slaves was inevitable given what can be determined about mass enslavements in this period. Moreover, Appian's evidence consists with Cicero's reference to a legal point—whether the offspring of a female slave was to count as *fructus* and to belong to the usufructuary or the owner—supposedly debated by the three founders of Roman jurisprudence, M'. Manilius, M. Junius Brutus, and P. Mucius Scaevola, who all flourished in the second century. The point may have been hypothetical, but it cannot have been devoid of all contemporary significance. While, therefore, warfare continued to generate new slaves, and trade networks provided the practical mechanisms by which slaves were filtered from one region of the Mediterranean to another, servile reproduction within Italy itself was much more than a subsidiary component in the overall supply of new slaves. Indeed, the servile population was maintained and expanded by a combination of complementary sources of supply, the effect of which was the creation of a strongly differentiated slave population whose attitudes and behavior, and whose responses to slavery in particular, cannot be assumed to have been always identical.[12]

One of the principal characteristics of the fully developed Roman slavery system of the late Republic and early Empire was an intense degree of job specialization among slaves. The situation in the second century is less clear, but slaves even then were probably used in a variety of jobs and entrusted with many specialized tasks. The broadest division lay between urban and rural labor, but within each category a hierarchy of servile statuses is likely to have emerged from the kinds of work slaves did. And in the rural sector especially, where the bulk of the slave population was contained, differentiation was encouraged by the types of farming with which slaves were associated. To be precise, allowance has to be made for "slavery in familial agricultural units, slavery in extensive pastoralism and cereal culture, and slavery in intensive 'plantation' agriculture." Moreover, slave workers incorporated in the villa system needed to achieve greater specialization and sophistication in their work than their pastoral counterparts, and it seems likely as a result that owners were prepared to make them certain concessions—forms of family life, for instance. There can be little doubt, therefore, that the diversity of the slave population was further increased by the range of occupations in which slaves found themselves.[13]

For agricultural occupations the vital testimony of Cato's *De Agricultura*, composed in all probability toward the end of Cato's life, allows a more detailed picture of slave life to emerge. Slave labor is taken for granted of course as a constituent element of the total labor supply available to the estate owners Cato addresses, and in his remarks on the slave workforce a marked degree of differentiation appears. Cato makes several references to the basic slave *familia*, recommending rations of food and wine and clothing allowances for its members; he gives details of their sleeping arrangements, and the slaves are included in the prescriptive prayers he lists. Cato understands, as noted above, that some slaves will be *compediti*, kept in chains, and it was perhaps such men to whom the severest laboring jobs were to be assigned—drainage work or olive pressing for example. But other workers are not simple *operarii* or *factores*, and their functional titles connote a greater feeling of status even if the work they did was not always highly skilled. In the ideal workforces specified for an oliveyard of two hundred and forty *iugera* and a vineyard of one hundred *iugera*, there appear *bubulci* (ploughmen), a *subulcus* (swineherd), an *opilio* (head shepherd), an *asinarius* (donkeyman), and a *salictarius* (osier manager), all of whom can be presumed slave workers, as too the *pastores* (shepherds) to whom Cato elsewhere alludes. While other workers mentioned are not part of the permanent labor complement but are hired (the *politor* [cleaner], various *custodes* [overseers], the *capulator* [oil drawer], *leguli* and *strictores* [olive pickers]), and while some of these were undoubtedly free men, it is likely that the jobs of all such people were at times filled by slaves, not least because slaves could be leased from one owner to another on a temporary basis. Over the permanent slave body, however, Cato allows for the provision of a *vilicus* (bailiff), the most elevated slave worker on the farm, one of whose essential responsibilities was the close supervision of the slave workers, both at work and in the material sphere. The duties of *vilicus* and *vilica*, who might in fact be husband and wife, are carefully set out.[14]

The evidence of Cato is complemented by that of Plautus's comedies, the historically realistic substratum of which is not open to question even if Plautus's debt to Greek models of comedy has to be taken into account. For obvious reasons Plautus is little concerned with rural slavery, but within his plays there are various allusions that are consistent with what is visible in Cato. Such slave workers as the *opilio* and *pastores* appear, for instance, together with *piscatores* (fishermen), the hired *operarius*, and *muliones* (mule drivers). Metaphorically, Plautus can refer to the *sator* (planter), *sartor* (hoer), and *messor* (reaper), periphrastically to the *bubulcus*. The chain gang (*genus ferratile*) is known; and certain slave characters are farm workers—Grumio the farmhand, the bailiffs Pistus and Collybiscus. The finest example of the *vilicus*, however, is Olympio in *Casina*, whose authority on the farm is made very plain: his sphere of command is a *praefectura* or *provincia*; he is able to appoint a deputy in his absence, to assign jobs on the farm, to supervise the hands' food and sleeping arrangements; and his threats to put Chalinus in the yoke or make him a water carrier serve to illustrate how any *vilicus* might maintain discipline. Further, Olympio can clearly expect to marry Casina and to take her to the country as his wife where she will have the modest comforts of heat, hot water, food and clothing, and where she will raise his children. Olympio has much in common therefore with the *vilicus* of Cato, and although Plautus does not use the term *vilica*, that is surely what Olympio imagines Casina will become. Moreover, the reliability of the *vilicus*, of concern to Cato, emerges in Olympio's reference to the *pietas* of his ancestors (*maiores*), so that altogether it seems undeniable that Plautus drew this character in large part from real life. Finally, it is worth noting that certain functional terms appear in Plautus not in reference to slave workers (*auceps* [fowler], *holitor* [market gardener], *fartor* [poultry and game fattener]), but they are terms nonetheless that are associated with slaves in later evidence. Whatever Plautus's debt to Greek comedy, therefore, there can be no hesitation in stating that his evidence on slave work and workers fully corresponds with the picture supplied by Cato: each author reflects the reality of the second century appropriate to his own medium of writing.[15]

Given this fact, there is every justification for exploiting Plautus's material on domestic slavery as evidence for contemporary historical conditions. There is, however, nothing comparable to Cato's book on agriculture to use as a control, but the functions Plautus assigns to slave characters are again consistent with servile domestic jobs well attested in subsequent periods of Rome's history, and this provides sufficient reason for accepting what is available in his plays. Also, the Plautine material on slave women in particular accords with and substantiates the earlier demonstration of a significant female presence in the servile population of the second century as a whole. So when slaves are found marrying in Plautus, when they identify their parents, and when references to *vernae* appear, such details only confirm the reality of servile natural increase.[16]

The world of Plautus is indeed one in which the ubiquitous presence of female slaves is simply taken for granted. Maidservants (*ancillae*) regularly appear in the plays, sometimes as rather more than incidental characters, and as slaves they address their masters appropriately, are bought

and sold (sometimes as captives from overseas), become victims of kidnapping, are put in bonds, given as gifts, and take refuge in temples. It is
expected of the Plautine slaveowner that he furnish his wife with a lavish
supply of maidservants and that he maintain them (and he recognizes the
economic value of manumission). But supervision of the *ancillae* is the
responsibility of his wife, who expects in turn to have an entourage of
servants and gives orders accordingly. The female slaves perform a variety
of domestic tasks, cleaning latrines, running errands and taking messages,
sweeping the house, working for the *familia*, baking, cutting wood, weav-
ing, and woolcarding; they also serve as their mistress's personal attendants, assisting in the toilette and even attending her in childbirth and
nursing children. In this world a robust Syrian or Egyptian girl is preferable
for menial work to someone of good looks; the slave women have their
own living quarters (as in Cato's household), and even farm work lies
within their sphere.[17]

In addition, various job titles usually associated with slave women are
used by Plautus: *cantrix* (singer), *cistellatrix* (wardrobe keeper), *ianitrix*
(doorkeeper), *nutrix* (nurse), *obstetrix* (obstetrician), *pedisequa* (attendant), *tonstrix* (hairdresser), *vestiplica* (clothes folder). Of these functionaries the *nutrix* is especially noteworthy, because the social importance
attached to the nurse in later times already seems to be well established
in Plautus's day to judge from the number of appearances she makes in
the plays. Phaedria, the daughter of the miser Euclio in *Aulularia*, has a
nurse who, now that Phaedria is no longer an infant, has become her
pedisequa—a transition that must have been very common in the real
world. The parasite Curculio can remember his childhood nurse, a woman
who is expected to care for a freeborn child even if the child's mother is
herself theoretically available to do the job, though the *nutrix* can also
nurse *vernae*. The nurse seems to be an essential domestic figure: as the
courtesan Phronesium tells Stratophanes in *Truculentus* in reference to
his supposititious son, a mother needs not only food for her child and
herself but also a woman to bathe the infant and a nurse who has to be
given a quantity of wine to maintain an ample supply of milk. To be sure,
it could be objected that the Plautine nurse is merely an intrusion from
the Greek theatre. But the objection is easily dispelled: in *Poenulus* the
Prologue forbids nurses to attend the play in case they become dry, and
the real life situation is obvious. In *Poenulus* too, finally, the precise
picture of the nurse Giddenis ought to be noted: as a slave nurse she had
been sold with her two female nurslings when they were respectively
aged five and four.[18]

Male domestics are equally conspicuous in Plautus. The entourage of
the *matrona* comprises not only female slaves, but male servants as well:
the *unctor* (masseur), *auri custos* (jewelry attendant), *nuntii* and *renuntii*
(messengers), *muliones*, *pedisequi*, and *salutigeruli pueri* (pages). Her

male counterpart can expect to be accompanied by the *agaso* (groom) and *calator* (footman) and to have his own *pedisequi*, who were clearly common contemporary figures. Within the household the *atriensis* (steward) is an important figure, but also to be observed are the *cellarius* (storekeeper), the *paedagogus* (chaperon of children), and the *cursor* (messenger). The *coquus* (cook) is worth special note, because it has been shown that this character type is a truly Plautine creation in which original Greek elements have been contaminated by realistic Roman influences: in Rome of Plautus's day the cook was always of servile status. Accordingly, when Ballio in *Pseudolus* gives detailed, specialized instructions to his slaves—describing, incidentally, their work roles as *provinciae*—it is clear that Plautus is indulging in parody of the established upperclass Roman household of his era. At the beginning of the second century a household of this sort was already highly elaborate, large, and well stocked with ample supplies of male and female servants. The social reality is transparent.[19]

The point needs to be made too that the children born to slave women were not economically superfluous but could be put to work by their owners at ages that are very young by modern standards. From the late Republic and early Empire there is again considerable evidence of child labor in Roman society, a phenomenon that cannot, however, have been unique to the central period, despite the chronological limitations of the available material. Cato once gave a speech in which he claimed that young slave boys were more expensive than land, and as censor he imposed a luxury tax on male slaves under the age of twenty who had been purchased in the previous five-year period for sums in excess of ten thousand *asses*. Such sales may have been of imported or home-born boys, but in either case if children were available for sexual exploitation, so also for less humiliating kinds of work. Indeed, Plutarch states of Cato himself that he "used to lend money . . . to those of his slaves who wished it, and they would buy boys with it, and after training and teaching them for a year, at Cato's expense, would sell them again. Many of these boys Cato would keep for himself." So it is not the case that children were without economic value in the Roman slavery system; and in fact their presence and their labor added a further dimension of variegation to it.[20]

It has been said of colonial Antigua that "the broad spectrum of slave employment leads to the realization that slave occupations naturally bred and shaped a complexity of roles and a wider range of relationships with masters . . . that must have strongly influenced individual and collective responses to enslavement." The same might be expected of Rome. But at no time in Roman history—other than, to a limited extent, during the period of Roman rule in Egypt—is it possible to examine in detail the composition of individual slave holdings, for inventories of estates have simply not survived. A little help derives from the so-called Will of Dasumius, a lengthy but highly fragmentary record on stone of a will that belongs to the early second century A.D. and contains the names or occupational titles of almost forty individuals who appear to have belonged to the testator's *familia*. It is unlikely that the will in its complete form would have itemized all the members of the household, and in what survives, the emphasis falls on the owner's domestic entourage. Even so, the diversity of the testator's domestic staff at a specific time (when the will was drawn up) is very plain indeed, with the range of attested jobs extending from the managerial and secretarial to the mundane and personally indulgent. The document thus supports and enriches the evidence for the second century B.C. already seen. But while much of that evidence is anecdotal and indirect, in general terms at least the heterogeneity of the slave population of Rome and Italy in the second century B.C. is reasonably clear, as are the conditions controlling it: varying sources of recruitment, geographical differentiation in origins, different rates of inurement to slavery, the nature of and circumstances in which work was done—these were all influential factors.[21]

Beyond this, linguistic differentiation added another element of variety, and from the viewpoint of their own concerns with promoting order and security, slaveowners recognized the advantages of avoiding homogeneity among their slaves: "Nor should several slaves of the same ethnic origin be obtained," Varro dictated, for "household difficulties tend most frequently to arise from this cause." Yet what the owner termed "difficulties" the slave might have considered in a very different light. It is true that the Roman slave population, like that of colonial Brazil, was "the most disadvantaged element in society"—"unable to make contracts, dispose of their lives and property, defend themselves or their families from physical abuse by their masters, testify against freemen, choose their labor or their employer, and limited by law and practice in a thousand other ways." But the variables among the servile population meant that no coherent response to slavery lay within the sphere of slaves' expectations; and even with allowance made for the fact that their juridical status and their lack of freedom gave them a certain common bond, there is still no sign of class consciousness or class solidarity ever developing in the Roman slave body as a whole. Equally, however, there is no basis for assuming that the entire slave body reacted with simple passivity and acquiescence to the reality of servitude (and none at all in the fact that slavery was a well-entrenched piece of the social fabric of Rome by the second century). Thus the signs of resistance to slavery have to be sought and drawn out as necessary antecedents to the great rebellions. What, then, was the servile response to slavery?[22]

If the question is straightforward enough, an answer is not. For the second century, as almost always in the history of Roman slavery, no records are available from slaves themselves to provide evidence of the motivations that lay behind their acts of resistance. The very record of events inevitably derives from authors whose attitudes were those of the slaveowning establishment and who accordingly held little sympathy for servile interests. Any sense of a slave point of view, therefore, can only be inferred from a record controlled by what historians of modern slave societies would call a proslavery bias; consequently, distortion and partiality in the record must always be assumed.

To begin, it is necessary to leave the second century completely and to go forward in time to the autumn of 46 B.C. when Cicero, in Rome, addressed a letter to P. Sulpicius Rufus, who was then holding a command across the Adriatic in Illyricum. Cicero's letter contained a personal request for Sulpicius's assistance in locating a fugitive slave Cicero was anxious to recover. As in modern slave societies, willful escape by the slave was one of the most important acts by which resistance to slavery manifested itself in the slave society of Rome, but it is not often that relatively full accounts of individual case histories appear in the sources. Cicero's correspondence, however, offers a few exceptions to the norm. He wrote to Sulpicius Rufus as follows:

> There is another matter in which I would earnestly request you to put yourself to some trouble, in virtue of our friendship and your unfailing readiness to serve me. My library, worth a considerable sum, was in the charge of a slave of mine called Dionysius. Having pilfered a large number of books and anticipating a day of reckoning, he ran away. He's now in your province. Many people, including my friend M. Bolanus, saw him at Narona, but believed his story that I had given him his freedom. If you see to it that he is returned to me, I cannot tell you how much it will oblige me. In itself it is no great matter, but I am intensely vexed. Bolanus will tell you where he is and what can be done. If I recover the fellow thanks to you, I shall regard you as having done me a very great favour.[23]

The letter is of great interest. First, the slaveowner's concern with protecting his personal property has been responsible for the letter's very origin, a concern that is far more important than the apparent triviality of the event, perfunctorily hinted at by Cicero, suggests ("In itself it is no great matter"): the consul of 63 B.C. was not going to accept unanswered the *fait accompli* of Dionysius's escape, despite the fact that his household could not possibly have been seriously affected by the loss of a single slave. Secondly, Cicero's response was largely one of self-help. In the absence of any state mechanism for the recovery of his property, Cicero drew upon his own celebrity and his own personal contacts to initiate steps for Dionysius's capture, couching his request to Sulpicius Rufus in the language of friendship and obligation typical of his age and social class. Thirdly, Cicero gives a number of details about Dionysius himself: his former occupation in Cicero's household (which, it may be imagined, had required an educated slave of some skill and trustworthiness); a brief comment on Dionysius's reputation as a thief and the putative guilt that had provided the alleged motivation for his escape; and the information that Dionysius was currently passing for a free man, though Dionysius's claim offers no evidence in itself of the frequency with which Cicero practiced manumission. These details closely parallel the descriptions given in newspaper advertisements for fugitive slaves by their owners in later periods of history, though in Roman society there was no comparable medium by which news of this sort could be broadly and quickly disseminated. In spite of the lack of rapid communications, however, Cicero had still been able to keep track of Dionysius's movements and whereabouts, at a far remove from Rome itself, which is a strong sign of the determination he felt over the slave's recovery. The matter was important and could not be allowed to rest.[24]

The slaveowner's position is clear from the letter. But Cicero's interpretation of Dionysius's behavior is of course one-sided and strongly prejudiced, and his view of Dionysius's motivation in running away is not necessarily to be taken at face value. The charge of pilfering is not to be altogether discredited, because it recalls Columella's later complaint about the wanton dishonesty of rural slaves. But the moralistic judgments of the elite do not have to be taken as representing the morality of their slaves. The evidence of petty sabotage perpetrated against slaveowners and their property in modern slave societies is sufficiently extensive to show that behavior of this sort was undertaken as a form of resistance to oppression in contexts where more spectacular forms, such as revolt and rebellion, were impossible or undesirable. Dionysius's behavior here is part of the same pattern, and so there is no need to believe that he ultimately ran away out of a sense of guilt: self-extrication from slavery, as a form of protest and opposition, was a logical continuation of the resistance implicit in petty sabotage and a predictable step to take under the right conditions. From the servile point of view, flight was not associated with the noxious at all. Dionysius's determination to escape, it may be inferred, was as strong as Cicero's to recover him. He was resourceful enough to make his way out of Italy, to take refuge in a locality where his condition was not easily recognized, and to make a plausible case that he had been set free when his identity became apparent to people known to his owner. Dionysius's origins are not known; he may have been a *verna* or an imported slave. But a clue may be detectable in the fact that he chose to flee to Illyricum, and more specifically to the Dalmatian coast of the Adriatic. There had been Roman military action there as late as 78–77 B.C., and it is just possible that Dionysius had been taken to Rome as a young captive: as seen earlier, attempts to return to original homelands were characteristic of fugitive slaves' behavior in New World slave societies.[25]

In the event, Sulpicius Rufus was not successful in tracking down Dionysius. On July 11, 45 B.C., the proconsul of Illyricum, P. Vatinius, sent a letter to Cicero which mentions the slave, a letter full of confidence that Vatinius can find Dionysius no matter where he is, even if in Dalmatia; for Dionysius, it becomes clear, was no longer at Narona but had taken refuge among the tribe of the Vardaei. Was this tribe his original people? There can be no proof. But Dionysius's continued resourcefulness in making good his escape seems incontestable, as too a certain imbalance between slaveowners' determination to recover fugitives and actual realization of their intentions. The passage of time obviously worked to the advantage of the fugitive. Cicero himself wrote to Vatinius in December 45 B.C., by which time he had become quite exasperated by the whole affair: "Do please settle this affair of Dionysius. I shall honour any undertaking you make him. If he behaves like the scoundrel he is, you shall lead him captive at your Triumph." The jaundiced Cicero must have entertained some notion of negotiating with Dionysius for his return, but this was now a faint hope. The slave had become a frustration, an object of verbal abuse and a potential candidate for physical and public humiliation. A few weeks later, early in 44 B.C., Cicero heard again from Vatinius: nothing further had been learned of Dionysius and the search efforts had been foreclosed by harsh weather. Presumably therefore Dionysius's success was, in the end, complete.[26]

Dionysius's escape and his bid for freedom speak more for his personality than the unflattering comments of his former owner. Moreover, the physical and logistical aspects of this episode—Dionysius's voyage across the Adriatic first to Narona and then to the Vardaei, the time it took for correspondence to pass to and from Illyricum, the difficulties inherent in tracing the slave—all suggest that a fugitive attended by luck and daring could create a new life for himself out of slavery once the decision, dangerous in itself, to make the attempt for freedom had been taken. It may have been a factor in Dionysius's thinking in 46 B.C. that the contemporary political climate could aid his attempt. The main question his case history raises, however, is whether his behavior was representative of a servile response to servitude at large or simply an isolated episode.

Cicero's experience with Dionysius was not, as it happens, the first time he had had a problem with fugitive slaves. Several years earlier, in 59 B.C., he sent these remarks to his brother Quintus, who was then proconsul of Asia:

Furthermore, a slave called Licinus (you know him) belonging to our friend Aesopus has run away. He was in Athens with Patro the Epicurean posing as a free man, and passed from there to Asia. Later, one Plato of Sardis, an

Epicurean, who is a good deal in Athens and was there when Licinus arrived, having later learned that he is a runaway, arrested him and gave him into custody in Ephesus; but from his letter we are not sure whether the fellow was put into gaol or into the mill. However that may be, he is in Ephesus, so will you please search for him and take good care either to send him to Rome or to bring him with you? Don't consider what he's worth—such a good-for-nothing can't be worth much. But Aesopus is so distressed by the slave's criminal audacity that you can do him no greater favour than by getting him back his property.

Cicero was not concerned here with the recovery of his own property. The slaveowner, Clodius Aesopus, was a tragic actor who, ironically but significantly, was himself a former slave: the lack of cohesion among the servile classes in Roman society is thus made vividly clear, as is the inarguable fact that slaveowners of nonelite status—of whom there were many in Rome and Italy, such as Caesar's favored troops—shared precisely the same uncompromising attitudes to the ownership of property as their social superiors. Nevertheless, this letter is very similar to those Cicero wrote concerning Dionysius: the same tenacious resolve to recover the slave and to defend property rights, the same righteous indignation, the same moralistic denigration of the fugitive, all are present. Equally, it is plain enough that some knowledge of Licinus's movements had been gleaned in spite of the distance involved, but use of that knowledge had been impeded by physical factors.[27]

Licinus's name does not suggest that he was of Eastern origin, so his choice of first Athens and then the province of Asia as places of refuge cannot strictly signify that he was trying to return to an original homeland. He may simply have been on the run. But he used the same tactic as Dionysius in claiming to be free and perhaps found some collusive assistance in the person of Patro: that is, fugitive slaves as well as slave-hunting masters may have been able to rely on networks of parties sympathetic to their cause, but that can only be speculation. Still, there can be little doubt about the motivating force of freedom in prompting flight, though at the same time Cicero's comments on the possible consequences of arrest—jail or the mill—illustrate the dangers to which any fugitive was constantly exposed, no matter how far removed geographically he was from the site of his servitude and how great the passage of time since his escape. Distance and time were not automatic guarantees of freedom as long as owners could draw upon contacts and associates to keep a search alive.

As with Dionysius, the ultimate fate of Licinus is unknown. So also in a third case involving Cicero, that of the fugitive Amianus, a slave who belonged to his friend T. Pomponius Atticus. In this instance, Cicero was the searching agent during his proconsulship of Cilicia in 51 B.C.

Amianus at that time had found his way to the region of the Taurus in central southern Asia Minor, but his point of departure is not recorded. Cicero was dubious about locating him in the winter of 51–50 B.C., for the slave had apparently sought refuge with a local chieftain, Moeragenes, though the latter was dead by the time Cicero wrote to Atticus from Laodicea in February 50 B.C. The loss to Atticus, who, it can be recalled, is supposed to have used only *vernae* in his *familia*, may have been permanent. If indeed Amianus was a home-bred slave he must have tried to find refuge wherever possible and was not motivated by a desire to return to his country of origin; and any familial attachments he had known in slavery in early life had perhaps not been strong enough or currently important enough to offset his decision to run away. But his circumstances are really unknowable.[28]

Altogether, then, the evidence of Cicero's correspondence implies that individual slaves who displayed initiative could secure freedom with relative ease by absconding (and could traverse vast distances in the process), regardless of the pressures for their recovery exercised by the slaveowning establishment. There was after all nothing as blatant as skin color to prevent fugitives from melting into the general population of a distant city or region. Cicero's evidence is of a very high order, however, and nothing comparable exists for earlier periods of Republican history. But once some minor pieces of evidence are collocated, it becomes undeniable that the troubles with fugitives that Cicero commented on in detail were symptomatic of servile behavior as early as the age of Cato. In Plautus, for example, running away is clearly associated with the slave, and it is worth noting that *Fugitivi* was the title of one of Plautus's now lost plays. In *Captivi*, the point of departure is the flight of a slave with one of his owner's young sons, and escape is regarded there as a very natural activity for the slave; hence presumably the use of the term *fugitivus* as a form of insult. The obvious refuge for a Plautine runaway is his *patria*: it is as though Plautus's audience would easily understand that a first-generation Roman slave would ordinarily want to return to his country of origin as a matter of course, and something almost of the slave's mental state prior to the act of escape seems to appear in Peniculus's words in *Menaechmi*: "Men that bind prisoners of war with chains and fasten shackles on runaway slaves are awful fools, at least in my opinion. Why, if the poor devil has this extra trouble on his shoulders, too, he's all the keener for escape and mischief. Why, they get out of their chains somehow. As for those in shackles, they file away the ring, or knock off the rivet with a stone." Those words do not derive from the literary imagination alone.[29]

To set alongside this material from Plautus is the detail in the *De Agricultura* of Cato that when an absentee farm owner visits his estate he might well expect his *vilicus* to offer servile truancy as an excuse for unfinished work, a remark that gives a realistic ring indeed to the exchange in *Captivi* between the overseer and Philocrates:

Overseer: Ah yes, you're planning to run for it! I see what's afoot.
Philocrates: Run—we? Where should we run to?
Overseer: Home.
Philocrates: Get out! The idea of our acting like runaway slaves!

A fragment of Lucilius, for all its brevity, leaves no doubt about the habitual shackling of fugitives, and Livy's account of a fire in Rome in 210 B.C., in which it was alleged that a fugitive slave from Capua had brought charges of arson against his owners out of spite, is a credible indication at a relatively early date, even though not properly contemporary evidence, of slaveowners' expectations of flight. Moreover, the record of Roman diplomacy throughout the Republic suggests that slaves who accompanied their owners on military campaigns at times took the opportunity to escape afforded by the fluid situation of warfare in distant geographical settings, for it is a common element in treaties concluding wars that fugitive slaves were to be returned to their masters. The civil wars of the first century in turn provided similar contexts for the display of servile opportunism and initiative. But perhaps most interestingly of all, an unknown senator of the late second century considered it worthy of recording on an inscription that while praetor in Sicily he had rounded up and returned to their masters 917 fugitive slaves. Whether these individuals were slaves from Italy who had fled to Sicily, or, perhaps more likely, slaves who belonged to Italians resident in Sicily, is far from clear. But in either case the record of flight itself has an unmistakable significance.[30]

The early evidence on flight, therefore, though paltry in comparison with the fuller accounts of Cicero, is nonetheless fully consistent with the case histories he records, and there is no justification for denying its importance as a mode of resistance in the era of middle Republican expansion and beyond. Nor is it accurate to describe flight in the later period as only an intermittent problem for the Roman authorities, for all the indications point to exactly the opposite conclusion. The earliest legal definition of the fugitive belongs to the age of Cicero: "He is one who remains away from his master's house for the purpose of flight, thereby to hide himself from his master." In the same period, professional slave catchers begin to emerge in the record; while the stipulation in the aedilician edict that the seller of a slave must declare, if applicable, the slave's tendency to run away, although not formally attested before the time of Aulus Gellius, must equally be of Republican origin. Such legal prescriptions and means of redress are not likely to have developed in response to an intermittent phenomenon; nor is it plausible to imagine that flight by slaves, given the scale of slaveowning and the general importance of slavery in the second century, was peculiar to the better-documented first century: when the jurist Ulpian wrote his version of the aedilician edict he included pertinent material from the time of Cato.[31]

Escape was a direct form of resistance to slavery by means of which the slave rejected his subjection to the authority of his master in favor of securing or regaining his freedom. Success depended on a combination of propitious circumstances: a suitable moment for departure, the ability to elude detection and to find safe refuge (even in such unlikely sites as tombs), the capacity to cover terrain and to survive independently. The whole enterprise demanded certain practical skills and, one must imagine, a certain quick-wittedness. Moreover, the personal risks run by the slave were considerable. Capture could mean that the fugitive was returned to his owner and to the desperation of slavery that had led to flight to begin with, and little sympathy for the recaptured could be expected from an established order that accepted the proclamation of the praetor who restored the 917 fugitive slaves to their owners as a meritorious action. In extreme circumstances death might confront the slave, for when Q. Sertorius attacked Contrebia in Spain in 77–76 B.C. he ordered the local townspeople to kill the fugitive slaves; and indeed their throats were cut and their bodies flung down from the walls of the city. Despite the lack of case histories for the second century, therefore, the extent of flight determinable on impressionistic grounds must be regarded as a severe commentary on the harshness of contemporary Roman slavery.[32]

The practical goal of escape to a country of origin is comprehensible enough for first-generation slaves who were unwilling to submit to servitude. But many will not have known how to plan and effect escape over long distances, while those who were slaves from birth had no country of origin at all to dominate their thoughts. Some fugitives may well have preferred therefore to try to survive, as free individuals, by submerging themselves in the communities in which they had formerly been slaves. Aulus Gellius records an instructive anecdote, for example, derived from the Republican jurist Sabinus, of a man who was convicted of theft for having concealed a fugitive with his cloak when the slave's master once came within view, implying that such a chance encounter was not extraordinary. The resort to flight could easily assume an individualistic flavor, but at the same time it is possible that absconding slaves came to form in Italy something comparable to the maroon communities of fugitives and rebels known from the modern history of slavery, whose purpose, as seen earlier, was to provide sanctuary for runaways and whose continued existence depended in part on successive accretions of new fugitives. If the comparative evidence creates this expectation, however, there is no obvious parallel in the Roman evidence that springs to mind. But the limitations of the material can be offset to a degree by reference to an episode from the history of slavery in the Greek world that has a certain suggestive value.[33]

According to a story in Athenaeus, who quotes the earlier Nympho-

dorus of Syracuse, the slave Drimacus organized and led a community of
runaway slaves on the island of Chios probably at some point in the first
half of the third century B.C.:

The Chians' slaves ran away from them and made off into the mountains,
where they gathered in large numbers and did a lot of damage to their country
estates. The island is rough and covered with trees. There is a story which
they tell that a little before our own time there was a certain slave who ran
off to make his home in the mountains. Since he was a brave man who had
a lot of luck when it came to fighting, he came to lead the runaways in the
same way as a king leads an army. After the Chians had organised many
expeditions against him which failed to achieve anything, Drimacus (for
that was the runaway's name) saw that they were being killed for no good
reason, and he made them the following proposal: "Chian owners: what
you have been suffering because of your house-slaves is never going to stop.
How can it, since it is in accordance with an oracle that has been given by
a god? Now if you make a truce with me and allow us to live in peace, I
shall ensure that there will be many benefits for you." So the people of
Chios made a treaty with him and agreed on a truce for a certain period of
time, and he prepared some measures and weights and a special seal. He
showed these to the Chians and said that, "I am going to take anything that
I take away from any of you in accordance with these weights and measures,
and when I have taken whatever I need, I shall leave your warehouses sealed
up with this seal. And I shall interrogate any of your house-slaves that run
away about what their reasons are; and if anyone seems to me to have run
away because he has been treated intolerably in any way I will keep him
with me: but if their story does not convince me, I will send them back to
their owners." When the other house-slaves saw that the Chians were prepared to accept this arrangement, they ran away much less frequently, since
they were afraid of being interrogated by Drimacus. At the same time the
runaways who were with him were much more afraid of Drimacus than of
their own masters, and treated him with great respect, obeying him as
though he were their commanding officer; for he punished those who were
guilty of breaches of discipline, and allowed no one to plunder the fields or
to commit even a single act of injustice without having obtained his consent.
At festival time, he would set out and take from the fields wine and any
animals suitable for sacrificial purposes which their owners themselves
would [†not] hand over. And if he found out that anyone was plotting to
lay an ambush for him, he would take his revenge on them.
 The city of Chios had announced that it would give a lot of money to
anyone who captured Drimacus or brought them his head; and so, in the
end, when he had grown old, he called his boyfriend to a particular place
and told him that, "I have loved you more than anyone else and you are my
favourite and like a son to me, and so on and so forth. Now I have lived for
long enough, while you are a young man in the best years of your life. So
what ought to be done? You ought to become an upright and respected
citizen. And since the city of Chios is going to give a lot of money to the

man who kills me, and has promised him his freedom, it is you who must cut off my head and bring it to the Chians, take the money from the city and live happily ever after." Although the young man objected, he convinced him to do this; so he cut off his head and received from the Chians the money that had been promised, buried the body of the runaway and then went home to his own country. Later the Chians suffered a lot of vandalism and theft because of their house-slaves, just as they had before; and since they remembered how fair Drimacus had been to them when he was alive, they erected a shrine to him out in the countryside, and dedicated it to the Kindly Hero. And even today runaway slaves bring the first fruits of everything they steal to him. And it is also said that he appears to many Chians while they are asleep and warns them when their house-slaves are plotting against them; and those to whom he appears go to the place where the hero's shrine stands and sacrifice to him.[34]

If taken at face value, this account, quite remarkably, has many features characteristic of maroon life. It begins with the postulate that slaves are naturally prone to flight; makes clear the relevance of the geographical intractability of Chios; and specifies the emergence of a distinguished leader who became powerful enough in his own right to negotiate with slaveowners and to wield authority over his slave followers. The account shows that the community of fugitives was economically dependent on the estates of the free for its survival; that despite the negotiated settlement the slaveowners still attempted to destroy the leader by putting a price on his head; and that, though finally killed, Drimacus himself continued after death to exercise a psychological-religious hold over his slave supporters. The authenticity of all these details, it must be acknowledged, is open to question. But there must be a presumption that the story was sufficiently credible to an audience of about A.D. 200, when Athenaeus set it down, and so there is every reason to accept the account as evidence of how fugitive slaves might be expected to behave under certain conditions. Moreover, Athenaeus's general interest in slave activities is rather unusual among ancient authors as a whole, and it might therefore be urged that the story of Drimacus, as a demonstration of a particular mode of slave behavior, has a greater importance and wider applicability because of its rarity in extant literature. If that is so, an elliptical passage from Suetonius concerning C. Octavius, the father of Augustus, assumes considerable interest, for in 60 B.C., Suetonius reports, when on his way to Macedonia to take up the governorship of the province, Octavius first carried out a special command, wiping out "a band of runaway slaves [fugitivi], refugees from the armies of Spartacus and Catiline, who held possession of the country about Thurii." The statement shows very firmly that, in spite of the formal suppression of the two movements led by Spartacus and L. Sergius Catilina, all the elements of servile opposition associated with them had by no means been fully eradicated; instead, the mountainous hinterland of Thurii had continued to provide sites for the maintenance of armed resistance. It is singularly unfortunate that Suetonius's words lack further detail.[35]

If, then, forms of servile behavior akin to marronage might be anticipated in the Roman slavery system, so too might episodes of direct revolt. In reality, however, the record of revolt before the major insurrections themselves is very meager, a fact of some surprise at first sight but one that is paralleled in the slave society of the southern United States. The fallacy of course is to assume that a low level of direct revolt is a measure of servile contentment within the system, but the case of the United States rapidly dispels any thought of that kind. Before the second century B.C. only five episodes of apparent revolt by slaves are attested, ranging in time from 501–500 B.C. to 217 B.C., and little can be made of them, either because the evidence is too far removed in time from the events to have any credibility or because the events themselves seem not to be genuine slave revolts in any meaningful sense. For example, in 259 B.C., according to Orosius, destruction of the city was planned by three thousand slaves and four thousand Roman naval allies, but the plot came to nothing because of a timely betrayal. The evidence is very sparse, but the conspiracy was not a straightforward servile action and may have been fomented by Carthage, with whom Rome was then at war. So it has been suggested. Much earlier, in 419 B.C., there was an attempt by slaves to set fire to Rome and to seize by force various strategic points in the city, according to the record of Livy and Dionysius of Halicarnassus, but again the conspiracy was betrayed from within. This time the episode appears to have been an independent action initiated by slaves alone, and since slavery as an institution was now coming to have a higher social profile at Rome, it may reflect genuine protest against servitude. But the record is so spotty and late that further comment is valueless. The scale, purpose, and motivations of the affair are beyond recovery. Still, a point that is worth emphasizing in the pre-second-century episodes is the tradition that conspiracies often failed because of internal subversion. The organization and implementation of revolt were, in any circumstances, extremely dangerous strategies of servile behavior, likely, in the event of failure, to result in severe personal consequences for those implicated. To recognize that the possibility of betrayal from within could never be eliminated, therefore, is to appreciate better the hazardous nature of revolt and to understand why it was such a rare form of resistance to slavery. Conversely, however, the records of early Republican revolts have a significance outside their own chronological context, for they point to the existence, toward the end of the Republic, of contemporary anxieties over the possibility of new slave uprisings, anxieties for which there was every justification after the period 140 B.C. to 70 B.C.[36]

In the half century or so before 140 B.C. there were outbreaks of servile disaffection of more apparent substance. For the first, disturbances in Latium in 198 B.C., Livy gives a relatively full description, but his account is marred in some places by textual problems. He records, however, that at the town of Setia the slaves of some Carthaginian hostages under detention in the aftermath of the Hannibalic War collaborated with other Carthaginian slaves acquired by the people of Setia as captives in an attempt to foment slave insurrections in the region of Setia itself and in the neighboring towns of Norba and Circeii. Setia was actually captured by the insurgents, Livy says, but nothing so dramatic occurred elsewhere. News of the uprising was brought to Rome by some slave informants (and, it seems, a free man too), where the praetor L. Cornelius Merula was authorized by the senate to investigate and take repressive action. The praetor hastily raised a force of two thousand men and on arrival at Setia arrested the leaders of the uprising and despatched troops to pursue those who had fled. The informants were rewarded (the slaves were given money and their freedom, their owners were compensated by the treasury), but the matter was not yet fully resolved: some of the fugitive slaves seem to have tried to attack the town of Praeneste, but Merula himself gave chase and executed five hundred of them, thus bringing the revolt to an end. At Rome, Livy notes, it was believed that the whole affair was instigated by Carthaginians and so was not a true slave uprising; a list of precautions taken to preclude such manipulation in the future is then appropriately given. The explanation is credible enough, given that the Carthaginian hostages in Italy may have been confined in contravention of the treaty of 201 B.C. which had terminated the Second Punic War. But other points are to be noted concerning the insurgents themselves, who, as far as can be told, were very new to slavery, derived from a single foreign source, and could not anticipate quick release from enslavement. The desire to escape from slavery, in and of itself, may therefore have been sufficient cause for the uprising, apart that is from any political nuance, and the attempt may have been facilitated by the rebels' common origin (communication would be easy) and the absence of any familial or personal ties to act as deterrents. The uprising was certainly serious enough to warrant a punitive force of two thousand men, a sign of the scale of the movement and the successful organization achieved by those whose prominence led, in the event, to prompt arrest.[37]

If Livy's record of 198 B.C. is anywhere near accurate, Rome, whose military retaliation against the slaves at Setia and whose recourse to executions were both swift, must have been becoming increasingly sensitive to the problem of security posed by the slave population of Italy in the early second century. The situation in 198 B.C. was contained, as again in 196 B.C., when the praetor M'. Acilius Glabrio took a Roman legion to suppress trouble in Etruria. In this case too the leaders of a plot were identified and the reprisals severe, but the problem was rather different from that of two years earlier: "Livy makes it clear that this rising was not brought about by Carthaginian prisoners like the one in Latium in 198—it was too widespread, and the slaves whose lives were spared were afterwards returned to their *domini*. The rebels were clearly members of the local serf class, their position relatively strengthened by the Roman punishment of members of the class of *principes*." But another set of events a decade or so later, in 185 B.C., once more pointed up the continual need for vigilance wherever there were concentrations of chattel slaves. Livy's account is again tantalizingly brief:

> There was a serious slave insurrection that year in Apulia. Lucius Postumius the praetor had Tarentum as his province. He conducted a strict investigation into a conspiracy of shepherds who had endangered the highways and the public pasture-lands by their brigandage. He condemned about seven thousand men: many of them escaped, many were executed.

The intensification of pastoral farming in Apulia after the Hannibalic War and the associated expansion of the slave population created in fact a permanent security problem; for shepherds involved in transhumance had to be allowed freedom of movement, and supervision comparable to that recommended by Roman authorities for less mobile slaves was impossible to effect with any rigor. Thus, what representatives of the established order pejoratively termed brigandage (*latrocinium*) was a problem in the south of Italy of very serious proportions that spilled over at times into parts of Sicily as well. The potential for further outbreaks of violence like that of 185 B.C. was enormous, and the likelihood of total suppression, as also in 185 B.C., not great.[38]

Although it is possible that there were other slave revolts of which no traces have survived, the record as it stands is insubstantial, and its chief usefulness lies in showing the need to guard against a number of easy assumptions. There is no evidence, for example, to suggest that slaves' juridical status, their mere absence of freedom, was enough of a common bond to promote massive, geographically widespread revolt; or that large-scale revolts could be easily organized and brought to fruition; or that the slave population of Rome and Italy was a revolutionary powder keg waiting to be ignited. Given the nature of that population, there could be no unanimous response to slavery on the part of the enslaved, nor necessarily any unanimous opinion about slavery itself. In effect, the record shows a number of sporadic outbursts in local situations, implies that further local troubles might be anticipated at any moment, and suggests that the government of Rome was alert to danger. But it points up too the need, in investigating the more sensational events of the period 140 B.C. to 70 B.C., to focus attention on the specific details of local disaffection and especially on the kinds of slaves involved in revolt, their experiences of

slavery, their individual positions in the servile hierarchy, and their relationships with their masters. If revolt was always one of a number of
modes of resistance open to slaves it was by no means the most popular,
for slaves could understand as well as anyone that revolt invited retaliation and that retaliation might bring drastic and even fatal consequences.

In its various forms resistance to Roman slavery has a piecemeal character in which theoretical or ideological influences appear to have played
no role beyond the obvious fact that the pursuit of freedom was a motivating ideal for those who directly opposed the system by resorting to
flight or revolt. But the ideal was of limited application only: freedom
for those prepared to take action for their individual betterment, not for
the amorphous slave population in its entirety. Resistance, however, even
if sporadic, discrete, and diffuse, was also constant, which implies that
the slavery system itself was oppressive, harsh, and essentially brutal.
The implication is real and cannot be altogether offset by the undeniable
fact that, within the system, devices existed for softening oppression and
for making slavery more tolerable. As already seen, the capacity for the
slave to be set free at Rome is at least as old as the time of the Twelve
Tables, and slaves in the second century were no doubt often given their
freedom, even in theaters of warfare: contemporary evidence, for instance,
makes clear that on one occasion L. Aemilius Paullus, proconsul in one
of the Spanish provinces in 189 B.C., liberated on his own initiative people
the inhabitants of Hasta Regia, near Gades, had enslaved. But within the
servile constituency as a whole, manumission was a divisive tool, a
counterforce operating against any notions of servile cohesion and solidarity. Ex-slaves could and did integrate themselves into the mainstream
of Roman and Italian life, at times becoming owners of slaves themselves.
Thus the great divide between slavery and freedom was always blurred
at the edges by the transition that some made from one state to the other;
and yet although no statistics are available, it is beyond belief that that
transition was ever made by more than a small proportion of the full
servile population. Moreover, from the evidence seen on slave reproduction, it must be assumed that in many quarters in the second century the
slave family had come into existence and that it too served for some to
temper the harsher aspects of slave life. Indeed, the existence of familial
ties among slaves may well be one reason why the incidence of revolt
seems to be so low. But family life was also a concession for those who
enjoyed it, one that was revocable and not guaranteed to endure permanently. Individuals of course had to learn to accommodate themselves to
the realities of their condition, and many will have chosen to try to integrate themselves into established social modes. How this could occur
is perhaps best illustrated by the series of inscriptions, belonging to the
first half of the first century B.C., from the Campanian town of Minturnae

in which the names are commemorated with pride of the members of the colleges of *magistri* and *magistrae*, slaves and former slaves, men and women, who were responsible for making cult offerings to a sequence of divinities long established in the traditional pantheon. But none of these considerations necessarily means that slaveowners had any generic interest in the humanity of their slave property for its own sake. And, as for so much else in this age, it is the stern and uncompromising attitude of Cato, as described by Plutarch, that must stand as the paradigm of the Roman slaveowner:

He acquired many dependants; he generally bought young prisoners of war who were still able to be trained and educated like puppies or foals. None of them was ever allowed to enter another household unless he had been sent by Cato or his wife; and if he was asked how Cato was getting on, the only answer he gave was that he did not know. A slave was supposed either to be engaged on some essential household job, or else to be asleep; Cato was very pleased with those who would sleep a great deal, since he considered them easier to control than those who were energetic, and thought that those who enjoyed sleep were in every respect more useful than those who did not. Since he thought that what made slaves most troublesome was their sexual needs, he allowed them to get together with the female slaves for a fixed price, but forbad any kind of association with another woman. In his youth, when he was still poor and serving in the army, he never made any complaint about the way he was served, but said that it would be shameful to engage in a running battle with a slave about one's stomach. But later on, when he was richer, he gave dinner-parties for his friends and fellow magistrates; and immediately after the meal he used to whip any slaves who had imperfectly prepared or served anything. He continually tried to arrange for his slaves to quarrel and argue, and was suspicious and scared if they agreed amongst themselves. He would try those who were accused of a crime which warranted the death penalty in the presence of all the other dependants, and have them killed if they were found guilty.[39]

[III]

The First Slave War
in Sicily

The first slave war in Sicily had its beginning in Enna, a city ancient writers called "the navel of Sicily" in view of its central location in the island's mountainous interior. It was a city rich in religious associations, for it was close by, so the myths said, that Persephone had once been carried off to the underworld, and both she and her mother Demeter remained the focus of worship in the city well into historical times: the townspeople indeed believed that Demeter continued to dwell among them, and Cicero knew from personal experience in Sicily that Enna was still regarded in his day as the goddess's special sanctuary. He described Enna as a city "built on a lofty eminence, the top of which is a table-land, watered by perennial springs, and bounded in every direction by precipitous cliffs, round which are numerous lakes and copses, and flowers in profusion at all seasons," while to Livy it was a place of "remarkable natural defences," "perched on a lofty site with cliffs on every side." Myth might be invoked to explain the natural prosperity of the region in which Enna was located. But at an elevation of some nine hundred and fifty meters above sea level the city also enjoyed the advantage of commanding a strong strategic position, controlling swift lines of communication with the coasts of Sicily and forming in effect a natural mountain fortress. Before the slave war Enna had had little direct involvement with Rome: early in the First Punic War, in 258 B.C., it was captured from the Carthaginians, and in the Second Punic War, in 214 B.C., Enna was prepared to defect from Rome until the slaughter of its male population by the commander L. Pinarius prevented such an eventuality—and guaranteed notoriety for Pinarius well into the future. But almost another century was to elapse before the city again impinged on Rome's consciousness.[1]

Sicily had become Rome's first overseas province in the wake of the first war against Carthage (264 B.C.–241 B.C.). Yet at first the area of subjection did not comprise the whole island: in eastern Sicily the territory of the petty king Hiero, whose rule was based on the great city of

Syracuse, was left alone as a result of the king's loyalty in the war. But the subsequent revival of Carthage that led to the second long struggle against Rome (218 B.C.–201 B.C.) brought a logical Carthaginian ambition to recover its former interests in Sicily, and in the period from 215 B.C. to 210 B.C. Rome in effect was forced to conquer the island anew. As the massacre at Enna demonstrates, that process brought destruction and hardship to the Sicilian cities. But victory was followed by complete possession. Hiero died in 215 B.C., and Syracuse was captured in 211 B.C. The following year, after the fall of Agrigentum, the consul M. Valerius Laevinus reported to the Roman senate that Sicily was now fully in Rome's control and that all Carthaginians had been expelled; the land, he said, was again being cultivated so that Sicily could not only feed itself but supply Rome with grain as well. It was Sicily's enormous agricultural prosperity, earning it the soubriquet "Rome's storehouse," that was to prove the province's greatest material asset to Rome.[2]

The prosperity of Sicily drew comment from Diodorus Siculus and Florus in their accounts of the origins of the first slave war. A land "so rich in grain," the latter wrote, Sicily "was occupied by large estates [latifundia] in the possession of Roman citizens. The numerous prisons for slaves [ergastula] employed in tilling the soil and gangs of cultivators who worked in chains provided the forces for the war." As might be expected from knowledge of Sicily's continuing function as a supplier of grain to Rome in the second century and beyond, the emphasis in Florus's remarks falls on the cereal production aspect of the Sicilian economy; and from a later era Cicero's speeches against the corrupt C. Verres, governor of Sicily from 73 B.C. to 71 B.C., display a similar and consistent interest, with abundant and exhaustive detail. But Diodorus, who provides the fullest account of the rebellion, concentrates his attention on slaves used in pastoral farming: large numbers of slaves were bought up by the wealthy, and the young especially managed their herds of livestock, having to resort to brigandage in order to guarantee survival. It was from this source of slaves, in this version, that material for revolt came, and Strabo was equally confident about the widespread herding of livestock before the first slave war.[3]

The accuracy of Diodorus has been impugned and the notion of extensive pastoral farming in Sicily in the second century dismissed. But such a radical view is hardly necessary. Sicily had long enjoyed a reputation for sheep and cattle breeding and for the raising of horses, so Diodorus's specific statement that the rebel slave leader Cleon was a horse breeder makes perfect sense within that context. Moreover, Diodorus's information, given its truncated form, cannot be expected to provide anything like a complete picture of the Sicilian economy immediately before the slave war. Even so, Diodorus does not say that purchased slaves were used exclusively as herders but indicates that those who were not young were used in whatever ways their owners felt useful; the language is admittedly vague, but it surely allows for the use of slaves in arable farming as well as in domestic service. Like Florus, Diodorus knew that some slaves were kept in chains and so recognized the presence in Sicily of nonpastoral workers, since herders were simply unable to function if shackled. Further, the rhetorical nature of Cicero's evidence on the Sicilian economy in his speeches against C. Verres equally precludes a full description of local farming practices in the period of Verres's governorship. So despite the wealth of details Cicero gives on cereal cultivation, his casual allusions to pastoral farming and individuals who practiced mixed farming have to be given prominence. There is therefore no reason to doubt that Damophilus of Enna, among whose slaves revolt first broke out, was anything but typical of Sicilian magnates in using some of his slaves, as Diodorus says, in managing livestock and keeping others in chains and housed in *ergastula*, that is, as arable workers. Sicily in the second half of the second century was not restricted to a single mode of economic production.[4]

The unique evidence of Cicero's speeches provides a glimpse of the extent of slaveowning in Sicily some two generations after the first slave war. Cicero remarks that the Roman governors of Sicily customarily traveled through the island in midsummer on tours of inspection, because immediately after the grain harvest, at threshing time, the slave workers were all assembled together and could be easily counted. He mentions specific slaveowners: three brothers from Centuripe, victims of Verres's henchman Q. Apronius, who owned grain lands, livestock, and slaves; C. Matrinius, a Roman knight, whose *vilici* and *pastores* receive attention; and Apollonius of Panormus, whose wealth Cicero says was invested in, among other things, his slave *familia* and livestock and who was charged by Verres with having a *magister pecoris* who had fomented unrest among slaves—though no such person actually existed. Another slaveowner, Eumenides of Halicyae, had a *vilicus* who was charged on Verres's initiative with conspiring to rebel; and the slaves of Leonidas of Triocala—as too those of Aristodamus of Apollonia and Leon of Imachara—were also suspected of revolt, though Verres recoiled from punishing them. Perhaps about 97 B.C. the governor L. Domitius Ahenobarbus had executed a slave *pastor* for illegally carrying and using a hunting spear. These references convey a strong impression of the widespread use of slave labor in Sicilian agriculture, and the distinctions of servile status implicit in Cicero's terminology can be noted. But Cicero's evidence occasionally points to the use of slaves in domestic service in Sicily as well. He tells of high-priced slaves who were inherited by Heraclius of Syracuse and stolen by Verres (some were kept, others sold); and of Agonis, a former slave of Venus at Eryx, who became wealthy enough to own slave musicians until they were sold off and Agonis herself reenslaved by Q. Caecilius Niger, Verres's quaestor in 72 B.C. All in all, therefore, the Sicilian slave population of the late seventies must be understood to have been very multifarious in composition, its character being controlled by the types of occupation slaves fulfilled and the degree of their individual inurement to slavery.[5]

As far as can be told, an identical situation prevailed in the late second century, just as in Italy itself. The use of slave personnel in the two main branches of farming has already been noted, both in general terms and in the particular case of Damophilus, who also had a considerable retinue of domestic slaves according to Diodorus, including perhaps costly slaves comparable to those of Heraclius of Syracuse and the musicians of Agonis: so Diodorus says, "He would proceed about the countryside accompanied by a retinue of expensive horses and four-wheeled carts and a paramilitary escort formed by his own slaves. In addition, he thought it very prestigious to have lots of beautiful boys and a crowd of uneducated hangers-on." Damophilus had clearly assembled for himself a domestic entourage of the Plautine type, and Diodorus knew of the Italian influence that controlled his ostentatious display. Cicero has little to say about the origins of Sicilian slaves in his day. But a passing statement makes plain that traders regularly brought slaves from the eastern Mediterranean to the ports of Sicily, and it is likely that much of the Sicilian slave population at the time of the first slave war was in fact composed of first-generation slaves brought from overseas. Since continuous warfare and trade provided the means by which slaves were transported to the Roman heartland, it is perfectly credible that Damophilus, representing in microcosm general practices among his landowning peers in Sicily, purchased slaves for his own use who had been free in their countries of origin and reduced, as Diodorus says, to slavery by warfare. The details that the slave leader Eunus and his female companion were Syrians from Apamea-on-the-Orontes and that Cleon, another leader, and presumably his brother Comanus too, was from Cilicia form part of a larger pattern of servile recruitment that is unimpeachable. But the knowledge that Eunus had a female consort and that Damophilus's wife Megallis had maidservants in her household opens up the possibility that already servile reproduction was a vital means of producing new slaves in Sicily, again as in Rome and Italy.[6]

Slavery was not of course new to Sicily in the second century: in view of the island's cultural orientation within the Hellenistic world, the situation could hardly be otherwise. But after the Roman reconquest the scale of slaveowning in Sicily had increased dramatically, both as a particular result of the presence of settlers from Italy and under the general impact of Roman rule. In his remarks on the condition of Sicily before the first slave war, Diodorus comments on the extent of landowning and slaveowning by Roman knights and equates the lifestyles of the wealthy Sicilians with those of their Italian counterparts, Damophilus serving as his specific point of reference. The actual degree of Italian settlement in Sicily after 210 B.C. cannot be accurately measured, though the signs of a growing Italian presence are clear enough. As early as 205 B.C. Scipio Africanus had to judge disputes over the ownership of land at Syracuse and restored to Syracusans properties they claimed had been appropriated from them by Italians in the recent war. In 199 B.C. C. Sergius Plautus was authorized to distribute land to troops who had served in Sicily; and probably in 193 B.C. a body of Italians set up an honorific statue at Halaesa to the praetor L. Cornelius Scipio, presumably in return for his promotion of their interests. Yet apart from permanent settlers, Sicily in the second century was equally affected by increasing visits from the peninsula of *negotiatores* and by the constant intrusion of the Roman governor and his staff, who represented the permanence of Roman rule that guaranteed a peace conducive to economic revival. The net effect was the importation to the island of the contemporary pattern of Roman slaveowning, which could be emulated—both for reasons of social ostentation and economic purposes—by Sicilian magnates such as Damophilus or the later Q. Caecilius Niger (himself a Sicilian) who benefited from Sicily's overall success. In its scale and complexity slaveowning in Sicily, whether by Italian resident aliens or indigenous elites, fully matched the Roman model.[7]

Servile living conditions in Sicily immediately before the outbreak of the first slave war are described by Diodorus in very bleak terms, so bleak in fact that it is tempting to regard them as exaggerated in view of the "morality tale" nature of his account of the war, in which the overweening pride and arrogance of the slaveowners are judged the cause of their destruction. Specifically, Diodorus records that on one occasion Damophilus, in response to a request for clothing from his naked domestic slaves, encouraged them to steal clothes from travelers and had them flogged for their impertinence. In general terms, he stresses that the huge numbers of slaves bought on the open market were branded by their new owners, that some were put in shackles and others beaten, and that all suffered from insufficient supplies of food and clothing. His information cannot be controlled through comparison with the other sources on the slave war, since all are deficient on the topic of servile material conditions. Indirectly, however, his remarks can be set in perspective.[8]

Evidence of the habitual physical abuse to which slaves were subjected in later periods of Roman history is so abundant that a detailed demonstration of the fact is hardly necessary. Equally, sexual exploitation of slave property was a natural consequence of Roman slaveowning. In their own eras such sadistic figures as P. Vedius Pollio and Larcius Marcedo came to stand as stereotypes of the cruel slaveowner (much now like Damophilus), representing not necessarily a typical exercise of brutality but pointing up nonetheless a possible degree of excess open to any slaveowner, against whose arbitrary application of punishment slaves had little effective recourse under the law. In an earlier age the plays of Plautus are full of the language of beating, shackling, and otherwise maltreating slaves, and no serious doubt can be entertained that this terminology echoes a social reality familiar to Plautus's audience despite the comic effects to which he puts it. Moreover, it has already been seen that Cato assumed the presence on the farm of chained slaves and that he flogged negligent domestics; he also recommended the sale of old and sickly slaves. Altogether therefore there are no grounds for rejecting as implausible what Diodorus has to say on the violence with which slaves in Sicily were treated.[9]

As far as clothing is concerned, Cato gives some idea of what were acceptable allowances for slave workers in his day in the *De Agricultura*. He instructed the *vilicus* to make sure that the farm slaves did not suffer from the cold and advised that the members of the *familia* should be issued with a new tunic, mantle, and pair of wooden shoes every other year, a prescription that sounds spartan indeed. But the type of wooden shoe to which Cato refers was known also to Plautus, and the tunic and mantle appear in a list of clothing items for slaves in a later legal source. Cato's recommendations will not therefore have been untypical of real practice. In any case, such clothing was perhaps preferable to the skins of wolves and wild boars that Diodorus says were worn by the brigand *pastores* in Sicily, an improvised form of clothing rather than finished and regularly distributed garments. Certainly the dress of slaves must often have been of inferior quality, no more than adequate, and so very distinctive in appearance; otherwise, the various anecdotes found in Greek and Roman authors of free persons who disguised themselves as slaves have little point. Doubtless the domestics who made up the retinues of upper-class grandees like Damophilus were at times sumptuously rigged out in order to advertise their owners' opulence. But for rural slaves this was obviously an unnecessary extravagance.[10]

As for food, Cato recommended a monthly ration of four *modii* of wheat for each slave in winter and four and a half *modii* in summer. The *vilicus*, *vilica*, *epistata*, and *opilio*, however, were to receive only three *modii*, apparently because less physical labor was required of them in their jobs. The grain was used for making bread. But slaves who were kept in chains had no access to facilities for grinding and baking and so were apportioned amounts of bread already made, four pounds a day, so it seems, in winter, five pounds when working the vines. Cato also recommended allocations of low-grade wine, olives, oil, and salt, observing that ten quadrantals of wine a year and one *modius* of salt were sufficient for each person. Again Cato's *vilicus* was told to ensure that the slaves did not go hungry, so the coarse rations described may be considered reasonable if not generous: Cato was after all a frugal estate manager. Cato's grain rations compare favorably in fact with the three *modii* of wheat issued monthly to the legionary soldier of the middle Republic and the monthly allocation of five *modii* distributed to the *plebs frumentaria* in the late Republic. Moreover, Seneca also used the figure of five *modii* of grain to connote the standard food allowance for the slave. "In dietetic terms," it has been noted, "a ration of 5 modii per month may have been equivalent to 3,000–3,500 calories per day, which is close to modern ideals of 3,300 calories per day for male adults," though some historians believe that this allowance provided more than a single individual's minimal needs. The emphasis here, however, must fall on minimal needs, for the grain distributions at Rome were meant to supplement purchases of other foodstuffs, and Seneca's slave was paid as well as fed. What food supplies the slaves in Sicily received cannot be determined from Diodorus. But his statement that *pastores* had supplies of milk and meat available to them, presumably from the livestock in their charge, implies that this particular category of slave workers had to fend for themselves to a large extent without being able to depend on regular distributions of food; and when rations were supplied they cannot in all likelihood have exceeded the subsistence level of Cato's allowances.[11]

Somewhat surprisingly, Cato and even the later Roman writers on agriculture had little to say about the living quarters of the slaves whose labor they took for granted. Cato himself assumed that a newly built villa was to include cells for the slaves (*cellae familiae*), presumably rooms principally for sleeping purposes, whereas Varro simply spoke of a resting place that would allow for comfortable recovery from the fatigue of work or adverse weather without specifying its nature. In a little more detail, Columella drew a distinction between the accommodations of chained and unchained slaves in the *rustica pars* of the villa, the area devoted to storage and housing facilities for animals and the workforce: the latter were to be put in *cellae*, the former in a subterranean *ergastulum* with windows beyond hands' reach. Still referring to the *villa rustica* apparently, Columella also spoke of cells for herdsmen and shepherds that gave swift access to the animals they worked with. A barracks-like situation is implied, involving a certain communal way of life, especially when meals were taken in a large kitchen. Varro and Columella both recommended that the lodging of the *vilicus* should be so situated that the comings and goings of the slave workers could be supervised.[12]

Slaves' living space can be somewhat better understood from the plans of Italian villas produced from archaeological discoveries, though it has to be kept in mind that identification of slave quarters in excavated farmhouses must always remain conjectural, and unfortunately the most spectacular examples postdate the era of the first slave war. Thus the two separate sets of slave accommodations identified in successive phases of the grand villa at Settefinestre near ancient Cosa in southern Etruria belong to the period marked by Caesar and Trajan. Here a row of cells in the *villa rustica* housed first, so it has been proposed, a complement of between fifty and sixty slaves, with some of the individual rooms sleeping four or even six people; later the completely new slave complex, a rectangular block set around an independent courtyard, may have catered for twice that number. The rows of cells at Settefinestre clearly consist with the barracks-like impressions conveyed by the literary evidence, though the cells' dimensions (3.0 m × 3.0 m; 3.0 m × 3.5 m) seem slightly more generous than in other examples. Two villas long known from southern Campania, for instance, had more compact dimensions (2.8 m × 1.9 m; 3.0 m × 2.0 m, approximately): in the former, each room had a floor of beaten earth, plain plastered walls, one window, a place for a lamp, and a small hearth. The more recently excavated and relatively small farmhouse at Posto in northern Campania had similar units (3.0 m × 2.5 m; 2.6 m × 2.5 m), while at the neighboring villa of San Rocco a commons area in the *villa rustica* is thought to have provided space for slaves in which to work, eat, and sleep, a view in keeping with the sense of communal living noticed in the literary sources. Obviously enough, the housing arrangements at these and other sites imply little more than rudimentary facilities, with privacy, especially for familial intimacy, almost completely lacking. Moreover, the situation can have been little different at the time of the first slave war: the Posto villa and that at San Rocco, an equally modest working farm in its earliest stage, as well as the villa Sambuco northwest of Veii in southern Etruria all came into existence in the late second century or early first century, and all three villas have been regarded as reflections of the spread of slave-based agriculture in central Italy suggested by Cato's farming manual. The discovery of iron stocks in the two southern Campanian villas, almost certainly for the confinement of slave workers, affords grim corroboration of the literary allusions to chains and fetters.[13]

If then it is assumed that similar factors obtained in Sicily, it is not surprising that Diodorus saw a direct connection between the harsh material conditions of life enjoyed by the slaves in Sicily and the extent of brigandage in the province before the outbreak of revolt. Being physically strong, having at their disposal weapons such as clubs and spears (technically for the defense of their herds), and enjoying in the nature of their work considerable freedom of movement, the *pastores* in particular turned easily to murder and theft under the impulse of hunger and need, attacking travelers and raiding estates at night to obtain the necessities their owners denied them. Clothed in the skins of animals and invigorated by their diet of meat and milk, their packs of dogs accompanying them, the *pastores* presented a terrifying aspect and made travel at night utterly impossible. They came to operate throughout the island, so it seemed to Diodorus, like paramilitary or guerrilla forces, and although not directly comparable, since total independence from their masters had not been achieved, their activities quite clearly had much in common with the social banditry practiced by the maroons of modern slave societies. Further, attempts at repression on the part of Roman governors were of no avail: pressure exercised on them by the wealthy slaveowners preempted their efforts, and the owners simply connived at and encouraged the illegalities of their *pastores* because they themselves benefited from them.[14]

The development of pastoral farming in Sicily after the Roman reconquest was an extension of an identical trend in southern Italy, where, as seen already, an uprising of slaves had occurred as early as 185 B.C. According to Livy, the Bruttii had a generic reputation for innate lawlessness, and in one tradition their very origin as a people was to be found among bands of marauding fugitive slaves who had once carved out territory for themselves in Lucania by violent means. However that may be, the pastoral slaves of Lucania and Apulia have a long history of involvement in violence in the first century B.C. and the first century A.D. It seemed to the supporters of L. Sergius Catilina in 63 B.C., for example, that there was fodder here for their conspiracy, while in the civil war with Caesar, Cn. Pompeius did not hesitate to turn *pastores* into cavalry when at Brundisium. Nor was it simply a question of pastoralists: the *ergastula* could be opened and their inmates let loose in the service of political aspirants. But it was the *pastores* especially who were regarded as the natural fuel of altercations, to be manipulated by the elite for private gain as well as political support. In 71 B.C. Cicero delivered a speech, the *Pro Tullio*, that survives only in fragments. But its interest is considerable, for the speech "takes us into the wild hill-country of Lucania" where "we find cattle-barons and their hired hands, armed slaves that is, raiding and plundering each other's herds and homesteads." Cicero's client, M. Tullius, had in fact had his villa in the region of Thurii destroyed and his slaves murdered by an armed band belonging to a certain P. Fabius, though Tullius's own slave *pastores* were capable of similar atrocities. Later, in A.D. 24, an abortive uprising of pastoralists at Brundisium and neighboring towns was led by a renegade member of the praetorian guard, and in A.D. 54 the credible charge could be leveled at a member of the imperial family that her slaves in Calabria were threatening the peace of Italy.[15]

From the early second century onwards, therefore, there was a close association in the south of Italy between pastoralism and "chronic brigandage," and in view of the similarity of conditions and geographical proximity, Diodorus's description of lawlessness in Sicily before the first slave war is not to be distrusted. In many ways, *pastores* could be regarded as a "class apart." Varro knew that they had to be given arms and had to be able to use them as they moved their herds from one place of pasturage to another. The distances involved in transhumance were considerable:

Varro refers to the movement of sheep from Apulia into Samnium and speaks of flocks he owned spending the winter in Apulia and the summer in the mountains around Reate. The constant danger, however, was that on their travels the slaves would turn their axes, sickles, and javelins against free society, a point the landowner always had to keep in mind when contemplating construction of a new villa. In addition, those who tended the migrant herds could provide cover for fugitive slaves escaping from the towns and regions through which they passed, so an inscription from Saepinum of *circa* A.D. 170 suggests. According to Varro again, certain areas of Sardinia and Spain were not regions that were safe for development; he probably knew that the same was true of Sicily as well.[16]

The principal figure of the first slave war, however, was not a herder but the wonderworker Eunus, a domestic slave in all likelihood, who belonged to a certain Antigenes of Enna. By birth he was a Syrian from the city of Apamea-on-the-Orontes and so belonged in the xenophobic Roman view to a race of natural slaves. How he had come to be located in Enna is not known. Presumably he was the victim of piracy and the slave trade. How long he had been in Enna before the war began is also unknown, though he may at one stage have had some experience of life in the *ergastula*. But it is clear that Eunus had brought to Sicily with him a deep devotion to the Syrian mother goddess Atargatis (Astarte) that was not abandoned in his new locale. Diodorus describes him as follows:

> This man was something of a magician and wonder-worker. He pretended that he could foretell the future by means of commands that came to him from the gods when he was asleep, and because he was so good at this he managed to deceive a lot of people. He went on from there and did not just prophesy on the basis of dreams, but even pretended to have visions of the gods while awake and hear from them what was going to happen. Of the many fantasies he invented some happened to come true. Since no one refuted those that did not, while those that did turn out true were widely acclaimed, his reputation increased enormously. In the end he would produce fire and flame from his mouth while in a trance, by means of a trick of some sort, and in this way produce inspired utterances about the future. What he did was put some fire and the fuel needed to keep it going inside a walnut or something similar which had had holes bored into it at both ends; then he would put it into his mouth and breathe and thus produce sparks or even a flame. Before the revolt he said that the Syrian Goddess was appearing to him and promising him that he was going to be a king. He insisted on repeating this not just to others but even to his own master.[17]

Diodorus was obviously skeptical about Eunus's miraculous and prophetic powers. But it would be a mistake to assume that Eunus's contemporaries were all unimpressed by his claims and so to dismiss Eunus merely as a charlatan. Florus, though similarly incredulous, correctly perceived that the flame trick could be turned to advantage when a propitious time for inducing slaves to revolt occurred. The important point, however, is that such an advantage could only be realized because of a widespread belief in the miraculous in antiquity, and that within the religious framework of the Greco-Roman world the capacity of gods and men attended by the gods to work wonders was anything but exceptional. Miracles could of course be fabricated quite unscrupulously. Late in the second century A.D. Lucian of Samosata told the story of Alexander of Abonoteichus, who convinced the local townspeople and many others of the oracular powers of a miraculously discovered snake that was emblematic of the god Asclepius's apparent move to the city. In fact, the discovery of the amazing snake had been deliberately contrived by Alexander, who used a false head, operated in the manner of a puppet, to make the snake perform— not, in the sequel, without profit and fame to himself. More seriously, however, belief in the curative efficacy of the god Asclepius is well attested in the Hellenistic world, not least by the long sequence of inscriptions from the god's temple at Epidaurus preserving records of cures of various forms of illness and distress. The remedies were imagined to have been effected when patients, asleep at night in the precincts of the temple, were visited by the god through dreams or visions. Further, in the first century B.C. the physician Asclepiades of Prusa was credited with raising the dead, as too the philosopher-magician Apollonius of Tyana in the first century A.D. Such phenomena were not unusual, merely striking.[18]

The cult of the Syrian Goddess demanded of its adherents, especially those who became her priests, a degree of religious fanaticism far more extravagant than anything attributed to Eunus. The priests were typically eunuchs, and again Lucian gave an authentic description of how the act of castration was carried out in his essay on the worship of Atargatis at her main cult center at Hierapolis, close to Apamea:

On appointed days, the crowd assembles at the sanctuary while many Galli and the holy men whom I have mentioned perform the rites. They cut their arms and beat one another on the back. Many stand about them playing flutes, while many others beat drums. Still others sing inspired and sacred songs. This ceremony takes place outside the temple and none of those who performs it enters the temple. On these days, too, men become Galli. For while the rest are playing flutes and performing the rites, frenzy comes upon many, and many who have come simply to watch subsequently perform this act. I will describe what they do. The youth for whom these things lie in store throws off his clothes, rushes to the center with a great shout and takes up a sword, which, I believe, has stood there for this purpose for many years. He grabs it and immediately castrates himself. Then he rushes through the city holding in his hands the parts he has cut off. He takes female clothing and women's adornment from whatever house he throws these parts into. This is what they do at the Castration.

The frenetic dances of Atargatis's priests could be seen elsewhere than at Hierapolis. In an extract from Apuleius's *Metamorphoses*, set in Thessaly, the wild gyrations of a band of mendicant devotees, their garish female dress and facial make-up, the self-biting and cutting induced by their transports, are described in realistic fashion; under the possession of the goddess one particular devotee expiates his perceived offenses through self-flagellation, a variation on the behavior reported by Lucian. In a world, therefore, where the miraculous was unquestionable for most and the ecstatic trance an integral part of the religious fabric, the impact of Eunus on the local population of Enna, which must surely have been familiar with the kinds of events reported by Lucian and Apuleius, is not to be underestimated. At Enna, the fortress city, worship of Demeter was all important. But like Atargatis, Demeter was a manifestation of the Great Mother principle that by the late second century had a long history in the Mediterranean, and assimilation of identities was easy and natural. In a hymn to the Egyptian goddess Isis from *circa* 100 B.C. the point is made plain:

> All mortals who live on the limitless earth,
> Thracians, Greeks, and foreigners as well,
> utter your glorious name which all honour,
> each in his own language, each in his own land.
> Syrians call you Astarte, Artemis, Nanaea,
> the tribes of Lycia call you Queen Leto,
> men in Thrace call you Mother of the gods,
> Greeks call you Hera of the lofty throne, and Aphrodite,
> kindly Hestia, Rheia, and Demeter.
> Egyptians call you Thiouis because you, being One, are all
> the other goddesses named by all peoples.

Given this nexus, the effects of Eunus's transports and claims have to be taken seriously, both among those who worshipped the Great Mother in her local form as Demeter and those, like Eunus, from the eastern Mediterranean who still retained their own traditions of other powerful mother goddesses.[19]

The first slave war began as a small slave revolt, not dissimilar, in essence, from revolts in Italy earlier in the second century. There is no indication that a grand uprising of slaves in Sicily as a whole was contemplated at the outset. In generalized terms, Diodorus states that the slaves in Sicily, motivated by their miserable living conditions and the brutality with which they were treated, discussed revolt before violence actually erupted, a fact that should occasion no surprise because, as in any slave community, such discussions will have served as a device for the release of tensions engendered by slaves' subjection and maltreatment. But nothing is known in detail of these deliberations; nor do they seem to have resulted in comprehensive actions. At Enna, however, the opulent and self-vaunting landowner Damophilus—the owner of a large and diverse complement of slaves—had developed a reputation as a paradigm of the cruel slaveowner. His wife Megallis was equally sadistic in her treatment of the slaves they owned, and it was among the latter that general servile discontent came to a head. A plot was formed to kill the couple, but before translating their plan of revenge-seeking into action the slave dissidents sought and received divine approval for their enterprise from the wonderworker Eunus. The number and the identities of the slaves involved in this approach to Eunus are unknown, but acting on his advice of immediate action the slaves broke open some of the local *ergastula*, set free the inmates, rounded up other slaves, and assembled a force of some four hundred outside the city at night.[20]

The religious sanction for revolt provided by the authority and presence of Eunus was confirmed when the slave rebels took oaths among themselves and performed sacrifices. Then, with whatever arms they were able to acquire and with Eunus working his miracle of fire, the force burst into Enna in the middle of the night and set about murdering its slave-owning residents and their families. At once a large number of slaves from within the city joined the insurgents, attacking first their own masters then others. But Damophilus and Megallis could not be found. It was learned that they were in fact outside the city, probably in one of the several extra-urban residences they owned, so some of the rebels were sent to find them and brought them back to Enna in bonds. After the first wave of killings the rebels had congregated in the city's theater—the site, as it happens, of the slaughter of 214 B.C.—and there, not without effect, Damophilus began to speak in defense of himself and his wife, as though the couple were on trial. The authority of a slaveowner over his inferiors was not easily destroyed. But before matters could proceed further two slaves named Hermeias and Zeuxis, men particularly hostile to Damophilus according to Diodorus, killed him, one piercing him with a sword, the other decapitating him with an axe. In contrast, however, the daughter of Damophilus and Megallis was spared through the agency of the same Hermeias. The young woman had in the past been kindly disposed to the slaves abused by her parents, and so now she was not violated, as other women had already been, but was escorted under the leadership of Hermeias to the eastern coastal city of Catina where she had relatives. In a much later age Toussaint L'Ouverture is similarly said to have saved the wife of the manager of his plantation before embarking on revolt.[21]

While still in the theater at Enna the slave rebels next took the momentous step of declaring Eunus their king, an action that responded to the religious aura that surrounded him, his instigation of the first successful assault, and the rebels' anticipation that he would henceforward prove a beneficent leader. Eunus quickly consolidated his position, both through the exercise of terror and in a symbolic way. He called an assembly of the slaves and ordered further executions, sparing only those citizens skilled in manufacturing arms (they were put to work in chains) and those who, as Antigenes's guests in former times, had shown him sympathy and kindness when he had been compelled to entertain them with his magic (they were set free). Eunus also killed his own owners, Antigenes and Pytho, and permitted some of her maidservants to dispose of Megallis, who was tortured before being hurled to her death from a height. Beyond these savage reprisals, however, Eunus took a diadem and regal dress, called his female companion his queen, appointed royal councillors, one of whom was a Greek called Achaeus, and conferred on himself the Seleucid dynastic name of Antiochus. Three days after the initial attack on Enna an armed force of more than six thousand rebels was brought into existence, according to Diodorus, and attacks on the neighboring countryside began.[22]

The extent of marauding conducted by Eunus and his force, which was further increased by a number of slaves still relying on various tools and implements as makeshift weapons, cannot be determined from Diodorus's narrative. Equally vague is his statement that Eunus enrolled new adherents to the rebellion and defeated Roman commanders by virtue of his superior numbers, which were soon more than ten thousand. The whole of Diodorus's account of the course of events after the attack on Enna, although leaving a clear impression that the original revolt soon escalated into a serious and full-scale movement of servile resistance, lacks substantive details, especially of chronological matters; indeed, the very year in which the revolt at Enna took place is unknown, with every year from 141 B.C. to 135 B.C. being a possibility. But it is certain that the war to which the revolt led came to an end in 132 B.C., and on the most reasonable estimate, the first slave rebellion in Sicily covered an impressively long period of five years or so. Given the state of the evidence, however, any attempt to indicate the main lines of development through these years must in some measure be speculative.[23]

Nevertheless, one of the key elements in the process of escalation was a secondary revolt in southern Sicily, led by the slave Cleon, that began within a month of the uprising at Enna. An experienced brigand as well as a horse breeder, Cleon, as seen earlier, came originally from the Taurus region of Cilicia and had arrived in Sicily perhaps early in his life, accompanied by his brother Comanus, a figure later to die a heroic death in the war. Having heard of Eunus's revolt, Cleon persuaded other slaves to join him in a new outbreak and he immediately overran Agrigentum and the neighboring region with a force said by Diodorus to have numbered five thousand, a far more realistic figure than the seventy thousand given in the Livian tradition. There were hopes, presumably among the magnates of Sicily, that the two rebel groups would prove each other's undoing, and in view of the divisions naturally inherent in the slave population those hopes cannot have been ill-founded. But unpredictably Cleon acknowledged the superior authority of Eunus, acting as a general to his king, and their two forces combined into one united body.[24]

As revolt spread, various cities fell into the rebels' control, and rhetorical claims appear in the sources that all of Sicily was in danger of being overwhelmed. To accept those claims, however, is to share the assumptions of the sources on what the rebels hoped to achieve from their insurrection, assumptions that cannot be weighed against any evidence from the slaves themselves. The fact remains that apart from Enna, which must have remained the chief center of resistance throughout, only Tauromenium on the northeastern coast, Catina in the east (the refuge of Damophilus's daughter), and Morgantina in the interior are actually mentioned by name in the sources as bases of servile resistance. Of Agrigentum, nothing further is heard after Cleon's first attack, while Messana is specifically said by Orosius not to have been involved at all because of the slaves' good treatment there. Whether Syracuse was affected is an open question. A passage in Diodorus refers to people "who ate the sacred fish" finding no relief from their suffering because they were visited by the anger of the presiding deity. The passage could be explained by Diodorus's earlier description of the fountain of Arethusa at Syracuse, on the island sacred to Artemis, that contained large numbers of fish "considered to be holy and not to be touched by men." "On many occasions," Diodorus states, "when certain men have eaten them amid stress of war, the deity has shown a striking sign, and has visited with great sufferings such as dared to take them for food." Diodorus also signified his intention, when writing these remarks, to observe the various desecrations at the appropriate points of his work. The later passage may then refer to the theft of fish by rebel slaves and so indicate that Syracuse was brought within the sphere of the rebellion. On the other hand, since sacred pools and fish were common elements in the worship of Atargatis, there may have been places other than Syracuse in Sicily to which Diodorus's comment could apply. Therefore, although it cannot be denied that other cities may have been involved, the area certainly affected by the rebels appears to have been southeastern Sicily from a line drawn from Agrigentum in the south through Enna to Tauromenium in the north, approximately, that is, half of the island at most. That was not an inconsiderable area, however, and by 134 B.C., when the consul C. Fulvius Flaccus took command of the Roman response, the rebels had maintained the upper hand here against a whole sequence of praetorian governors who had tried to deal with the rebels in the previous four-year period. A brief but indignant notice in Florus states that the rebels captured Roman camps and drove the praetorian generals from the field of battle. The disgraced men were Manlius, perhaps A. Manlius Torquatus, who was later known to have uttered a brave witticism when besieging the rebels at an unidentified city; Lentulus, perhaps L. Cornelius Lentulus, the consul of 130 B.C.; Piso, that is, L. Calpurnius Piso Frugi, who as the consul of 133 B.C. was later to participate again in the slave war; and Hypsaeus, that is, L. Plautius Hypsaeus, who, when recently arrived from Rome and at the head of eight thousand Sicilian troops, is said by Diodorus to have suffered a defeat shortly after the time of Cleon's amalgamation with Eunus. At that point Diodorus gives the total number of slave rebels as twenty thousand, rising soon thereafter to two hundred thousand; he also reports other rebel successes, but without specific details.[25]

Despite the presence of a senior magistrate in Sicily in 134 B.C., and just possibly with the war affecting adversely the supply of grain to Rome, in 133 B.C. Rome sent another consul to Sicily, L. Calpurnius Piso Frugi. Although later Piso had the reputation of having liberated Sicily from the slave war, his campaigns were not successful in all respects. The subordinate cavalry commander C. Titius was at one point surrounded by rebels and compelled to surrender arms to them, an action that brought severe disciplinary measures from Piso for both Titius and the men in his command. But Piso, whose son fought under his command with distinction, was able to recover Morgantina, allegedly killing eight thousand rebel slaves; and he also laid siege to Enna, a fact known from the discovery there of slingshots bearing his name and office. When Piso's year of office expired, therefore, the Roman position appears to have improved significantly in comparison with previous years. But the war was by no means over, and the slaves continued to find ways to maintain their resistance.[26]

In 132 B.C. P. Rupilius, the third consul to lead the Roman effort against the rebels, finally brought an end to the slave war by capturing the two strongest centers of resistance, Tauromenium and Enna. Twenty thousand slaves are said to have died in consequence. Rupilius operated first at Tauromenium, heavily investing the city and reducing the rebels to cannibalism. At one point, so Diodorus records, Cleon's brother Comanus attempted to escape from Tauromenium but was captured; Valerius Maximus adds the information that the man he simply calls Coma was subsequently interrogated but persisted in his resistance by taking his own life. Valerius seems to place these events after the later fall of Enna, so perhaps Comanus was taken by Rupilius to the last site of rebellion once Tauromenium had fallen, an eventuality that, as in previous slave revolts, depended in the last resort on betrayal by a rebel, a Syrian slave named Sarapion in this case. The captives were tortured and executed. But the siege had been difficult, and a hint of Rupilius's lack of complete success may be contained in Valerius Maximus's further report that the consul ordered his son-in-law Q. Fabius to leave Sicily because through his negligence the citadel of Tauromenium had been lost.[27]

From Tauromenium, nevertheless, Rupilius proceeded to Enna, where the siege conducted the previous year by Piso may never have been interrupted. Florus credits a certain Perperna, probably M. Perperna, the future consul of 130 B.C., with responsibility for the final siege of Enna and, indeed, with the termination of the war, claiming that Perperna defeated the rebels, reduced them by starvation, and put the survivors in chains before crucifying them. The defeat may have been that suffered by Cleon, who left Enna during the siege with a small force to give battle but was killed. But apparently the Romans fought on two simultaneous fronts in 132 B.C., with Perperna continuing the work of Piso at Enna before Rupilius's arrival from Tauromenium. Even then, however, Enna remained impregnable and like Tauromenium only fell to Rome through betrayal from within. It was at this juncture presumably that the priests sent to Enna from Rome to expiate the murder of Ti. Gracchus, the radical tribune of 133 B.C., were able to gain access to the shrine of Demeter.[28]

In the company of a thousand bodyguards Eunus the king escaped. But knowing that Rupilius was in pursuit and that their fate was inevitable, the bodyguards beheaded each other in preference to capture. Then with four attendants, a cook, a baker, a masseur, and an entertainer, Eunus himself was extricated from the cave in which he had taken refuge and was put under arrest. He was not executed but later died an unpleasant death, at Morgantina in one tradition, at Rome itself in another, having contracted a wasting disease, perhaps scabies. After his capture, Rupilius is said to have quickly removed all remnants of the rebellion from the province.[29]

The record of the war's events is clearly imperfect, with the preponderance of information concentrated on its beginning. But the basic pattern observable in the early stages is that of disaffection in one household swiftly leading, against a backdrop of general discontent, to a wider revolt among the slaves of Enna once Damophilus's slaves had taken the initiative and, with the cooperation of Eunus, decided to act. The single motivation visible in Diodorus's account of events is the rebels' wish to secure violent revenge against their masters for the cruelty with which they were habitually treated and the desperation of their material conditions. Moreover, the account of Diodorus seems to indicate that slaves normally resident both within and outside the city were implicated, including women; and while a simple equation between urban and domestic, on one hand, and external and rural, on the other, is too simple, still the degree of servile alienation was deep enough to penetrate the boundaries of servile status. It appears too that spontaneity was the key ingredient in converting the attack of the four hundred into a more general uprising, for the original insurgents did not plan to extend their revenge-seeking beyond Enna. Weapons were at first in short supply and had to be improvised, and it was not until the objective of murdering the cruel slaveowners had been realized and the strength of the rebel force had become apparent that the need for a longer sighted strategy arose. Then, at a very significant point, the slaves reacted to their initial and rather easy success—the slaveowners at Enna seem to have been taken completely by surprise—by elevating Eunus to a much more formal position of leadership than he had enjoyed when Enna was first put under assault, and it was Eunus who saw that order had to be imposed on the insurgents. His concern to avoid indiscriminate slaughter of the citizenry at Enna, to set about the acquisition of newly made weapons for the rebels, and to draw on the insight of slaves like Achaeus, who correctly perceived that retaliation for the early murders was bound to occur, became possible only when the rebels achieved a position of strength at Enna. But neither Eunus nor any other of the original rebels could have foreseen that their assault on Enna would have led to total control of the city. The subsequent phase of the revolt's rapid escalation was therefore entirely unpremeditated and unplanned.[30]

As the geographical scope of the rebellion increased, however, the strategy developed by the rebels lay in occupying cities that could be defended against retaliatory forces and provide secure bases from which raids might be conducted. The inland city of Morgantina in the 130s was not perhaps as prosperous as it had been before 211 B.C., when by the authority of the Roman senate it was handed over to Spanish allies as a reward for their loyalty against Carthage. In the Hannibalic war Morgantina had twice revolted against Rome, on the first occasion, in 214 B.C., its inhabitants massacring the Roman garrison stationed there. But from Livy's statement that a large quantity of grain and other supplies had been stockpiled in the city for the use of Roman troops, the logistical potential of Morgantina comes clearly into focus. With its dominant acropolis six hundred meters above sea level rising over the ridge on which it was located, Morgantina was, like Enna, an important crossroads city, controlling the routes from Gela in the south into the northeast of Sicily and from Catina in the east into the mountainous interior. The choice of Morgantina as a rebel base was therefore no more likely to have been fortuitous, once the process of escalation was under way, than that of Tauromenium, another citadel city on the slopes of Mount Tauro, situated roughly at a midpoint on the eastern coastal road from Messana to Catina. In 36 B.C. Octavian was to find that Tauromenium was not an easy city to take. As harbor cities, furthermore, Tauromenium and Catina gave the rebels access to the sea should it be necessary. But the most significant aspect of the occupation of Enna, Morgantina, Tauromenium, and Catina was that it opened up directly to the rebels the rich plain of Leontini, from which continuing supplies of grain could be procured as new slaves joined the rebellion. The four centers could produce supplies locally: Enna and Morgantina had their own grain lands, and Morgantina, Tauromenium, and Catina were all important producers of wines. But it was the plain of Leontini that was renowned for its agricultural fertility, as Cicero makes plain, and control of this region must be regarded as one of the most vital means by which the rebellion was sustained over time.[31]

The duration of the war depended also, however, on the great numbers of rebel forces that came to be involved and on the difficulties Rome's armies had in subduing them. Tauromenium and Enna were captured only by betrayal, at times when practical problems of supply were making themselves felt, and for several years Rome's military efforts appear to have been singularly ineffectual. The actual dimensions of the slave uprising are in the last analysis unknowable of course: the highest figure given by Diodorus for the total of rebels is two hundred thousand, far in excess of the seventy thousand and sixty thousand given by other sources. But unfortunately these numbers are difficult to assess because neither the size of the overall population of Sicily nor that of the servile proportion of the overall population is known. In summary statement, "modern estimates of the total population of Sicily in Cicero's time range between 600,000 and 1,000,000." Since the servile proportion of the Italian population in 225 B.C. can be approximated at 15 percent and in 31 B.C. at 35 percent, on these figures the servile population of Sicily in the 130s might have ranged anywhere from ninety thousand to three hundred and fifty thousand if the overall population were assumed to be approximately the same as in Cicero's age. A rebellion of two hundred thousand slaves is therefore very unlikely. The source tradition, however, is at least internally consistent in conveying the straightforward impression that unprecedented numbers of slaves rose in rebellion, and it seems relatively safe to say that tens of thousands were involved.[32]

Even though a very rough finding, a rebellion of tens of thousands of slaves can be put into some perspective by comparing the approximate scale of the Roman military response. The tide did not begin to turn against the rebels until Piso was put in charge of the war in 134 B.C. In the previous years, the praetors who led the Roman military effort can have had at their disposal no more than a single legion, the normal size of a praetorian army, together with a complementary force of Italian allies. A garrison army was not permanently stationed in Sicily, and Diodorus's statement that Hypsaeus, on his arrival from Rome soon after the revolt at Enna had broken out, used a force against the rebels made up of eight thousand Sicilians implies that he had no regular Roman troops available to him at all. Given the fact that Rome experienced sporadic difficulties of recruitment in the period from 151 B.C. to 133 B.C., together with the range of military dispositions maintained in other theaters of warfare, that inference is not as impossible as it might first seem. The exact size of the Roman legion and of the allied complement in the second half of the second century is disputed. But the legion contained in the order of five thousand troops and the allied contingent was at least as large and probably larger. So the praetors who operated in Sicily before 134 B.C. will have had armies of no less than ten thousand troops, together with cavalry detachments and whatever forces could be raised locally. On any estimate, consequently, the rebel forces substantially outnumbered their opponents, and it is not altogether surprising that Roman commanders suffered a succession of defeats, even if their soldiers were in theory better trained and equipped than the rebels. With the appointment of a consular commander, itself a very strong sign of the seriousness of the slave war, the Roman army automatically doubled in size; and if M. Perperna as propraetor in 132 B.C. headed a separate force from that of the consul Rupilius, the army may have been even greater. At a minimal strength of two legions, however, the army in Sicily from 134 B.C. to 132 B.C. was comparable to those probably serving in the usually more demanding regions of Gaul and Illyricum in the period from 140 B.C. to 136 B.C. and in the Spanish provinces in 132 B.C. The decision to commit and maintain consular armies in Sicily, therefore, reflects not only the scale of the opposition against which they had to contend, but also the rebels' success in sustaining organized resistance over a period of several years.[33]

On any account, then, the first slave uprising in Sicily was of vast proportions, and even in the late stages of the war no real crisis seems to have developed over a shortage of adherents. In fact, it was in all likelihood the size of the slave forces that proved the undoing of the rebellion. There is very little firm evidence to indicate that continuous recruitment of new rebels was consciously adopted as a deliberate policy by leaders such as Eunus, only that efforts were made to organize and harness the energies of those slaves who in the main chose independently to flee from their servitude and to ally themselves with the first dissidents from Enna. The practical forms those efforts took over time, to be examined in detail a little later, must in consequence be viewed as the means by which the nature of the rebellion is best explained. Now, it is sufficient to emphasize that as the numbers involved in the rebellion increased, so too did the problems of feeding, arming, and maintaining coherence among the rebels. The spontaneous growth of the uprising, in other words, created for the slaves of Sicily as many difficulties as their rejection of slavery solved.

[IV]

The Second Slave War
in Sicily

A generation after the upheaval to which the revolt at Enna had led, a second servile insurrection took place in Sicily of equally dramatic scale. The first episode of violence in this new set of events, which are known again chiefly from Diodorus Siculus, occurred in the far west of the island near Halicyae, a small city that lay some thirty-three kilometers east of the major coastal center of Lilybaeum. Unlike Enna, Halicyae was not a city of any especial distinction, and few details survive of its relationship with Rome before 104 B.C., the year in which revolt again broke out. The people of Halicyae had joined the Roman side at the beginning of Rome's first war against Carthage, and it has been suggested that the city was soon made free and exempt from paying tribute to Rome in consequence. Without doubt Halicyae was one of the five Sicilian cities to enjoy such a status in Cicero's day. But in actuality it is highly unlikely that the status was conferred as early as the middle of the third century. Nevertheless, Halicyae was presumably a city of some prosperity: like all of western Sicily it had not been adversely affected by the devastations of the first slave war, and in the first century it was wealthy enough for at least one of its prominent citizens, a certain Eumenides, to become a victim of C. Verres's extortionate demands when his *vilicus* was accused of fostering revolt. The charge brought by Verres was false. But in 104 B.C. the revolt led by thirty slaves who belonged to two other wealthy landowners—they were brothers—was very real indeed.[1]

The thirty slaves, led by a man named Varius, first killed their owners one night while they were asleep and then went to neighboring estates to gather more support for their cause. In all, one hundred and twenty slaves were brought together, and as soon as they had occupied and strengthened a defensible site they were joined by eighty others, who brought weapons with them. P. Licinius Nerva, the Roman governor of Sicily in 104 B.C., responded to these developments by quickly putting the slaves under siege, delayed perhaps only by having to travel across Sicily from Syracuse, the governor's normal seat of residence, and by having to raise troops, apparently local militias, beforehand. Licinius found, however, that he could not capture the rebels' base and so put his hopes of solving his problem in subterfuge. He found aid in the figure of a convicted criminal and brigand, one C. Titinius Gadaeus, who was promised immunity in return for his services. Titinius's reputation for being sympathetic toward slaves was great enough to allow him, accompanied by a band of slaves he could trust, to approach the rebel camp on the pretense that he wished to join the revolt. He was welcomed as an ally and made a rebel general. But Titinius then betrayed the slaves, some of whom died fighting in an engagement, others by their own hand, preferring death to the punishments they anticipated if captured. The revolt at Halicyae thus abruptly ended, and Licinius was able to disband his army.[2]

The revolt at Halicyae was a failure. But obviously servile discontent in Sicily in 104 B.C. was strong enough to impel a serious attempt at violent resistance; and although the slave population cannot generically be assumed to have been ready to give support, the revolt might well have proliferated had it not been for the timely intervention of the governor, who astutely followed earlier precedents of responding promptly to servile disorders. The situation in Sicily as a whole this year, however, was indeed tense, the likelihood of other violent outbursts high; and it was Licinius himself who, in the short run, was mainly responsible for creating a volatile climate of feeling among the slaves on the island. For hopes of a swift release from slavery had been encouraged in some sections of the servile population toward the end of the second century by the passage at Rome of a senatorial decree that banned the maintenance in slavery in a Roman province of any citizen of an allied state. The decree was passed in answer to the claim of the Bithynian king Nicomedes, when a request was put to him for assistance in Rome's war against the Germanic Cimbri, that the bulk of his population had been carried off into slavery by Rome's tax agents. Doubtless the claim was exaggerated: a contingent of Bithynians was soon to be sent to Sicily to fight in the slave war. But at Syracuse Licinius had subsequently begun to implement the decree by listening to petitioners alleging false enslavement—access to the governor must have been readily given and owners compelled to comply—and within a few days some eight hundred persons were set free. Other slaves' expectations of release, however, were cut short when Licinius brought a swift end to his manumission hearings, bowing to pressure exerted on him by Sicilian slaveowners presumably alarmed about the effects on their slave holdings of the governor's actions. They may even have bribed Licinius to further their personal interests. Those slaves still waiting for their cases to be assessed, therefore, were simply dismissed by the governor and ordered to return to their owners. But the petitioners, perhaps having assembled at Syracuse from many points throughout Sicily, fled en masse instead to the shrine of the Palici, about fifty-five kilometers to the northwest in the territory of Leontini, where they entered into discussions of revolt. A minimal hope of manumission, in Sicily as in any community of slaves, served to induce servile compliance and obedience. But when hopes of freedom were raised only to be dashed, the psychological impact on the victims of official inconsistency was disastrous. Licinius had clearly miscalculated his capacity to control the rising expectations of that element of the slave population that had only recently been subjected to slavery.[3]

The Palici were twin deities believed to represent the mysterious force inherent in a volcanic lake and were understood to be deadly "avengers of perjury," yet "friendly powers, promoting the fertility of the land and helping the native population." Most important of all, the shrine of the Palici was a traditional site of asylum for brutalized slaves, the authority of which was still in full force in Diodorus's day:

> This sacred area has also been recognized for some time as a place of sanctuary and has been a source of great aid to luckless slaves who have fallen into the hands of brutal masters; for if they have fled there for refuge, their masters have no power to remove them by force, and they remain there protected from harm until their masters, having gained their consent upon conditions of humane treatment and having given pledges, supported by such oaths, to fulfil their agreements, lead them away. And history records no case, out of all who have given slaves such a pledge as this, of a violation; so faithful to their slaves does the awe in which these gods are held make those who have taken the oath.

It is not known whether those who sought refuge at the shrine benefited from its ancient powers, though their actions are perfectly comprehensible in view of Licinius's culpable behavior. It is possible that negotiations defused the situation, because as seen already it was in the west rather than the east of Sicily that servile discontent first took a violent direction: a connection between the revolt of Halicyae and Licinius's conduct at Syracuse should certainly be granted. But on a longer view the revolt at Halicyae—as too the events that unfolded in the sequel—must also be seen in the context of Sicily's total recovery as a slave society in the generation following the conclusion of the first slave war; for the potentially explosive climate of 104 B.C. was the result above all of the swift restocking of the island with new slaves to replace those lost in the course of the first insurrection.[4]

To mark his success in bringing the first war to a conclusion, P. Rupilius may well have been awarded the honor of a triumph when he returned to Rome from Sicily; certainly M. Perperna is said by Florus to have been granted the lesser but still impressive award of an ovation. If so, Rupilius was the first of a long line of triumphant Roman generals in the interval between the Sicilian slave wars, for from 129 B.C. to 104 B.C. the triumphal records list no fewer than eighteen celebrations of the military distinction, commemorating Roman victories over a variety of external enemies. In the middle and late 120s Rome conducted a series of campaigns against the tribes of southern Gaul, and after 119 B.C. fighting persisted in the Balkans for much of the period. Such efforts accounted for the bulk of the triumphs. But victories were also celebrated in Spain, Sardinia, and the Balearic Islands, as well as eventually over the Numidian prince, Jugurtha. The significance of these successes for present purposes lies in the fact that Roman warfare in the late second century continued to make available for the market large numbers of enslaved war captives. During the first slave war the rebels suffered enormous casualties, so that replacements for those who had died were sorely needed by landowners who hoped to recover economically from the setbacks the war had occasioned. In 104 B.C. there was no shortage of slaves in Sicily ready to embark on revolt again, and it must be supposed that many of these new rebels were slaves who had been imported to Sicily in the aftermath of the first war, acquired in the course of Rome's victories from 132 B.C. onward. That is to say, the earlier pattern of mass enslavements after successful Roman warfare continued, with Scipio Aemilianus selling off the survivors of Numantia in Spain at the beginning of the period and C. Marius following suit at Capsa in North Africa, at least, toward the end. And even though the literary record of mass enslavements is now less explicit than for earlier periods, the action of C. Sextius Calvinus, the consul of 124 B.C., in permitting a Roman sympathizer named Crato to save himself and nine hundred other Gauls from enslavement, should be taken to mark the exception rather than the rule. Nor was it Rome alone that created new slaves from warfare. About 127 B.C. the Parthian tyrant Himerus is reported to have sent a large contingent of Babylonians to Media, together with their families, for disposal as slaves, and it was presumably dealers and pirates and those, such as Roman agents, in collusion with them who directed these captives to centers such as Sicily where they were needed. Moreover, even in areas of Sicily unaffected by the first war, natural attrition will have helped to keep demand high.[5]

Whether conveying prisoners or victims of kidnapping, there can be no doubt about the important role played by pirates in maintaining the level of the Roman slave supply in the second century, especially those who from their bases in Pamphylia and Cilicia operated throughout the eastern Mediterranean. According to Strabo, piracy in Cilicia Aspera had developed in the middle of the second century as a result of the attempt of Diodotus Tryphon in 145 B.C. to usurp the Seleucid throne: Delos served as a convenient point of despatch for the pirates' kidnapped victims, and demand for slaves in the Roman heartland fueled their activities. Strabo was of course wrong about the origins of Cilician piracy, because there is clear evidence that the phenomenon long antedated Diodotus Tryphon; and it was a problem for the Hellenistic communities to deal with themselves, not one for Rome's attention at the earliest possible opportunity: about 140 B.C. Scipio Aemilianus, on a tour of inspection in the East, paid some attention to the problem but attributed the dimensions of piracy to the inefficacy of the Hellenistic ruling powers. Further action by Rome was avoided. However, the scale of piracy certainly increased throughout the second century under the impact of Antiochus the Great's loss of claims to the regions of southern Asia Minor after the Treaty of Apamea, Seleucid decline after the reign of Antiochus Epiphanes, Ptolemaic inertia toward policing the seas, and the inability of Rhodes to act as an instrument of coercion after 167 B.C. From Rome's vantage point it may not have been until the years following the bequest of Pergamum in 133 B.C. that recognition of the necessity or desirability of intervening began to emerge; and it was only in 102 B.C. that Rome took the initiative by directing the praetor M. Antonius to undertake military action against the Cilician pirates and by the passage soon after of a law to guarantee freedom on the seas.[6]

The reason why precisely in 102 B.C. a naval command against the pirates was entrusted to M. Antonius remains obscure. But by that date the second slave war was well under way, and the two events may therefore not be unrelated. Despite the demand for new slaves in Sicily in the generation after 132 B.C., the difficulties caused by the new rebellion may well have prompted Roman government to try to control one of the sources of the slave supply that, while efficient, brought with it the pernicious disadvantage of making all sea traffic dangerous. However that may be, the measures taken by Rome at the end of the second century point up the extent of piracy then in existence: the piracy law in particular instructed the consul of 100 B.C. at Rome "to send letters to the kings and city-states of mediterranean Anatolia, Syria and Egypt, requiring them to prevent the use of their harbours by pirates, either as markets or as bases, and to see that all members of the Roman alliance in Italy should enjoy the freedom of the seas without let or hindrance." Given this all-embracing context, it is inconceivable that Sicily had remained unaffected by the activities of the pirates in the period between the two slave wars, and indeed Sicily had its own defenses against piratical raids. Warfare by itself may not have been able to supply all the slaves sought by landowners in Sicily, and dealers collaborating with pirates will have helped make up the shortfall. It is clear from Licinius Nerva's manumission hearings in Syracuse that first-generation slaves were abundant in Sicily in 104 B.C., and Athenion, one of the leaders of the second slave war was, like

Cleon earlier, a Cilician in origin. To a significant extent, their presence in Sicily must have been due to the supply provided by the pirates.[7]

That there was a continuing demand for slave labor in Sicily after 132 B.C., in domestic service and agriculture, can scarcely be questioned, for there were no radical changes to Sicily's economic structure. During the governorship of P. Rupilius, a senatorial commission of ten men had been set up at the conclusion of the first war to make recommendations on the future management of Sicilian affairs. The recommendations were implemented in due course by a law known as the *lex Rupilia*. Knowledge of the law's contents is confined to judicial and constitutional details; and while Rupilius was responsible for introducing new settlers to the city of Heraclea Minoa, there is no evidence to suggest that he brought about, through the *lex Rupilia* or any other means, major changes to the economy of Sicily that had an impact on the patterns of slave ownership. Some historians have maintained that Rupilius established a policy designed to reduce the extent of pastoral farming in Sicily in the decades following his governorship. But this view is highly improbable. Rather, a mixed pattern of farming persisted in Sicily in the late second century, as earlier and in the age of C. Verres, and it is only the partiality of the sources that seems to indicate change. Immediately before the outbreak of the second slave war the extent and structures of slaveholding in the island should be regarded as essentially the same as in the middle of the second century.[8]

Lawlessness outside the cities also continued largely unaltered, not least because the traditional association of brigandage with pastoral farming could not be eradicated. Diodorus's remarks on C. Titinius Gadaeus illustrate what was possible. In 106 B.C. this man had been sentenced to death for an unknown offense but had escaped punishment and spent the two years until seconded by Licinius Nerva living the life of a brigand. To judge from his name, Titinius was a Roman citizen, but the oddity of the *cognomen* Gadaeus might suggest that he was in fact a former slave. In any case, he had murdered many free people, so Diodorus reports, but had done no harm to slaves, a detail reminiscent of Diodorus's general statements on brigandage and the insecurities of travel in Sicily before the first slave war. A further incident, undated but perhaps falling in the interval between the wars, concerns an individual named Gorgus of Morgantina who, together with his father, was killed by fugitive slaves while on a journey. The incident represents the kind of behavior with which Titinius will have been associated. Even after the *lex Rupilia*, therefore, Roman rule in Sicily was not sufficiently firm to prevent the emergence of a figure like Titinius who, foreshadowing as an outlaw the resourceful Kwasi in eighteenth-century Surinam, was able to move with ease between the world of established authority and that of slave dissidents.

Moreover, for slaves who simply refused to obey their masters and, as in 104 B.C., withdrew to the shrine of the Palici for asylum, there was little other alternative for survival than banditry, and officialdom was virtually powerless to prevent it. With the slave population always being fermented by new arrivals and rural lawlessness remaining unabated, consequently, it is not surprising that the war which broke out in 104 B.C. was only the culmination of a series of revolts which had sporadically manifested themselves elsewhere since 132 B.C. Details are sparse. But the general record of servile rebellious activity is impressive enough to warrant the belief that the potential for violent resistance by slaves in the late second century was both enormous and constant, with opportunity and resolve being all that were necessary for the potential to be realized.[9]

Altogether eight or nine episodes are attested. Contemporaneously with the first war in Sicily an outbreak of trouble at Minturnae, on the border of Latium and Campania in Italy, resulted in the crucifixion of four hundred and fifty slaves, and some four thousand slaves were suppressed nearby at Sinuessa. Even Rome was not exempt from revolt: one hundred and fifty slaves there are reported to have rebelled at approximately the same time. All three uprisings were swiftly put down by the authorities, that at Sinuessa being eradicated by Cn. Servilius Caepio and Q. Metellus according to Orosius. If these men were the respective consuls of 141 B.C. and 143 B.C. their appointment to deal with a slave revolt is an important sign of the dangers it raised. However, slave resistance was not limited to Italy: in the eastern Mediterranean a further uprising of more than one thousand slaves occurred in Attica, in addition to revolts on the island of Delos and perhaps other places. These too were immediately crushed by local forces. Before the second slave war there were also more incidents of unrest in Italy, first at Nuceria, where thirty slaves entered a conspiracy and were quickly punished; and secondly at Capua, where two hundred slaves briefly revolted. In the East there may have been also a second insurrection of slaves in the mines of Attica. But most remarkable of all is the story—which recalls the world of Cicero's *Pro Tullio*—of the Roman *eques* T. Minucius, who is said to have purchased on credit the freedom of a slave girl with whom he was in love and, when he was unable to pay his debt, to have armed four hundred of his own slaves, inciting them to revolt in order that he might kill his creditors. As a self-proclaimed rebel king, Minucius succeeded in his aim and then broadened the scope of the revolt by attacking neighboring estates and increasing the number of his followers. Eventually he came to control an army of thirty-five hundred slaves. On receiving news of these events the senate at Rome authorized the praetor L. Licinius Lucullus to suppress Minucius, and with an army of four thousand infantry and four hundred cavalry assembled by the time he reached Capua, the city where the uprising had probably begun, Lucullus engaged the rebels. Unsuccessful at first, he was soon able to secure the help of a renegade named Apollonius and achieved Minucius's downfall. The king and his adherents preferred in the end to kill themselves rather than be captured by Lucullus.[10]

The revolt of T. Minucius belongs to 104 B.C., the year of Lucullus's praetorship. But the precise date or dates of the incidents at Capua and Nuceria cannot be determined. Diodorus, however, saw the three episodes as intimations of the war that was to come in Sicily soon afterwards, just as he believed the earlier revolts in Italy, Attica, and Delos were triggered by news of the first war. Similarly, Orosius wrote of sparks flying from Sicily to ignite servile unrest in Attica and Delos. With the benefit of hindsight such connections were easily made. But they are not credible. Most of the incidents are better understood as purely isolated responses to slavery of the sort that could occur at any time, as indeed had happened earlier in the second century, in places where slaves, especially those new to slavery, were densely concentrated and their living conditions aggravated by difficult local circumstances. The extensive use of slave labor in appalling working conditions in the mines of Laurium, the rapid passage of huge numbers of deracinated slaves through the trading center of Delos, the use of Capua as a training ground for slave gladiators, and the density of the slave population at Rome itself comprise a mesh of circumstances sufficient by themselves to explain independently the incidence of revolt by slaves in the late second century without any need for recourse to assumptions of external stimulus or provocation. The possibility of revolt in this period was always more than theoretical, and thoughtful slaveowners must have been constantly aware of the threat to social stability at the local level that their ownership of slaves brought. The revolts indicate above all the inadequacies of slaveowners in failing to control growing slave populations to whose members' interests relatively few concessions were made.[11]

Altogether, then, the revolt at Halicyae was one more of a foreseeable train of events in which the servile determination to resist the hardships of slavery through violent methods is visible. It is unfortunate that so few details have survived of those events. But they show well enough that the oppressed were consistently prepared to withstand oppression, and they suggest that a protracted form of resistance might easily follow, under the right mix of circumstances, from a succession of spontaneous, localized reactions to the horrors of slavery.

As soon as the revolt at Halicyae was suppressed, the troops of P. Licinius Nerva were dismissed and returned to their homes. But the news was at once brought to the governor that another band of slaves, eighty in number, had now risen in revolt: they had murdered a Roman *eques* named P. Clonius, and their numbers were increasing. Hesitating under conflicting advice and lacking a full complement of troops, Licinius at first took no action at all and so allowed the initiative to remain with the rebels. He may have reasoned that immediate action was in fact unnecessary, since the revolt at Halicyae had been dealt with efficiently. So, using what forces remained available to him, Licinius journeyed to Heraclea on the south coast, bypassing en route the rebel slaves who had taken up a position on Mount Caprianus. Since he had again avoided an encounter, Licinius gave the rebels the opportunity to claim that he was afraid of them, and within a week their numbers are said to have risen to eight hundred and shortly after to two thousand, the slaves as always arming themselves as best they could. Licinius decided ultimately to entrust his subordinate, M. Titinius, with the command of six hundred men summoned from the garrison at Enna. Titinius attacked the rebel base, but his troops were routed, and the rebels captured much of their weaponry. Titinius's service in Sicily may not have been altogether unremunerative, if a silver drinking cup thought to bear his name is truly illustrative of his plundering activities. But his defeat also increased further the size of the rebel forces, which soon rose to over six thousand.[12]

Diodorus's description of this phase of revolt gives no indication that the insurgents had any plans to incite a widespread uprising of slaves throughout Sicily but only that, as on other occasions, a small group responded to a localized situation of oppression and subsequently fled to a defensible stronghold that, once established, became a focal point of attraction for other groups of discontented slaves. However, with their strength soon equal to that of a Roman legion the rebels set about imposing a structure on their activities that had originally been unnecessary. They held an assembly and selected a king, a man named Salvius who, like Eunus before him, had a certain religious presence that helped mark him out as a rebel leader. According to Diodorus, Salvius had a reputation for being skilled in the arts of divination, though unlike Eunus he was not credited with miraculous powers. He was also a musician, a flute player who performed at women's festivals, and so was probably a domestic slave rather than an agricultural worker. Moreover, Salvius was an individual of some acumen who, once events were in motion, perceived the need for imposing order and looking to the future. Accordingly he prevented the rebels from indiscriminately attacking cities but instead divided them into three contingents, each with its own commander, with orders to meet at a certain place and time after raiding the countryside. How long these preparatory measures took is unknown. But their intent was to provide the insurgents with resources for protracted resistance and to train them for warfare. As a result horses and other animals were acquired, and the slave army itself rose to a total of twenty-two thousand, with two thousand slaves set up as a cavalry unit.[13]

As far as can be told, the slaves' sphere of operations so far was confined to western Sicily. But with their forces now well prepared, the slaves suddenly shifted the focus of the revolt by moving across the island and encamping near Morgantina in the southeastern interior. They attacked the city and put it under siege. It thus seems that the rebels had decided to secure control of one particular site that could serve indefinitely as a center of resistance, and their choice of Morgantina was perhaps influenced by the fact that the city had been one of the main centers of servile attention in the first war because of its strategic location and the access it gave to the grain lands of the southeast. Licinius was compelled to give chase. He traveled at night and endeavored to relieve Morgantina with an army of ten thousand Italians and Sicilians. Some of these troops may have been quickly brought in from the mainland, but most were again probably local garrison forces or militias: names of some Sicilians who fought against the rebels survive in fact in inscriptions discovered on slingshots used in the fighting. In any case, Licinius found the rebel camp hardly protected at all and easily captured it. But as he proceeded to Morgantina itself the slaves counterattacked and defeated him. Then, pulling off a master stroke, Salvius announced to the enemy that those who cast down their arms would not be harmed, and many are said to have immediately taken him at his word. Salvius recovered his camp and took possession of the weaponry abandoned by Licinius's troops, keeping his promise toward those who surrendered: four thousand captives are reported to have been taken but no more than six hundred to have died. This second victory led, so Diodorus continues, to a doubling of the rebel forces. But while completely dominating the surrounding countryside, Salvius was still unable to capture Morgantina. He attempted to weaken the city by offering the slaves within their freedom. But these urban slaves—a considerable proportion being domestic servants presumably and so on greater terms of intimacy with their owners—opted to accept a similar offer made by their masters in return for their assistance in repelling the rebels. The urban slaves were obviously in a difficult situation. Yet the lack of solidarity among the servile population of Sicily as a whole at this point is very noticeable and important. Licinius later overturned the manumission of the slaves at Morgantina, prompting them to join the rebel cause. But for the time being, the city held out against the siege.[14]

The events of 104 B.C. so far described are known only from Diodorus, and it is somewhat surprising that no other ancient writer ever mentions Salvius and the siege of Morgantina. The reason perhaps is that the new slave king, despite his great success in converting the early insurgents in the west into a coordinated and well-regulated army, never seems to have become as charismatic a figure as the wonderworker Eunus before him. In addition, Salvius did not survive until the end of the war, and command of the rebel slaves was ultimately to fall to the Cilician Athenion, whom later writers remembered as the dominant figure of the rebellion.[15]

Athenion emerges into history, indeed, much like Cleon in the first war, as the leader of a subsidiary local revolt while Salvius was still in full control of the main uprising. According to Florus, he was a Cilician and a *pastor*, who killed his own master, set free the slaves in his owner's *ergastulum*, and shaped them into a military force. Besides agreeing on Athenion's Cilician origin, Diodorus gives other details: he was the *vilicus* of two brothers and a skillful astrologer; he first secured support for revolt from the two hundred slaves in his charge and then from others on nearby estates, so that within five days he collected a following of more than one thousand men. Athenion therefore should be regarded perhaps as a *magister pecoris* belonging to a substantial slave *familia* that comprised both agricultural workers, housed at night in an *ergastulum*, and pastoral herdsmen; and some sense of the kind of individual he was can be gleaned from the agricultural writers. Cato, for example, required of the ideal *vilicus* that he be deferential, industrious, sober, trustworthy, efficient, literate, and a strict disciplinarian toward the slaves in his charge; for Varro too the *magister pecoris* was to be literate, a man physically strong but somewhat older and more experienced than his subordinates. Such slaves, exercising managerial functions, could perhaps be viewed as symbols of a certain upward progression in the servile hierarchy that was open to others if diligence and compliance to the master's will were displayed, and the more spacious living quarters they enjoyed, to judge again from the evidence of Italian villas, made their advancement highly visible to other slaves. Not least as repositories of their owners' trust, consequently, they could strengthen and reinforce the system of slavery. More important in the present context, however, is that, like any estate manager, Athenion must have been used to operating as an intermediary between the orbit of the slaveowner and that of the slaves he managed (and to which he ultimately belonged in spite of his privileged status). As a fomenter of revolt Athenion was obviously not the Catonian ideal. But there must be a presumption that he used his knowledge of his owners to judge when the moment was ripe for revolt; that he was used to commanding authority and to being obeyed; and that whether or not he had any formal education he was shrewd enough to be able to convert his owners' trust of him into actions of seeming advantage to those who took instructions from him. At any rate, the uprising he fostered was again in the far west of Sicily, in the area of Segesta and Lilybaeum, where the earlier revolts led by Varius and Salvius had by no means exhausted the potential for violent resistance on the part of the slaves who remained there.[16]

Like Salvius, Athenion had the sense to understand that revolt, once in motion, could not endure without systematic measures. Thus as another slave king—one who assumed all the external appurtenances of monarchy, a purple robe, silver scepter, and a crown and one whom the gods, he claimed, intended to rule all Sicily—Athenion used some of his adherents as troops and kept others in their customary occupations, prevented comprehensive pillaging of the land and its products, and was thereby able to provide his army with a secure food supply. At the head of ten thousand troops he ambitiously laid siege to the coastal city of Lilybaeum, but not surprisingly in view of Lilybaeum's past record in holding out against sieges, Athenion was forced to withdraw. Nonetheless, he kept up morale among his followers with the argument that to continue the siege would be to invite disaster and that retreat was the order of the gods. His credibility was confirmed when a force of Mauretanian troops arrived to relieve Lilybaeum and worsted the rebels as they were retreating. The appearance of the Mauretanians cannot of course have been fortuitous, and it may be that in the sequel to Rome's defeat of Jugurtha the year before the senate had appealed for assistance from African allies in response to information from Licinius on the uprisings in western Sicily. However, nothing further is heard of the Mauretanians or of Gomon their general.[17]

Meanwhile in the east Salvius appears to have abandoned the siege of Morgantina and to have concentrated his efforts on plundering raids. Moving his army, now said to be thirty thousand strong, into the plain of Leontini, where the rebels' slingshots have also been found, he made sacrifice to the Palici and offered them a Roman toga in thanks for his recent victory in battle. Further, although already a slave king, Salvius at this point assumed the name of the Seleucid usurper Tryphon, an action perhaps intended to strengthen his authority over his supporters and to convince his enemies that the rebellion was far from over. In addition, his religious and ceremonial actions may also have been undertaken in direct response to the emergence in the west of the new king Athenion, that is, to prepare for a possible confrontation over the questions of rebel leadership and rebel plans. There is no evidence whatsoever that the revolts of Salvius and Athenion were anything but uncoordinated, entirely separate uprisings. But a problem was now in the making, since Salvius intended to return to the west—at this stage the sphere of Athenion—and specifically to the natural fortress of Triocala near Heraclea. A show of superiority was therefore necessary, and as with Eunus and Cleon in the first war, Salvius summoned Athenion to him, as a general to a king. Athenion deferred, meeting Salvius at Triocala with three thousand troops, the rest of his force having been left to extend revolt in the far west. Hopes that the two kings might prove each other's undoing were once again thus confounded. Salvius then proceeded to fortify Triocala with a wall and moat; it was a site that could be defended and was well supplied with water and fertile land. He also built a palace and an agora in his new headquarters, selected intelligent men to give him advice, and added Roman magisterial trappings to his monarchical paraphernalia. His suspicions of Athenion, however, were not allayed, and the latter was held under arrest. The authority of Salvius, it appears, was firmly established.[18]

The impact on Sicily as a whole in 104 B.C. of the two revolts led by Salvius and Athenion, following hard on the episode at Halicyae, is difficult to judge but must have been considerable. Thousands of slaves were in rebellion; at least two major cities had been invested; the rebels had joined forces; and the governor, Licinius, had been utterly unable to prevent the escalation of the isolated revolts into a serious insurrection. Diodorus indeed has a highly rhetorical account of the widespread brigandage and damage to property the war occasioned—in which not only the slaves participated but the free poor as well—and he creates the impression that anarchy came to fill all Sicily, with the slaves of the cities (again, in the main, domestics) preparing to join those who commanded the open areas of the island. But the whole of Sicily had by no means fallen to the slaves, and Diodorus's view must be regarded as tendentious and exaggerated. The forces of Salvius and Athenion had affected a corridor linking Lilybaeum in the west with Leontini in the east and had doubtless wreaked havoc along it. But nothing is heard of problems in regions to the north of this corridor, which appear to have remained immune to the effects of the rebellion so far. Moreover, the assaults on Morgantina and Lilybaeum had failed, and a potentially divisive conflict over rebel leadership had barely been averted. At the end of Diodorus's record for the first year of the slave war, Salvius's strategy still seems to have been to find one impregnable site to hold as a bastion of freedom for the rebels against authority forces. The strategy was proving difficult to implement, however, and there is nothing to suggest that a plan of any greater compass was in place.[19]

As the rebellion entered a second year the situation in Sicily was evidently considered acute enough by Rome to justify the despatch of a substantial military force to stamp it out. Sixteen thousand troops were accordingly sent to Sicily in 103 B.C. under the command of L. Licinius Lucullus, the man who as praetor the year before had effectively crushed the revolt of T. Minucius in Italy. Lucullus's army consisted mainly of Roman citizens and Italian allies, but Diodorus specifies that contingents of Bithynians, Thessalians, Acharnanians, and Lucanians were also included. It was probably as large as the army that had fought in Sicily in the late stages of the first war. Salvius, knowing that a contest with Lucullus was inevitable, at first planned to remain within Triocala and to undergo a siege. But eventually he followed the advice of Athenion, who was no longer under detention, and favored an open engagement. The rebel army of forty thousand thus took up a position near the neighboring town of Scirthaea, and a major battle ensued. Athenion himself commanded a cavalry detachment of two hundred men but was incapacitated by the wounds he received and only survived by pretending to have been killed. Salvius and his forces finally fled in defeat, and twenty thousand slaves, that is, half the army they had put into the field, are alleged to have been killed by the Romans. The survivors retreated under the cover of night to Triocala and considered giving themselves up to their former owners. But the spirit of resistance prevailed, and when Lucullus arrived to besiege them, having waited nine days before following up his victory, the rebels were able to drive him off. Moral weakness and venality were alleged as the causes of Lucullus's ultimate failure. But whatever the truth, his error in not swiftly pressing the advantage gained at Scirthaea was grave.[20]

It cannot be categorically stated that Lucullus made no further efforts to combat the rebel slaves during the remainder of his term in Sicily. The record is simply deficient. Florus states in his pitifully brief account of the war that at one juncture Athenion captured Lucullus's camp, which, if accurate, could refer to some development in the main battle at Scirthaea or to some other engagement before or afterwards. Nonetheless, it seems that the rebels were permitted the chance to regroup and reorganize after their defeat, and indeed the incredible actions attributed to Lucullus at the end of his year in office gave the rebels a far greater opportunity for recovery than they could possibly have hoped for. According to Diodorus, Lucullus was accused of wishing to enlarge the scope of the war before he left Sicily; and so in order both to offset the charge and to guarantee the disgrace of his successor, C. Servilius, he ensured that Servilius would not be immediately able to oppose the rebels by transporting his army to Italy, disbanding his troops, and burning his camp. The sequel was later played out at Rome itself, with Lucullus being tried for peculation, while in Sicily the slave rebellion continued into a third year.[21]

In 102 B.C. the advantage, despite their losses, seems to have remained with the slaves, for C. Servilius is credited with no success against the rebels at all. But the record of Diodorus at this point is very brief, and exactly what Servilius tried to do is irrecoverable. Florus again remarks that Athenion once captured his camp, so presumably Servilius tried to engage the rebels as would be expected. Yet Diodorus states merely that he did nothing to stop Athenion besieging cities, overrunning the country, and securing control of many places. No details survive to lend substance to this generalization. However, it may have been in 102 B.C. that Athenion extended the geographical range of the rebellion by launching an assault on the city of Messana in the extreme northeast of Sicily, an event known from an undated fragment of the history of Cassius Dio which reports that, although the people of Messana were not expecting to be attacked, they stored all their valuables in the city for safety's sake (a sign no doubt of the panic caused by the war) and that Athenion, learning of the store of valuables, attacked the citizens of Messana while they were holding a public festival outside. Dio continues that Athenion murdered many of these people and came close to taking the city. It is known too that Athenion fortified a site called Macella, the precise location of which is unclear but which seems to have been close to Messana, and used it as a base to ravage the surrounding countryside. A possible indication of these raids might be found in the discovery of slingshots used by the slaves—some of them actually bore Athenion's name—at the modern centers of Bronte, Troina, and Assoro, all to the northeast of Enna in the direction of the northern promontory; and it could be assumed that Athenion's appearance in the northeast had something to do with Lucullus's evacuation in 103 B.C. However that may be, it seems legitimate enough to associate the attack on Messana with Diodorus's account of 102 B.C. If in this year, then, Athenion was conducting pillaging raids on a broader geographical scale, a change in rebel strategy emerges that must have been due to Salvius's death and his replacement by Athenion as the supreme slave leader. These developments apparently belong to 102 B.C. also, but they cannot be fixed, in time or circumstance, more specifically. Salvius's death, however, must have brought an end to the tensions experienced earlier over the questions of leadership and tactics, but at the same time Salvius's original adherents who were still alive in 102 B.C. must have regretted the loss of one who for several years had done much to sustain the momentum of their rebellion.[22]

On the Roman side the final stage of the war was conducted by M'. Aquillius, who arrived in Sicily in 101 B.C. as one of the consuls of that year. Aquillius ended the war. But more than a further year's efforts against the rebels were needed, and it was not until late in the year 100 B.C. or even early in 99 B.C. that Aquillius returned to Rome, having remained in Sicily as proconsul, to celebrate the ovation granted him for his victory. The opposition of the slaves was thus not easily overcome, and a sign of the disruption the war produced in Sicily may be reflected in the fact that Aquillius once found it necessary to lend grain, presumably taken from the amounts collected for tax payments, to some of the Sicilian cities. Plutarch believed that in one of the slave wars in Sicily a plague of locusts caused by rotting, unburied corpses destroyed grain supplies throughout the island: he does not say in which war the plague occurred, but it may well have been the reason behind Aquillius's emergency measure.[23]

In another full-scale battle Aquillius finally defeated the rebels, and although he suffered a wound to the head in the fighting, later to be put to dramatic effect by his defense counsel when Aquillius was tried in Rome for peculation during his governorship, it was actually Aquillius himself who killed Athenion. After their defeat the rebels' numbers are said to have fallen to ten thousand, and Aquillius gradually sought out and captured the refuges into which the survivors retreated, perhaps, as

Florus seems to suggest, reducing the slaves to starvation by intercepting their supplies in the manner of M. Perperna during the first war. Eventually, no more than a thousand rebels were left, a group headed by a certain Satyrus who is known only from this last phase of the war. The slaves surrendered to Aquillius and, as proof of his success, were taken by him to Rome to fight the wild beasts of the amphitheater. The second slave war in Sicily was over. Yet the grim defiance that had provoked it was not quite fully subdued, for in preference to a death in the amphitheater the slave prisoners killed each other in front of the public altars at Rome until only Satyrus remained alive. Satyrus then took his own life—as Diodorus says, heroically.[24]

Over a second substantial period of time, then, slaves in Sicily had been able to sustain resistance and withstand Rome's retaliation with remarkable success. The synopsis of the course of the rebellion shows that much more is known about its earliest stage, in 104 B.C., than about developments in subsequent years. Yet despite the imperfections of the evidence, a number of points can safely be made about the insurrection as a whole. First, for example, the great importance of slaves' desires to acquire freedom is evident in the record of Licinius Nerva's handling of the senatorial decree on illegal enslavement and in the record of Salvius's appeal to the slaves of Morgantina. For those who made the difficult choice in favor of flight and rebellion, the pursuit of freedom and rejection of servitude were powerful motivating forces that reflected the absence in society of well-defined principles by which manumission might be peaceably and cooperatively obtained and the impossibility, in normal circumstances, of most slaves ever being set free. Brutal treatment does not receive prominence as a causal factor in revolt this time—there is no counterpart to Damophilus of Enna in the record of the second war—but cruel treatment on the part of masters must have added to the desperation bred in slaves by the hopelessness of their manumission prospects: for the abuse of slaves was undeniably a permanent feature of the slavery system in the Roman heartland and is implicit here in the several episodes of slave suicide—extreme behavior that can only have been precipitated by slaves' fears of punishment upon capture. Further, the episodes of slaves murdering their masters have to be predicated on the assumption that revenge for maltreatment was being sought.

Secondly, the discrete groups of rebellious slaves led by Varius, Salvius, and Athenion rose up in revolt on the lines of a well-established pattern of small-scale resistance and did not deliberately aim to engage the whole slave population of Sicily in a general insurrection. Although there are signs that the second slave war involved different categories of slave personnel, the hierarchical structure of slavery naturally precluded any assumption of complete solidarity among all slaves, so that such a design was unthinkable, no matter how much various groups of slaves may have talked about revolt on various occasions in reaction to their own personal circumstances. The narrow strategy adopted by Salvius, of confining his followers to as secure a location as possible in order to protect the rebels' tenuously held liberty, could succeed only if the rebellion were kept within certain limits of control; while Athenion's looser and more opportunistic strategy of sporadic attacks over a wider area, clearly grounded in the tradition of brigandage, was also founded on no more than the need to guarantee the rebels' survival. The rebels knew that to capture and hold indefinitely numerous cities across the whole of Sicily was beyond the realm of the possible or desirable. The divergent strategies of Salvius and Athenion therefore represented two different solutions to the problem of how the momentum of rebellion was to be maintained over time once the early revolts had escalated into a larger movement.[25]

Thirdly, the growth of the rebel numbers in 104 B.C. was again a largely spontaneous phenomenon, the logical sequel to a cluster of localized, violent revolts taking place against a background of long-standing servile resistance to slavery by flight. As in the first war, the process was facilitated by the absence from Sicily of a permanent Roman military force and the inability of local troops to police adequately the slave population. With the appointments of Lucullus and Servilius in 103 B.C. and 102 B.C., it became possible, in theory, for a Roman legion to take away the military advantage from the rebels. But political factors and personal weaknesses seem to some degree to have nullified this potential. In these years, however, when Rome's military resources were predominantly invested in a more demanding struggle against the Cimbri in Transalpine Gaul, to place a larger army in Sicily was probably not feasible. Yet when Lucullus and Servilius met with failure Rome was compelled to send a consular army to Sicily in spite of other demands on its manpower, and it was only when the army had doubled in size that the rebels were defeated, clear evidence of their organizational success in the years beforehand.[26]

Throughout the war, finally, constant attention was paid by the rebels to procuring an adequate material base of arms and food with which to continue their resistance against authority forces. Allusions to this reality are frequent in Diodorus's narrative and elsewhere, as are allusions to the emergence of strong leadership and the ability of Salvius and Athenion to impose order on groups of slaves who had achieved their immediate objectives of killing slaveowners and extricating themselves from slavery. The details of this reality will be seen presently. It is enough at this point to assert, without ambiguity, that while the slave leaders responded to the need for discipline and order that the proliferation of numbers dictated, in the long run the practical demands presented by the scale of the rebellion were too great for even the most energetic and resourceful of individuals to overcome.

[V]

The Slave War of Spartacus

In 211 B.C., the year in which Syracuse was reduced in Sicily, the Campanian city of Capua was deprived of political independence by Rome as the price required for its defection to Hannibal five years earlier. But in spite of its loss of autonomy, the city that in many respects had previously been Rome's equal in Italy and that Polybius described as "once the richest of all the cities in this area" was still to reach its highest point of economic development; and in the period from the middle of the second century B.C. to the middle of the first century A.D. great prosperity accompanied Capua's subjection to Rome. In part this success depended on Capua's role as a center for bronze manufacturing, the making of textiles, perfumes, and other commodities. But above all the primary foundation of Capuan prosperity lay in agriculture and the extraordinary production of grain, wine, and olive oil that the exceptional fertility of Campania made possible.[1]

Naturally enough in such a situation Capua relied on a large servile population, the varied character of which has been revealed through study of Capuan epigraphy. For example, inscriptions commemorating *vernae* and servile names indicating order of birth (Primus, Secundus, Tertius) provide evidence for a degree of natural reproduction as one means of supply, while names of foreign origin point to the continual arrival in Capua by trade of new slaves from all across the Mediterranean. But the combination of homeborn and first-generation slaves is only one aspect of the diversity. For just as at Rome and in Sicily, slaves at Capua could be found in a multiplicity of activities, the most striking of which, civic government, emerges from the records of Capuan *magistri*, the boards of local officials who carried out various administrative functions in the city. The appearance here of slaves and ex-slaves, sometimes side by side with the freeborn, presupposes that some slaves at Capua had access to a certain amount of wealth and that manumission was sufficiently practiced to allow the assimilation of some slaves within established frameworks of authority. Thus collaboration with the status quo was one response to servitude that could at times lead to real social advancement.[2]

This avenue of progress, however, cannot have been available to the majority of Capuan slaves, and a distinction should properly be drawn between the slave *magistri* and their kind, on the one hand, and the bulk of the slave population, on the other, whose constant potential for acts of violent resistance is illustrated by the two episodes of revolt that occurred at Capua in the late second century B.C. Moreover, it was in this flourishing city that the last and greatest of the Roman slave wars began, with a revolt in 73 B.C. of gladiators led by a foreign slave named Spartacus. In the two years following, tens of thousands of dissidents again joined the original insurgents and large regions of the Italian peninsula were affected by their activities. Indeed, the war had a much greater territorial impact than the two previous wars in Sicily, even though it did not last as long, and a punitive force equal to that with which Caesar was later to conquer Gaul was required to suppress the rebels. But in the first instance it was purely to local conditions of enslavement at Capua that the gladiators responded, their behavior assuming an utterly different character from that of the slaves who aspired to civic administration.[3]

In their fully mature form in the Imperial period, the gladiatorial contests of Rome can be understood, from a sociological perspective, to have operated as psychic and political safety valves that, within a cultural context of discipline, violence, and bloodlust, provided a mechanism for the release of social tensions and for instilling a sense of law and order into the crowds of spectators who witnessed them. At the time of the uprising led by Spartacus, however, gladiatorial contests were still in the process of becoming a prolific form of popular entertainment at Rome, and exhibitions of gladiators remained as yet sporadic: in the half-century from 94 B.C. to 44 B.C. only twenty-five exhibitions by named individuals can be attested, and some of these are dubious cases. Training schools for gladiators may well have existed at Rome in the late Republic, but it was only with Imperial initiative and direction that fully permanent institutions were later established. In actuality it was Capua in the first century B.C. that served as the main entrepôt for the training and housing of Roman gladiators, a legacy of the fact that gladiatorial combats originated in Campania and the south of Italy in the fourth century and arrived at Rome not less than a century or so later. Hence in the Catilinarian crisis of 63 B.C. the senate decreed that troupes of gladiators in Rome were to be removed to Capua and other Campanian towns in order to relieve Rome of the potential dangers their presence represented; and it was from Capua too that C. Marcellus was expelled the same year, apparently for soliciting the support of gladiators. In 49 B.C., as civil war began, Caesar had five thousand gladiators located in Capua, a body that the consul L. Cornelius Lentulus contemplated using as troops but whose members were subsequently distributed, two per household, among the city's population for safety's sake.[4]

Spartacus and his immediate followers in 73 B.C. broke out of a gladiatorial training school owned by the manager (*lanista*) Cn. Lentulus Batiatus. The man is otherwise unknown. But a strong distinction between this kind of slaveowner and that represented by Roman and Sicilian magnates must be assumed, for in respectable society the *lanista* was a figure of very low esteem, and his occupation as a trafficker in slaves, much like that of the slave dealer, was held in contempt. Martial derided the type for his capacity to grow rich, comparing him with informers, cheats, and sexual profiteers. More soberly, but in complementary fashion, the recently discovered senatorial decree of A.D. 19 from Larinum, prohibiting members of the Roman upper classes from publicly appearing on the stage or in the arena, classes the *lanista* with such other undesirables as actors, procurers, and gladiators. Similarly, in the earlier Table of Heraclea, *lanistae* are banned, like convicts, actors, and gladiators, from being enrolled in the councils of Italian municipalities. There could therefore be little opportunity for the emergence of anything resembling paternalistic bonds between *lanista* and slave gladiator: the social status of each was virtually the same; their relationship must often have been only of short duration; and the one was in business at the constant risk of the other's life. The absence of loyalty to the master on the part of the slave gladiator was consequently an important precondition of revolt.[5]

In the extant narrative accounts of the Spartacan war there is little to suggest what life was like in the training school or in first-century Capua at large for gladiators. But something of their social and material circumstances can be reconstructed. The mixed origins of the gladiatorial population, for instance, cannot be doubted. Spartacus himself is said to have been a Thracian who, having once seen military service with the Romans, was later sold as a prisoner at Rome itself, while his followers, it is reported, were mainly Gauls, Germans, or other Thracians who had been kept imprisoned in the school by their owner. It appears therefore that gladiators tended to be first-generation slaves, acquired either as war captives or through the slave trade, an impression with which Cicero's generic description of them as desperate and barbarian is consistent. More specifically, Cicero thought it unusual if gladiators were sought in *ergastula* rather than on the open market, and for Livy too the slaves provided by *lanistae* were normally acquired by purchase. The later evidence of sepulchral inscriptions commemorating gladiators confirms the impression, for at Rome and other cities in the West, individuals are encountered whose tombstones preserve details of birth in Thrace, Greece, Egypt, Arabia, and so on. Gladiators, then, were often men whose experience of slavery had been brief and who can be expected to have wished to recover their freedom as a matter of course. It is true that not all gladiators were slaves, so in theory it is possible that some of those who accompanied Spartacus in revolt were free men. But in view of the evidence that Spartacus himself was sold at Rome, his servile status is unquestionable; and it seems implausible to believe that men from out-lying areas of the Roman world should have volunteered themselves for gladiatorial careers in central Italy as others sometimes did.[6]

One probable result of lumping together in a gladiatorial training school numbers of slaves who derived from many different and distant points of origin was that communication among them was at times difficult. And, indeed, slaveowners have always appreciated the advantages provided by this situation for minimizing the potential for dissidence among their slaves: the following passage from William Smith, the captain of a slaving vessel employed in the African slave trade, only elaborates the comments of Varro quoted earlier:

> As for the languages of *Gambia*, they are so many and so different, that the Natives, on either Side the River, cannot understand each other; which, if rightly consider'd, is no small Happiness to the *Europeans* who go thither to trade for slaves. . . . I have known some melancholy Instances of whole Ship Crews being surpriz'd, and cut off by them. But the safest Way is to trade with the different Nations, on either Side the River, and having some of every Sort on board, there will be no more Likelihood of their succeeding in a Plot, than of finishing the Tower of Babel.

More to the point, however, the inability of multiracial slave populations to communicate easily in antiquity, except in the language of their own-ers, has been urged as the explanation of why slave revolts in the ancient world as a whole were so infrequent. But the argument is untenable, glossing over as it does the necessary presumption that if foreign slaves and their Italian masters had to establish basic forms of communication in order for work to be accomplished, then such communication could be exploited by slaves for their own purposes. Moreover, the development of pidgin and creole languages in modern slave societies proves that lan-guage barriers between slaves were problems that could be surmounted, and the same must be imagined for ancient slave populations in which the will to resist slavery was strong.[7]

A more harrowing result of the slave gladiators' diverse origins was the social deracination necessitated by their geographical dislocation. Never-theless, gladiators were sometimes able to create for themselves new lives in slavery, not least through marrying and establishing families. Epitaphs again provide a useful medium of evidence here, because inscriptions commemorating deceased gladiators commonly show the existence of familial ties. Thus the Greek Beryllus was commemorated by his wife

Nomas on an inscription from Nemausus, and a certain Paeragrinus by his wife Prisca on a stone found near Puteoli; again, the gladiator Urbicus, whose inscription comes from Mediolanum, left at his death a wife, Laurica, to whom he had been married seven years, and their five-month-old daughter Olympias. It is not a complete surprise, therefore, that when Spartacus was sold as a slave he had with him a wife, a woman also Thracian by birth who remained with him after his transfer to Capua and participated in the revolt he led. The family lives of gladiators, however, as of other categories of slaves, were controlled by the wishes of their owners and so were subject to possible disruption at any moment in time, particularly through the adverse effects of sale. Cicero's casual reference in 56 B.C. to Atticus's purchase of a troupe of gladiators conceals, from the servile perspective, the harsh reality that the sale of slave property brought no guarantee that slave families would survive intact over time. But when not separated by sale, married slaves in the school of Lentulus Batiatus may have been allowed to live with their wives to judge from the gladiatorial barracks excavated at Pompeii, which resemble in some ways the slave quarters of Italian villas. One of the skeletons found at Pompeii was that of a woman—evidently wealthy, since items of jewelry were discovered with her—who is sometimes considered to have been a gladiator's mistress but who could just as easily have been a gladiator's wife; the remains of a newborn infant were also found in a jar in one of the rooms of the Pompeian barracks. Gladiatorial competitions after all were lucrative for the star fighters, and the woman's ornaments could be explicable as the rewards of her husband's successes in the arena. Yet even if the assumption is correct, the material conditions for family life in the school must have been severe because the individual cell-units in which the gladiators are thought to have been domiciled measured, on average, only ten to fifteen square meters; and given the identification in the barracks of a large mess kitchen, life was obviously organized on a communal basis that diminished opportunities for conjugal privacy and intimacy. The situation at Capua is hardly likely to have been any better.[8]

The fact that some gladiators gained wealth from their successes in the arena may have served to encourage rebelliousness among them, for "in slave societies, the ability to accumulate . . . becomes a symbol of freedom; where patrimony can lend dignity to genealogy, individual accumulation can mean individual identity." The more so when, despite the accumulation of rewards, the living conditions of gladiators were in many respects primitive and not rendered more palatable by the knowledge that the urban indigent of Roman society fared no better. From the evidence of housing at Ostia and Rome of the early Imperial period it is clear that the poor tended to live in rented apartments comprising only one or two sparsely furnished rooms, while in the late Republic "most of the inhabitants of Rome," it has been said, "lived in appalling slums." The

circumstances of gladiators therefore may have been no worse than those
of other elements of the lower-class population, but that can hardly have
made their conditions more tolerable. Consideration of such an essential
matter as food illustrates the point further. To feed a troupe of gladiators
required outlays of cash that at Rome even men of the senatorial order
could not always afford, and at a time of famine, such as that of A.D. 6,
gladiators could be among the first, as a disposable commodity, to find
themselves expelled from the city in order to reduce pressure on what
stocks of supplies remained. In normal circumstances, so literary references suggest, gladiators were fattened up before combat with plentiful
amounts of food. But the quality of the food was probably poor. The elder
Pliny implies that barley was long thought to be the traditional staple
cereal of gladiators; and while it would be naive to assume that all gladiators always relied exclusively on a single source of food, Pliny's association of *hordearii*, a term used of gladiators, with the Latin word for barley
(*hordeum*) cannot be meaningless. Consequently the far inferior nutritional value of barley, compared with wheat, needs to be noticed, as does
the fact that in Roman antiquity barley was grown in large quantities
especially for feeding animals and the impoverished. Sallust suggests that
slaves' food was never very good. On the other hand, a healthful location
may have afforded some compensation for a low quality diet: speaking
of Ravenna, Strabo remarked that gladiators were to be fed and trained
there because of its favorable climate, a circumstance that Capua similarly enjoyed.[9]

The lives of gladiators were of course dominated by a climate of violence, but not merely the violence of the amphitheater with the risks of
injury or death any gladiatorial contest entailed. The management of
gladiators required the exercise of discipline, and it is clear from the
discovery of stocks compelling those constrained to lie down or else sit
in discomfort that one of the rooms in the Pompeian barracks served as
a prison or guardhouse. The gladiators imprisoned at Capua in 73 B.C.
therefore were not receiving special treatment. Further, since slave gladiators were not only disposable but also manipulable commodities, their
professional associations with violence and killing could be directed toward highly unsavory ends. In 57 B.C. P. Clodius used his brother's gladiators as a private armed force to block passage of the bill to recall Cicero
from exile, and in the preparations made for the murder of Caesar in 44
B.C., the conspirator D. Brutus arranged for gladiators to be available to
protect the assassins if help were needed. Prominent Romans of the late
Republic commonly used their gladiators as personal security guards,
almost as if the men formed part of their domestic servile entourages.
But under such circumstances, gladiators became a perpetual threat to
public safety, and on occasion the volume of their presence at Rome had
to be restricted. So in 65 B.C. when Caesar as aedile gave magnificent

gladiatorial games—and when the memory of the Spartacan war was still fresh—a law was passed to curtail the number of gladiators any individual could maintain in the city because of the fears that Caesar's gladiators engendered. Later, in 22 B.C., Augustus restricted the praetors from giving more than two gladiatorial shows a year and from using more than one hundred and twenty men on each occasion.[10]

The willingness of gladiators to participate in acts of political violence and civil war is explained by the attractiveness of manumission as a motivating impulse. When in 49 B.C. Caesar's gladiators at Capua were approached by L. Cornelius Lentulus, it was promises of freedom in return for their support that he brought. But such participation is also a sign of the desperation induced in gladiators by their material conditions, desperation that at times found outlets other than collusion with politicians and militarists. Thus gladiators committed suicide as the ultimate means of resistance to slavery, as Seneca for instance shows in telling of the deaths of two gladiators who killed themselves before entry into the arena: the first, a German, and so notably a first-generation slave, choked himself to death in a latrine, the only place he could escape detection, using for the purpose a sponge-tipped piece of wood kept there for hygienic reasons; while the second, when being conveyed to the arena in a cart, pretended to fall asleep, put his head between the spokes of one of the cart's wheels, and allowed his neck to be broken by the wheel's rotation. A comparable incident is known from a much later period: Symmachus noted the death by self-inflicted strangulation of twenty-nine Saxons fated to become gladiators.[11]

Open revolt was another extreme form of resistance theoretically available to gladiators, though before Spartacus there are no instances of this kind of activity in Roman history on record. Yet the revolt Spartacus led was not altogether unique. In A.D. 21 slaves training to become gladiators at Augustodunum joined the rebellion against Roman rule of Gauls led by Julius Sacrovir, but this event was not solely a reaction against slavery. Again in A.D. 64 gladiators at Praeneste began to rebel, and their actions produced a panicky response at Rome itself, evoking fears of a new Spartacan uprising. The gladiators, however, were quickly suppressed by Roman troops. Of course, to engage in revolt was a dangerous enterprise, and the intrinsic risks may well have deterred many slaves from even contemplating such drastic behavior. But in their careers, gladiators confronted the likelihood of physical harm every time they fought, and Cicero's rationalization that gladiatorial combat was praiseworthy for the training it gave in withstanding pain can hardly have been of much comfort to them. (Nor did it prevent Cicero from commenting on the essential barbarism of the sport.) However, when gladiatorial contests by their very nature thrust slaves into situations where their lives were threatened, revolt may well have seemed to many no less hazardous an alternative.

In cities where gladiators were kept, the possibility of insurrection must always have been a preoccupation of their owners.[12]

The gladiatorial population of Capua on the eve of the Spartacan revolt, then, is likely to have been a highly volatile community. It consisted chiefly of first-generation slaves brought to central Italy from peripheral areas of the Roman world whose enslavement had probably brought, in most cases, an abrupt and recent transformation of their lives. Their material amenities were spartan, their opportunities for family life meager. There were prospects before them of rewards for success in the arena, and perhaps even of eventual manumission. But the possibility of contrived involvement in civil unrest was just as strong, and all sense of stability in their lives was lacking. Above all, their existence was fully permeated by the violent ethos of the age.

That ethos affected the lives of many other slaves too, which helps to explain the participation in the Spartacan war of the thousands of rebels who followed the gladiators' lead. Late in the second century Ti. Gracchus is said to have been disturbed by the gravity of the first slave war in Sicily, and—a sure sign of how the memory of the second war lingered—when L. Cornelius Sulla was demanding the surrender of C. Flavius Fimbria in Asia in 85 B.C., Sulla's soldiers conferred on Fimbria the opprobrious name of Athenion in mock honor of the erstwhile slave king. By 73 B.C., however, the servile population of Italy was not just a potential source of further unrest and disturbance in its own right (that is, on the Sicilian pattern), but a segment of the overall population whose support could be enlisted by political leaders engaged in civil clashes. A tradition, that is, of general servile involvement in political and civil strife had now come into being, following the sequence of civil wars and other commotions that had affected Rome and Italy in the previous sixty years. For example, Appian records that in 90 B.C., during the Social War, the Italian commanders C. Papius and C. Vidalicius enrolled in their armies slaves made available to them when they captured certain towns in southern Campania and Apulia; and that in 87 B.C. the consul L. Cornelius Cinna used slave troops drawn to his cause by his offer of manumission. Cinna, however, was unable to control the men, who indiscriminately killed and destroyed property until the order was given for their massacre. Incidents in Rome's political history of this kind created an atmosphere in which servile violence came to be taken for granted. But for slaves themselves the dividing line between participation in acts of violence contrived by members of the political classes and self-centered violent revolt had become a very narrow one to cross.[13]

Moreover, Roman and Italian slaves took part in acts of violence that arose from private as well as public concerns, the incidence of which was aggravated by the longstanding Roman tradition of recourse to self-help at moments of perceived personal grievance. As early as 138 B.C., it was charged, slaves belonging to the company controlling the production of pitch in the Silva Sila in Bruttium were implicated in murder; and in 83 B.C. Cicero's client P. Quinctius was said to have been forcibly expelled by slaves from estates in Gallia Narbonensis owned by Sex. Naevius, his adversary in court, and Quinctius's recently deceased brother. Episodes of this kind led in 76 B.C. to the issuance of an edict by the praetor M. Terentius Varro Lucullus that sought to restrain the violence armed gangs of slaves perpetrated. For, according to Cicero, "it was said that many forces of slaves in remote estates and pastures were armed and committing murders and . . . this practice seemed to affect not only the property of private persons but the highest interests of the state." The Lucullan edict complemented the establishment two years earlier, following the insurrection of M. Aemilius Lepidus, of a permanent court for cases of public violence. But actions in which slaveowners used their slaves to defend lands against men with rival claims to ownership—a feature that has later parallels in the slave society of Brazil—brought the delivery, in 71 B.C. and 69 B.C. respectively, of Cicero's speeches *Pro Tullio* and *Pro Caecina*.[14]

There was no difficulty in this period in keeping up the level of the slave supply. Two incidents illustrate how natural reproduction continued to provide new slaves. First, again during the Social War, in 90 B.C. the army of Q. Servilius Caepio was ambushed by the Italian leader Q. Popaedius who had duped Caepio into an alliance by bringing him as evidence of his trustworthiness two infants Popaedius claimed were his sons; in reality the infants were conveniently available slave children. Second, at about the same time, the *princeps senatus* M. Aemilius Scaurus paid what became a notoriously high price, HS 700,000, for the grammarian Daphnis, a slave known to have been born into slavery. In addition, warfare continued to contribute captives to the slave markets. In 97 B.C. in Spain, Q. Sertorius enslaved the surviving population of Castulo, which had revolted against Roman rule, and over twenty years later he likewise enslaved the inhabitants of Lauro, also in Spain. During Rome's war against Mithridates of Pontus, C. Flavius Fimbria in 86–85 B.C. allowed his troops to engage in random acts of enslavement as he marched through Thrace, and in 86 B.C. Sulla sold the remaining population of Athens into slavery after his capture of that city. The pattern was repeated in the cities of Asia in the following year. Evidence of the bitterness such enslavements involved—apart from the simple deprivation of freedom itself—emerges from the report that when Mithridates's general Zenobius enslaved the Chians in 86 B.C., the men were deliberately separated from the women and children before being shipped to Pontus.[15]

Shortly before the Spartacan revolt Cicero stated: "For when, every hour, we see or hear of an act of cruelty, even those of us who are by nature most merciful lose from our hearts, in this constant presence of trouble, all feeling of humanity." In the previous twenty years or so the fabric of the Roman state had been shaken by the Social War, the first armed march on Rome of Sulla, the bloody reaction of C. Marius and L. Cornelius Cinna, Sulla's dictatorship, and the insurrection of M. Aemilius Lepidus. Against this background it is hardly surprising that the slave population of Italy, consciously maintained at a high numerical level and steeped in violence, should eventually have been prepared to turn against its masters: the violence of revolt was the product of the violence slave-owners themselves had long fostered in their slaves and for which they themselves had set the example. In the two years of the Spartacan war, the slave rebels were remarkably successful in withstanding the Roman forces sent to deal with them. But although information on the war is available in many sources, from almost contemporary notices to items written in late antiquity, the source tradition as a whole, like that for the Sicilian wars, is not copious enough to permit reconstruction of the course of events on anything like a day-to-day basis. The essential progression of the war is not seriously in question, however, and, predictably, correspondences with earlier events in Sicily are noticeable.[16]

One such correspondence concerns Spartacus himself and it requires emphasis before the events of the war are described. As other commentators, Plutarch was aware of the Thracian origins of Spartacus. But Plutarch used that point of detail to introduce a comment, unique in the source tradition, that is very striking: Spartacus, he says, was "a Thracian from a nomadic tribe who was not only very brave and physically powerful, but also more intelligent and more humane than one would expect of someone whom Chance had made a slave, and he was far more like a Greek than was normal for his race." The comment implies that to a Greek author of the late first century A.D. Spartacus could be considered to have overcome the natural inferiority produced by the twin handicaps of foreignness and servile status by sheer force of character; and the prejudice underlying it is similarly detectable elsewhere: Florus makes clear the uncontested point that merely to be a slave was stigmatic in and of itself, and Diodorus Siculus unambiguously brands Spartacus as "barbarian." Nevertheless, Spartacus was always remembered as the supreme leader of the slave war, and it appears that his leadership was in part grounded in the same type of charismatic appeal earlier commanded by Eunus and Salvius. After remarking on Spartacus's moral worth, Plutarch recounts the following anecdote:

> The story goes that when he was first brought to Rome to be sold, a snake appeared and wound itself round his face as he was asleep, and his wife, who came from the same tribe as Spartacus and was a prophetess and ini-

tiated into the ecstatic cult of Dionysus, stated that it signified that a great and fearful power would accompany him to a lucky conclusion.

That the story is literally true is of course highly unlikely. But it indicates that Spartacus was thought to have been a figure who was surrounded by an aura of religiosity, insofar as he is portrayed here as the elect of supernatural forces, and there is no reason to believe that such a characterization was not perceptible to the slaves who attached themselves to him. The possibility will emerge later that Spartacus has to be regarded as following in the tradition of the Sicilian slave leaders in drawing on and manipulating religious associations for the purpose of promoting resistance to slavery.[17]

It was perhaps in the summer of 73 B.C. that about seventy slaves escaped from Batiatus's training school at Capua and established a defensible position on Mount Vesuvius some thirty kilometers away. As the gladiators broke out of the school, they are said to have seized kitchen implements for use as makeshift weapons—the detail recalls the kitchen in the barracks at Pompeii—and to have intercepted a wagonload of gladiatorial equipment en route to another city. Their actions appear to have been improvised at short notice, the result perhaps of the betrayal of a much larger eruption that had earlier been discussed. Spartacus soon emerged as the rebels' leader, it seems, and may have been the driving force behind the initial outbreak. But once the gladiators had begun to engage in pillaging raids from their mountain base, at least two other men, the Gauls Crixus and Oenomaus, figured as individuals of some initiative and authority. If the band of gladiators had any concrete plans beyond effecting their own escape from Capua they are not recorded. But news of their actions must have spread quickly, for once entrenched on Mount Vesuvius they became a focal point of attraction for other slaves who, not least because some were normally kept in *ergastula*, can in the main only have been rural slaves from the neighboring villas and estates of Campania. Thus the gladiators' revolt began to develop into a broader servile insurrection, and Spartacus's practice of equally dividing the spoils of the pillaging expeditions may have been a special inducement for encouraging discontented agricultural workers to join the growing movement.[18]

The scale of the revolt at this preliminary stage cannot be determined precisely. Florus, even before mentioning Mount Vesuvius, claims that the rebel numbers had already reached ten thousand. Exaggeration must be suspected. But while Mount Vesuvius was still serving as the rebels' base, the revolt was deemed serious enough to warrant the despatch from Rome to stamp it out of one of the praetors of 73 B.C., Claudius Glaber.

It is possible that retaliation against the rebels had first been attempted by local forces from Capua, but if so they had been repulsed. As a praetor, however, Glaber should be expected to have had under his command a full legion of troops, a probability supported by Plutarch's reference to an army of three thousand serving under him, and it can be assumed that such a force was the appropriate complement to the flight and rebellion of several thousand slaves.[19]

Claudius Glaber's policy was to lay siege to the rebels' mountain stronghold, but the tactic did not work. The rebels first escaped from the position to which they had been confined by descending the mountain on ladders made from wild vines, and then with a surprise attack they destroyed the Roman camp. Frontinus believed that several Roman cohorts gave way on this occasion to a force of only seventy-four gladiators, a figure obviously reflecting the tradition of the number of gladiators who originally left Capua but one that cannot represent the full size of the slaves' numbers in view of the size of Glaber's army. After this initial rebel success, however, potential for escalation of the revolt was certainly created, and Plutarch indeed speaks of many herdsmen and shepherds now joining the rebellion. Moreover, although the sources continue to leave the impression that the expansion of the rebels' numbers was more fortuitous than contrived, there are hints too of a more deliberate pattern of organization that previously had not been needed: some of the new adherents were provided with arms, and others were deployed as scouts and light infantry. A disciplined slave force was thus being formed.[20]

To be sure, the ordinary individuals who made up this army cannot be identified in any way; only their leaders have left a personal trace or two in the extant record. But from Varro's remarks on *pastores* in the agricultural treatise he published in 37 B.C., near the end of his life, a sense of what they were like in type can be gleaned, for there is no reason to think that slave herdsmen and shepherds will have been generally different a generation earlier. Preferably, Varro says, herdsmen who pastured livestock for sustained periods without returning daily to the farmstead were to be physically mature (boys were of no use for this work) and well above average in fitness, in view of the rigors of their work and the terrain to which they were exposed. "You should choose men," he stated, "of powerful physique, fast-moving and nimble, who are not clumsy when they move their limbs, and are not just able to follow after the flock but also to defend it from predatory beasts or brigands, who can lift loads up onto the backs of the pack animals, are good at sprinting and at hitting their target." As seen earlier, familiarity with weapons was standard for these men, and *pastores* were in fact usually armed. Varro observed further that certain Spanish tribesmen were not at all suitable for becoming *pastores* but that Gauls were, a remark implying that even late in the first century B.C. herdsmen were often new slaves. So like their counterparts in Sicily, enjoying considerable freedom of movement though answerable to a chief herdsman, as they moved their animals along the drove roads between summer and winter pasturage such men, new to slavery, used to a certain independence and to relying on their own resources for survival, might well be thought ripe for revolt when the opportunity arose. As early as 213 B.C. during the Hannibalic war, T. Pomponius Veientanus had raised in Bruttium an "ill-trained mob of slaves and peasants."[21]

After the Roman reverse at Vesuvius and still in 73 B.C., a second praetor, P. Varinius, was put in charge of Rome's operations against the rebels. Although his troops were not all seasoned veterans, his army may have been larger than that of Glaber: Furius, one of his subordinate officers, alone headed a contingent of two thousand troops, and L. Cossinius, another officer, also headed a sizable force. But in separate encounters both men suffered setbacks, and Cossinius in particular, although avoiding capture, lost his camp and supplies to a surprise attack from Spartacus at a site called Salinae. Varinius too suffered defeats, at one point ignominiously losing his lictors and horse to the rebels, though he too escaped. Sallust suggests that his army was weakened by desertions and the effects of autumnal disease, and at one point Varinius found it necessary to send his quaestor, C. Toranius, who had also suffered defeat by Spartacus, to Rome with the news of the army's discomfiture and its mutinous disposition. Another commander, P. Valerius, was despatched, with hastily recruited troops, to oppose the rebels.[22]

This second phase of the war seems to have extended into the winter of 73–72 B.C., and during Varinius's command the geographical scope of the rebellion broadened considerably. Besides evidence of ravaging attacks in Campania, with specific assaults on the prosperous cities of Cumae, Nola, and Nuceria, there is also evidence that the rebellion now affected the south of Italy, with the coastal towns of Metapontum and Thurii, on one hand, and Cosentia, deep in the heart of Bruttium, on the other, as objects of eventual attack. Not that these southern towns attracted the rebels as possible centers of occupation, however, for they were not at all the equals of the wealthy cities of Campania. From the time of the Hannibalic occupation, the south of Italy had witnessed a steady but serious decline of its free population, of which widespread urban decay is the strongest indication. By contrast, the intrusion of slaves occupied in agriculture offset the erosion and guaranteed successful use of the land; so Strabo knew in his day of the good wines that came from the regions of Thurii and Cosentia, and large estates lay around Metapontum. But likewise in Strabo's day Thurii was a very weak city, and Metapontum itself actually vanished. While Cosentia could still be characterized as the metropolis of Bruttium, therefore, it was the rural hinterlands of the towns, offering supplies of food and a remote environment, that controlled the rebels' movements. Thus Sallust preserves the detail that the rebels at-

tacked farmers (*coloni*) at Abellinum on the southern migration. Moreover, given the associations of the region with chronic brigandage, it
comes as no surprise to learn of further increases in the numbers of rebels.
Oenomaus may now have been defeated and killed. But Crixus is reported
to have had ten thousand followers under him, and Spartacus three times
that figure. In total, at this point, Appian puts the rebel numbers at seventy thousand.[23]

Whatever the accuracy of these figures, the proliferation of the rebellion
they imply is genuinely reflected in the appointment against Spartacus
in 72 B.C. of both the consuls for that year, L. Gellius Publicola and Cn.
Cornelius Lentulus Clodianus. The step was a major one for Rome to
take, and it leaves no doubt of the successes thus far enjoyed by the rebels
or of the fact that the initiative still lay very much with them. The praetor
Cn. Manlius and the former praetor Q. Arrius also participated in the
campaigns of 72 B.C., and with its army now at a strength of at least four
legions, the military tide at first turned in favor of Rome. For it was in
this year that L. Gellius, notwithstanding his rather advanced years (he
was in his early sixties), defeated and allegedly killed twenty thousand
slaves in the region of Mount Garganus in northwestern Apulia after a
surprise attack on a body of rebels under Crixus that had become separated
from the main forces. But this shift in fortunes was short-lived, perhaps
because, as Plutarch suggests, the command of Gellius was open to re-
proach: the high reputation gained in the war by M. Porcius Cato, who
had volunteered for service out of devotion to his half-brother, the military
tribune Q. Servilius Caepio, formed at least a signal contrast to Gellius's
leadership. Still, although the details are not fully known, both the consuls and C. Cassius Longinus, the governor of Cisalpine Gaul and head
of an army of two legions, were defeated in the course of 72 B.C. This
means that after the earlier southward push, Spartacus had reversed and
marched north, his purpose perhaps being to allow his followers to leave
Italy altogether so that they could disperse to other lands. After the defeat
of Longinus, at Mutina, an exit across the Alps was presumably open to
them; but unanimity of purpose was absent. So again the slaves changed
direction, and at one juncture contemplated attacking Rome. Yet in the
event they returned to the south of Italy and eventually occupied Thurii
instead. Throughout the year, therefore, it appears that despite maintaining the military edge the rebels had no single policy or long-term aim
to pursue. Spartacus, rather, hampered by an inability to control all the
dissidents, was only able to react to a series of immediate situations by
which he found himself confronted.[24]

Consequent upon their failures, the consuls of 72 B.C., probably late in
the year, were recalled to Rome in disgrace. In what had become a critical
situation, however, Rome showed no hesitation about embarking on a
new phase of engagement with the rebel slaves, and in the most drastic

move of the war so far the future triumvir M. Licinius Crassus was given an extraordinary military command of ten legions, six of which were new—and perhaps raised only through the admission of older men—the rest taken over from Gellius and Lentulus. Beneath the appointment of course lay Crassus's political ambition and rivalry with Cn. Pompeius. Crassus's operations, however, did not begin auspiciously. As the rebels were making their way south, Crassus took up a position in the region of Picenum and ordered his subordinate Mummius to follow but not to engage Spartacus. But Mummius disobeyed his orders, attacked, and was overcome with the two legions in his charge. Immediately thereafter Crassus imposed on the army the humiliating punishment of decimation and then moved to face Spartacus. In turn, Spartacus retreated across Lucania to the sea, and it was now that the military balance began to tilt firmly against the rebels. The details provided in the source tradition are again discrepant. But defeats of distinct rebel contingents are recorded, such as that of thirty or thirty-five thousand slaves led by Castus and Gannicus—leaders previously unheard of—an engagement in which the legates Q. Marcius Rufus and C. Pomptinus played a conspicuous role by executing a surprise attack. Spartacus himself may even have been worsted by Crassus. Despite the lack of detailed knowledge, therefore, the losses inflicted by Crassus must have been substantial as the superior might of his army began to prevail.[25]

In the winter of 72–71 B.C. the rebel forces found themselves trapped near Rhegium in the peninsula of Bruttium, where Spartacus had withdrawn after considering (again in reactive fashion) but abandoning the idea of an evacuation to Sicily. Crassus installed fortifications and besieged the rebels, whose deep southern position became increasingly perilous through the winter months. Whether the defeat of Castus and Gannicus preceded or followed the implementation of the siege, it is certain that attempts the slaves made to break through Crassus's defenses met with few positive results, and on one occasion Spartacus is said by Plutarch to have been driven in retreat toward the cover of the mountains of Petelia on the eastern coast of Bruttium. He was pursued by the cavalry commander L. Quinctius and the quaestor Cn. Tremellius Scrofa but won a victory against them, the wounded quaestor only narrowly escaping. Finally, Spartacus succeeded in penetrating Crassus's barrier, planning, it appears, to make for Brundisium in another bid to leave Italy altogether. But if that was the intention, it was nullified by the arrival at the port city of M. Terentius Varro Lucullus, who had been ordered to return from his province of Macedonia in order to bring aid to Crassus. Spartacus turned to face Crassus for the decisive encounter, in desperation according to Appian, overconfident in the version of Plutarch because of the gains made against Crassus's officers on the retreat to Petelia. The final battle was probably fought at the head of the river Silarus in northwestern Lucania. The slaves were defeated, and Spartacus was killed. Those who survived fled to the mountains, with Crassus in pursuit. Six thousand captives were crucified along the Via Appia from Capua to Rome, and Crassus was rewarded for his victory with the honor of an ovation.[26]

The details of the last phase of the war are no less certain than those of the earlier stages. Yet the senate's summons of Lucullus from Macedonia strongly suggests that early in 71 B.C. the issue of the war was still in suspense; nor was it Lucullus alone who was ordered to bring Crassus assistance: returning from his victory over Q. Sertorius in Spain, Pompeius was also instructed to engage the slaves, and in due course—probably in the spring in the wake of Crassus's success—he cut down a band of fugitives. By the spring of 71 B.C., indeed, after six months' campaigning by Crassus, the Spartacan war was over. From its origins as a revolt of gladiators at Capua, the insurrection had grown to incorporate an immense mass of slave rebels, who for close to two years found ways to continue their resistance against slavery over an immense area: to the south, Campania, Lucania, Bruttium, and Apulia were all affected by the war, but the rebels' abortive drive to the north had meant for a time that virtually no region in the peninsula was immune to their depredations. The severities of slavery presupposed by those bare facts hardly stand in need of further emphasis.[27]

It does, however, require stress that the escalation of the revolt of gladiators into a sustained war of servile resistance cannot possibly have been what Spartacus and his immediate companions had hoped to achieve when they made their escape from Capua. The sources have little to say about the motivations of the rebel slaves, but everything that is said pertains only to the gladiators' circumstances. Plutarch sets the idea of breaking out of the gladiatorial school against the background of the harsh treatment the slaves received there: "they were forcibly kept imprisoned to fight as gladiators, not because they had done anything wrong, but because of the wickedness of the man who had bought them"; Appian makes the blunt statement that Spartacus "persuaded about seventy of them to gamble for their freedom rather than be put on show at a public spectacle"; Florus adds that a wish for revenge manifested itself once the gladiators had received their first infusion of additional servile support. The desire to avoid incarceration, to gain liberty, and to take revenge for injuries suffered is comprehensible enough in sheer human terms. But no matter how similarly arduous the living conditions of other slaves, there is no evidence to suggest that Spartacus and his followers, any more than the slaves at Enna or Halicyae in Sicily, purposely set out from the beginning to raise a general rebellion of slaves throughout central and southern Italy. Indeed, the peculiarity of their circumstances, once contrasted with those of other slaves, precludes any such thought.[28]

Still, whatever the reliability of the recorded figures, the escalation of the rebel numbers occurred on a massive scale, such that even commentators in late antiquity were surprised: "historians have hardly found a satisfactory answer to the question how a conflict begun by a very small number, that is, fewer than seventy gladiators, was expanded into a servile war by the addition of a huge number of fierce and cruel men, who thereafter defeated many a general of the Roman people and devastated cities and whole districts." But the cause of the proliferation lay at root in the willingness of large numbers of discontented rural slaves in Italy to risk rejecting their conditions of servitude in favor of a precarious, but freer existence under the leadership of men who had already proved both that escape was possible and that, after the defeat of Glaber's army at Mount Vesuvius, the forces of Rome were not necessarily strong enough to return them to slavery. The growth of the rebel movement was not a deliberately contrived or carefully orchestrated phenomenon, therefore, but an example on the grand scale of traditional patterns of flight and revolt.

It is true, admittedly, that hints of recruitment for the slave army can be found in the sources: as Sallust suggests, for instance, when rebellion was in progress and casualties were suffered, reinforcements were certainly needed. But this particular situation aside, the hints are usually unreliable or occur in contexts where considerable spontaneous escalation had already taken place. It is true too that there is evidence of individuals who were not slaves participating in the rebellion: explaining his decision not to march on Rome, Appian records that Spartacus "did not think he was powerful enough for that yet and his army as a whole was not yet properly armed—for not a single city had cooperated with him: they were all slaves and deserters and generally an indiscriminate rabble." But the desertions from Rome to Spartacus are symptomatic only of the self-interested opportunism encouraged by any period of warfare, and there is no reason to believe that they were numerically great or of undue significance. Appian also claims that "some free persons from the countryside" joined Spartacus while he was still based on Mount Vesuvius. But again the number of such persons cannot be estimated and in any case hardly seems great enough to justify categorizing the whole uprising as a peasant revolt. In this regard, Sallust's notice of the flight of *coloni* before the advance of Spartacus's force is of especial importance. It could be urged that some of those who were attracted in 63 B.C. by the proposal of L. Sergius Catilina to cancel debts—veteran soldiers, for example, who had failed as farmers and peasants the settlers had displaced—were already suffering by the late seventies and so were inclined to violent disaffection. But as Catilina knew, the interests of Roman citizens were not those of restless slaves, and the notion of a coalition thus makes little sense. In 63 B.C., furthermore, Catilina is expressly said to have spurned the support of rural slaves. The argument might be made that Spartacus had once hoped to exploit the general tendency of slaves to resist servitude by flight and to convert the original revolt of gladiators into a wider slave rebellion. But there is no evidence of such aspirations. There can be no reasonable doubt, therefore, that widespread revolt, whether of slaves or of slaves in alliance with other social elements, was not at all the best means by which the gladiators from Capua might hope to convert their act of flight into a state of permanent freedom, for the greater the rebel numbers, the greater the prospect of Roman retaliation in kind.[29]

Accordingly, it is not surprising that the strategies devised by Spartacus during the course of the war for leaving Italy completely have all the signs of having been hastily determined responses to the unanticipated problems posed by the growth of the rebel numbers. In 72 B.C. Spartacus, according to Plutarch, first "considered what the most likely outcome would be, and did not suppose that he could break the power of the Romans. Consequently, he led his army towards the Alps, thinking that they ought to cross over them and go to their homelands, some to Thrace and some to Gaul." Whatever the merits of the plan, Plutarch's statement suggests that it was no more than a response to a predictable military situation caused by the rebellion's own development, and certainly the notion that the plan was abandoned because Spartacus's army contained many free Italians from the south who wanted to return to the regions they had first come from lacks conviction. Why had they gone north to begin with? Later in 72 B.C., Plutarch again records, Spartacus by chance fell in with some Cilician pirates as he withdrew to the deep south and secured their agreement to help transport two thousand slaves to Sicily in order to seize the island: a recent slave war there had not long ended and could easily be renewed; but in the event Spartacus was deceived by the Cilicians, who proved of no use to him. Plutarch is careful to note that Spartacus on this occasion intended to evacuate only a detachment of his forces, not the full complement. But Florus speaks of a more all-embracing plan, devised in critical circumstances: "being cut off in the angle of Bruttium and preparing to escape to Sicily, but being unable to obtain ships, they tried to launch rafts of beams and casks bound together with withies on the swift waters of the straits." It could be said that the strategy was justifiable given Sicily's earlier history; and the potential for further servile unrest there is substantiated by the measures taken by the governor, C. Verres, to prevent Spartacus's arrival in Sicily. Spartacus may indeed have considered extending the rebellion into the province as a means of protecting his beleaguered forces, but the proposed evacuation was not part of a carefully meditated master plan and cannot be regarded as anything more than an improvised tactic designed to solve the difficulties of sustaining resistance with large numbers of followers. Moreover, the logistical difficulties involved in evacuation, both in the north after Mutina and in the south with the plan to reach Sicily, may simply have been underestimated.[30]

Within the rebel movement, therefore, a coherent set of objectives never existed. To some degree that may have been due to Spartacus's inability to control fully his vast following, for the signs are plentiful that disagreements undermined the insurgents' efforts to maintain their struggle. In the context of Varinius's pursuit of Spartacus, Sallust records that "a difference over policy had brought them near to quarrelling: Crixus and his fellow Gauls and Germans wanted to go and meet Varinius and offer battle of their own accord; on the other hand Spartacus [opposed an attack?]." Plutarch attributes Gellius's success against the Germans to the latter's presumptuous separation of themselves from the main body of rebels and refers to a dispute that led to some of the slaves taking up a separate position at the Lucanian lake (or marshes) under Castus and Gannicus. Toward the end of his narrative, Plutarch further speaks of the rebels' refusal to obey their leaders, while Appian specifies that the ten thousand slaves Crassus defeated had camped away from the main contingent of Spartacus's forces. On a generous view, it might be thought that what commentators saw as disunity was in reality the result of tactical decisions made to increase the rebels' chances of survival. There may equally have been, however, genuine dissension arising from divergent aspirations on the part of the rebel leaders. But it was the sheer size of the uprising itself that made it impossible to render permanent the freedom the slaves acquired by their acts of revolt. Their only option was to withstand Rome's retaliation for as long as was practicably possible by resorting to whatever methods of survival could prove effective. Once the details of those methods are brought out, and with the causal context of the rebellion kept in mind, it becomes impossible to view the Spartacan movement as being in any way dominated by abstract or ideological imperatives: freedom from slavery was the intent of the fugitives; the slavery system itself remained unaffected.[31]

[VI]

The Maintenance of Rebellion

In the middle of the first century A.D., more than a hundred years after the insurrection of Spartacus had been crushed, the Stoic philosopher Seneca formulated the most liberal set of doctrines on slavery that had ever been articulated at Rome—as far, that is, as the extant corpus of ancient literature allows of judgment. Advocating that masters should treat their slaves with lenience, for instance, Seneca broke down the artificial distinction between slave and free and insisted that all men shared a common origin and a common mortality. Thus the true worth of the individual was to be evaluated not from the criterion of social rank, which was simply the result of accident, but solely from that of moral standing. Hence the condition of slavery was not an impediment to the slave's achievement of freedom of spirit. Seneca believed indeed that the slave had the capacity to confer on his owner a kindness or benefit, and since the slave could thereby demonstrate his virtue, he had access to an equality of moral character with other men. Slavery being a condition of the body only, the human mind could transcend physical bondage and exercise for good that freedom of spirit which lay beyond subjection and was available to all.[1]

Given these ideas, it could be assumed that Seneca advocated the humane treatment of slaves on the basis of a genuinely held belief in the equality of all mankind, a concern for the worth of the individual as an individual, and a recognition of the slave's essential humanity. But Seneca did not reach the point of calling for an end to slavery as the logical outcome of his thought, and all that he sought from slaves themselves was a respectful, loving attitude toward their masters. Abolition of slavery never presented itself to him as a seriously viable possibility, and in reality Seneca's *humanitas* was not prompted by an interest in the plight of the slave as a slave or as a fellow member of the human race; instead, Seneca's object was to secure Stoic moderation among slaveowners, whose exercise of lenience upon their slaves would elicit unswerving loyalty and obedience in them. The resultant social harmony between slave and free would permit the Roman system of slavery to continue without interruption or jeopardy. The notion of spiritual equality was not to be converted into practical form, altering in any way the hierarchical structure of Roman society.[2]

Belief in the spiritual brotherhood of mankind was not unique to Seneca of course, but had long been a central tenet of the Stoic tradition Seneca adapted and developed. However, since that belief, even in its most advanced expression, never came to weaken or erode the concept that slavery was an integral component of society, it cannot be said that the three slave rebellions of the period 140 B.C. to 70 B.C. occurred under the influence or against the background of a "revolutionary atmosphere": for whatever view may be taken of shifts in the geopolitical balance of the Mediterranean world or in the political life of Rome in this period, without an intellectual dynamic to impel and effect massive social change (such as that of modern abolitionism), any concept of a widespread "revolutionary climate" is inappropriate for explaining the outbreak and course of the slave rebellions. Certainly the rebellions took place in an age of political turmoil and civil commotion, the products of a nexus of social and economic ills long festering and aggravated by the expansion of slavery. Hence the proposal of Ti. Gracchus in 133 B.C. to redistribute land in Italy is said to have been influenced by both his personal observation of large numbers of foreign slaves in rural Etruria and the impact of the first Sicilian slave war; and a subsidiary aim of the proposal may well have been "to reduce the number of slaves employed on the land in order to lessen the danger of slave uprisings." But the significant point is that neither Ti. Gracchus nor any of the subsequent politicians who advocated agrarian reform in the last century of the Republic extended their attempts to tackle contemporary problems by adopting the truly revolutionary tactic of eliminating slavery from Roman society.[3]

Moreover, the distinction between rebellion and revolution that the earlier survey of resistance in modern slave societies made clear must underscore the impossibility in classical antiquity of rebel slaves themselves ever hoping to effect a radical transformation of the social and institutional structures around them. In contrast, an uprising of slaves on the Engenho Santana in Brazil in 1789 was followed after two years of sustained unrest by an offer to return to servitude if certain demands were met: improved conditions of labor, land for the slaves' own development (with guaranteed time to farm it), their own selection of overseers, and uncontrolled intervals of rest and relaxation. In the event the demands were rejected. But they represented all the same a revolutionary threat to the institution of slavery of a kind that is without parallel in the Roman world. The history of resistance in modern slave societies suggests in fact that the rebel slaves of Sicily and Italy sought only to restore, or in some cases to acquire for the first time, a personal liberty that was otherwise completely closed off to them; and the motivations for revolt given in the sources are consistent with this expectation, for nothing else is attributed to the rebels than the desire of an originally small group of dissidents to grasp their freedom and to take revenge against cruel masters. To the members of a social grouping devoid of all political personality, the issues of Roman politics—"the rights of citizens, the location of sovereignty in the state, the control of foreign relations and military affairs, and the access of individual citizens to a share in the resources which the state had at its disposal"—were meaningless and irrelevant. Personal experience of brutality and degradation, not ideological imperatives, prompted the initial acts of revolt.[4]

Naturally, it has to be recognized that the information available on motives comes from nonslave sources—authors who rationalized the behavior of the slave rebels in their own way—and that because the rebels have left no statements of their aspirations and intentions, their views of events, as of all their experiences in slavery, must always remain irrecoverable. In theory therefore the possibility that in all three episodes slave insurgents premeditated insurrection of the oppressed on an enormous scale can never be disproved. But given the surviving evidence, together with the general pattern of slave resistance available for the Roman world—in which a constant leitmotif of individual flight was punctuated by occasional small-scale revolts aroused by local circumstances—the balance of probability must lie against this. As far as can be told, the great escalation of all three movements was unforeseen, unplanned, and unexpected. Once a reality, however, the rapid growth in the numbers of the dissidents demanded a positive reaction from the slaves themselves if the immediate gains of flight and revolt were not to be forfeited at once. That demand was met in all three cases, as order and organization emerged among the amorphous masses of slaves. From a comparative perspective, the actions slaves took should have served only the purposes of protecting their freedom and sustaining the momentum of rebellion. What can be termed a maroon dimension to their resistance is indeed detectable in the historical record, and, once exposed, it confirms the absence of any ideological theory or impulse behind the slave movements.

Violent revolt by disaffected slaves could not take place without access of some sort to weapons, to be used at the least for self-protective purposes. But the lack of any systematic planning for rebellion on a major scale by the original dissidents in Sicily and Italy is indicated by the haphazard fashion in which they were compelled to equip themselves, for none of them appear to have been able at the outset to rely on any but improvised weapons. This is true of the four hundred slaves at Enna in the first Sicilian rebellion, while still at an early stage of developments some of Eunus's followers were using "axes and hatchets, or slings, or sickles, or fire-hardened stakes, or even kitchen spits." The cruel Damophilus, it will be recalled, was killed with a sword and an axe. Similarly, the rebels who based themselves on Mount Caprianus during the second Sicilian rebellion are said by Diodorus to have armed themselves in whatever way was possible. And when Spartacus's revolt began, kitchen utensils, axes, and spits were again the main weapons used by the gladiators. Once escaped from Capua, they improved their situation, quite fortuitously, by taking "wooden stakes and swords" from travelers, in the account of Appian, or by seizing gladiatorial equipment they found in transit, in the account of Plutarch. Velleius has them seizing swords in Capua, Frontinus using shields made from osiers, covered with the hides of animals, and Florus remarks that the rebels "made themselves rude shields of wicker-work and the skins of animals, and swords and other weapons by melting down the iron in the slave-prisons [ergastula]." Details may differ, but the theme is the same. The herdsmen who joined the revolt of Eunus may have been better prepared for armed resistance, since various weapons ("clubs and spears and hefty sticks") had become standard equipment for rural brigands. But to rely on thefts of tools and domestic implements or on windfall acquisitions of more regular arms was not an obvious way of preparing to raise a large slave army, whatever the degree of ingenuity demonstrated by slaves.[5]

Signs of more measured attempts to secure other than purely makeshift weapons become evident once the rebellions began to escalate. Eunus, after his elevation to the status of a slave king, refused to sanction indiscriminate slaughter of the citizen population at Enna and purposely spared those who could make weapons for the growing numbers of rebels. When Salvius had been made a king during the second Sicilian uprising, his preparations for the attack on Morgantina must also have included arming his adherents. According to Appian, Spartacus had weapons made for what had become a force of seventy thousand rebels after the defeat of P. Varinius, while at Thurii his followers "bought lots of iron and brass and did not do anything to harm the people who traded in these metals. In this way," Appian adds, "they came to be well supplied with a lot of war material." A fragment of Sallust referring to Spartacus's campaigns against Varinius tells of the slaves' need "to harden their spears in the fire, and give them (apart from the necessary warlike appearance) the capability of inflicting almost as much damage as steel." Weapons had not only to be acquired but readied to produce the maximum effect in battle.[6]

Nonetheless, the most fruitful sources of ready-made arms were the Roman armies and local forces confronted by the rebels, and a string of details in the narrative accounts suggests that the slaves' ability to continue military resistance always depended, as in modern maroon situations, on the maintenance of a predatory relationship with the forces intended to suppress them. So the defeat of M. Titinius in the second Sicilian rebellion resulted in the slaves collecting weapons from Titinius's dead or deserting troops. At Morgantina, Salvius gained possession of "a large quantity of weapons" from Romans he urged to save their lives by abandoning their arms. The gladiators from Capua willingly exchanged their gladiatorial equipment for weapons taken from the local garrison at once sent against them and defeated. Subsequently the Spartacan rebels captured a Roman camp after their early descent from Mount Vesuvius; their successes against L. Cossinius (near Salinae) and Cn. Cornelius Lentulus produced more acquisitions, while after their victory over Mummius, Roman troops again deserted, leaving their weapons as the rebels' prize. The plundering of weapons from establishment forces was an essential device for supplying the rebels' practical needs.[7]

A clearer sense of the equipment actually secured in this way can be gleaned from the sixth book of Polybius's *Histories*, composed *circa* 150 B.C., in which the contemporary Roman legion is described in considerable detail. The legion in battle formation was divided into four lines of troops: first the *velites*, the youngest and poorest of the soldiers, who functioned as a light screen; then the *hastati*, the first of the three main lines, men somewhat older and financially better off than the *velites*; next the *principes*, the prime troops; and finally the *triarii*, the oldest and most experienced of the combatants. At full strength the infantry numbered forty-two hundred, with a complement of three hundred cavalry. As for weapons, the *velites* used swords, short javelins, and small circular shields, whereas the main lines used the shorter Spanish sword, for cutting and thrusting, a larger oval shield, and the long throwing javelin (except that the *triarii* used an alternative type of thrusting javelin). As for armor, the main lines were equipped with bronze helmets, pectorals, and greaves, with some troops wearing mailcoats. The cavalry, Polybius says, were now armed in Greek style, using long lances, round shields, and linen corslets. Between the time of Polybius's description and the rebellion of Spartacus, a number of modifications occurred in Roman legionary tactics and organization. The use of greaves was abandoned, for example, and the *triarii* came to use the same kind of javelin as the other main troops. Also, the *velites* disappeared as a separate line and became armed in more standard fashion. Most importantly of all, the legion came to be arranged in cohorts rather than the older units called maniples, the change, as all the others, taking place gradually through the later second century and culminating in the reforms associated with the name of C. Marius. Consequently Polybius's account of the legion cannot reflect in every detail the appearance of the armies variously sent to deal with the rebel slaves in Sicily and Italy. With appropriate allowances made, however, there is no reason to doubt that the rebels acquired,

in bulk and on several occasions, armaments and weaponry of the sort
Polybius describes or that the exploitation of such formal fighting material was vital to their practical maintenance of resistance.[8]

Still, the process of maintaining armed resistance was always problem-
atic, and one indication of the disadvantaged position the rebels must
constantly have faced, no matter how successful their piecemeal plundering of defeated Roman armies may have been, emerges from Appian's
account of Spartacus's attempt to march on Rome in 72 B.C. After his
victories over the consuls of that year, Appian reports, Spartacus began
the march at the head of one hundred and twenty thousand infantry. In
preparation he had destroyed what he judged to be unnecessary equipment—some of which had presumably been taken from the consular
armies—and in order not to impede the movement of his forces he had
killed his prisoners and slaughtered a number of pack animals. After again
defeating the consuls in Picenum, however, Spartacus then abandoned
the march because he believed his forces to be deficient in numbers and
weapons. The problem of supplying the rebels with arms involved delicate
calculations over the most effective purposes to which they could be put,
and clearly the problem could not always be satisfactorily resolved.[9]

During the course of the three rebellions the slave rebels adopted various methods of fighting. A category of surprise attacks can be observed
first, in which the advantage plainly lay with the slaves. So when Eunus,
leading the four hundred slaves, first fell upon Enna, the rebels' intention
of exacting vengeance resulted in the killing of some local slaveowners
and mutilation of captives that could not be immediately countered in
the sudden press of events. Likewise, the unexpected nature of the actions
accounted for Cleon's success in his attack on Agrigentum, the rebels'
occupation of a fortress and of Mount Caprianus early in the second Sicilian rebellion, and the gladiators' outbreak from Capua in 73 B.C. The
slaves quickly learned how to adapt and to take advantage of any situation
in order to protect themselves or to gain a psychological edge over their
enemies. Spartacus's descent from Mount Vesuvius when his force was
under siege from Claudius Glaber was effected by the use of ropes made
from locally collected osiers, and the ruse was at once followed by a
sudden assault on the Roman camp, producing a response of panic. When
later surrounded by P. Varinius, Spartacus stole his army away at night,
having created the impression that his camp was under normal nighttime
guard. But the sentries posted, regularly clothed and armed, were fresh
corpses tied to stakes, whose object, together with the fires that had been
lit throughout the camp, was not only to provide cover for the rebels'
withdrawal but also to terrify the Romans into flight. Later still, Spartacus
was able to cross M. Crassus's lines at Rhegium by filling the surrounding
ditch with both natural materials (earth, wood, branches) and the corpses
of slain prisoners and cattle. A Roman camp might be bombarded with

stones—or taunts of cowardice; or a very elaborate scheme might be devised to instil fear in the enemy: thus at one stage of the first Sicilian war, Eunus, safely stationed some distance away from the Roman forces, "put on a show of mimes for those in the city, in which the slaves performed the story of how they had revolted from their own particular masters, reproaching them for the arrogance and inordinate pride which was now leading them to their destruction." Tactical ingenuity, or what even might be called guerrilla-style methods of fighting, on the maroon model, played a large part in the rebels' survival over time.[10]

Before a fully organized response from established society was possible, surprise attacks could be further capitalized by plundering raids such as those carried out after Eunus's initial assault on Enna, those by which Salvius gathered supplies before the investment of Morgantina, and those conducted by Spartacus from Mount Vesuvius and Thurii. Alternatively, the rebels might exploit local terrain to gain a victory in warfare, as when the occupants of Mount Caprianus defeated M. Titinius. But rebel success was less assured in direct confrontations with retaliatory forces, and here the record shows no more than mixed results. In the first real battle of the first Sicilian rebellion, when slave numbers were still expanding, the slaves were successful against L. Hypsaeus (Diodorus alludes to some other victories also), and in the second Sicilian rebellion Salvius's army was able to recover its camp from Roman occupation before Morgantina. But in the later stages of the war, when the slaves were under the sole command of Athenion, they lost pitched battles in open country to L. Licinius Lucullus and M'. Aquillius, perhaps predictably: for the longer the rebellions continued and the larger the Roman forces became, the odds of repeated successes in direct engagements correspondingly turned against the slaves. Thus in the Spartacan rebellion, in spite of the impressive sequence of slave victories in battle against Roman commanders, the sheer weight of Crassus's army was eventually too great for the diminishing numbers of rebels to withstand.[11]

The slaves' record in siege warfare is equally mixed. Diodorus vaguely credits Athenion with taking cities by siege, but the most detailed descriptions of events at Morgantina and Lilybaeum in the second Sicilian war show that the rebels' attempts at siege operations failed in their ultimate purpose. In the first Sicilian war, however, the slaves did much better in resisting sieges at Tauromenium and Enna, both of which were finally lost only by betrayal, while in the second war, Triocala remained impregnable. Betrayal was one variable in ancient siegecraft that was frequently of more relevance to the issue than any of the other elements over which a military leader exercised control. So no significant weaknesses in rebel solidarity should be assumed on this score. Yet it should be recognized that for any army, let alone forces raised as a result of slave revolts, siegecraft was a complex, even scientific business in the late

Hellenistic age, requiring careful planning on the part of the offensive leadership, access to food supplies for the duration of the operation, resources, especially timber, for constructing increasingly sophisticated siege engines, and the guarantee of discipline among the rank and file of the soldiery. In spite of Salvius's preparations before the siege of Morgantina, therefore, it is not altogether remarkable that the slaves' initiatives in this area proved unsuccessful. On the other hand, their capacity to withstand siege for limited periods is comprehensible. For if an assaulting enemy forfeited the advantage of surprise and allowed a city's population to store up supplies, bringing within the city walls livestock and recently harvested crops, the besieged might well be able to oppose the enemy vigorously for a time, countering attacks on the city's defenses with raids and foraging expeditions, deploying defensive machinery against catapults and sappers. During the three slave wars no Roman commander was apparently able to organize as systematic and relentless a siege as that of Scipio Aemilianus at Numantia in 134–133 B.C., where after a year or so the enemy was gruesomely starved into submission. But by the time the betrayal of Tauromenium occurred, the slaves had fallen into a perilous state: "conditions of unspeakable and extreme hunger had been forced upon the insurgents—so that they began by eating their children, then their womenfolk, and in the end they did not even hesitate to eat each other." Appian's account of the cannibalism to which the Numantines were reduced is enough to lend plausibility to Diodorus's remarks here. Similarly, Spartacus may have been affected by food shortages when besieged on Mount Vesuvius, and he was certainly driven to break through Crassus's lines in Rhegium by that problem. Again, therefore, resisting siege over protracted periods was a difficulty the slave rebels could not surmount, and they were compelled to discover the truth of the axiom that "the most miserable fate in war is to endure a siege."[12]

In coping with siege, as indeed in much else, provision of food for vast numbers of insurgent slaves was as critical a matter as the provision of arms and the devising of suitable strategies for warfare. Once more, various pieces of the narrative accounts of the rebellions suggest that this aspect of maintaining resistance was not neglected. It was normal of course for any ancient army to live off the land in wartime conditions (or else to exact appropriations from communities too powerless to demur), and with the slaves often moving from one locale to another, windfall acquisitions of food must have made up a major portion of their requirements. Slaves used to working on farms and *pastores* used to habitual living off the country will obviously have known what to take for their immediate needs. Random plundering raids such as those Spartacus carried out from Mount Vesuvius will have guaranteed short-term rations, even supplies of wine; and the animals collected by Salvius prior to the siege of Morgantina can be understood to have included livestock for the rebels' consumption as well as horses for their force of cavalry. But under such circumstances—as Spartacus discovered when opposed by P. Varinius and again in the peninsula of Bruttium—the prosecution of resistance could hang on a very slender thread, since the need to plunder for food exposed the rebels to enemy attack. Therefore, as the rebellions grew into long campaigns extending through difficult winter months, a more efficient method of providing food was desirable in order to complement the gains of simple pillaging, and the point was understood. The extreme recourse of feeding on animals sacred to divinities had to be avoided. But Diodorus makes the general observation in his account of the first Sicilian rebellion that the slaves, astutely giving some thought to the future— which can only mean continuation of their struggle—refrained from wanton destruction of farm buildings, equipment, and crops in storage, as well as from attacking the free population working as farmers. It is difficult to tell how consistently this line was followed or how elaborately it was developed, and it has to be noted that it was offset to some degree, so Diodorus says, by the vengeful behavior of the free peasantry who, hostile to wealthy landowners, engaged in destroying property. The record as it stands, however, offers valuable evidence of the emergence of a rational, even sensible and enlightened, character in the slaves' actions, and it is paralleled by Diodorus's subsequent comments on Athenion's rising in western Sicily. Here, remarkably so it seems, Athenion refused to accept all rebellious slaves as troops in his embryonic army but instead kept many of them at their customary occupations, the result being that his fighting force was well supplied with food. Athenion maintained indeed that he was to become the ruler of all Sicily: land, livestock, and crops were thus his private property and not to be damaged. Whether genuinely believed or not, the claim functioned as a deterrent against willful destruction of property by rebels who were being shaped into a military force.[13]

The suggestion has already been made that in launching assaults on cities the rebel slaves intended to gain control over the cities' hinterlands for the supplies of foodstuffs they contained. But it should also be emphasized that in addition to offering potential batches of weaponry, the opposing Roman armies also possessed other supplies that were attractive to the rebels, including food, for the armies normally included baggage trains of pack animals and wagons transporting tents and other camping material, artillery, and food rations. Polybius again refers to the ways in which Roman troops and cavalry were deployed for the sake of protecting supplies when the army was on the march and when camp had been made at night (with cattle and booty inside). He gives details too of the standard allowances of food the soldiers received: three *modii* of grain per month for the infantryman, nine *modii* of grain and thirty of barley for the cavalryman. During the slave wars the Roman camps may not have degenerated like those allegedly found in Spain by Scipio Aemilianus in 134 B.C. or in Africa by Q. Caecilius Metellus in 109 B.C. Metellus found that "camp-followers and soldiers roamed about together at all hours of day and night, plundering the fields, taking forcible possession of farmhouses, and trying which of them could carry off most cattle and slaves to barter with traders for imported wine and other commodities. They even sold their grain rations and bought what bread they needed each day." Scipio, in order to restore discipline among the soldiery, is said to have been forced to expel hucksters, prostitutes, and seers; to order the sale of many pack animals and wagons and their useless contents; and to insist on the troops using only a minimum of cooking utensils. Moreover, reform by C. Marius in the interval between his suppression of Jugurtha and his departure against the Cimbri and Teutones may have resulted in a truncated convoy: the legionary soldier was now supposedly more responsible for carrying his own baggage, food, cooking implements, and other tools. Nevertheless, the fact remains that "stocks of armour, weapons, horses, and every sort of war material, including an abundance of provisions—everything, in fact, that is commonly needed in operations on a big scale and of mixed character" was there for the taking by a shrewd enemy. Appian and Plutarch were struck by the details that Spartacus captured the horses and lictors of Roman generals. But exhaustive plundering of defeated Roman armies and their camps will have produced many more prosaic items that fueled the slaves' resistance in a very vital way.[14]

By examining in detail the rebel slaves' methods of fighting and sustaining themselves the emergence of a maroon aspect to the Roman slave wars thus becomes perceptible, and characterization of the slaves as dissidents comprising communities continuously at war has a justifiable attraction. In modern maroon societies, however, a sense of community frequently developed among slaves not merely as a result of commonly held strategic and economic goals, and the concerted activities required to gain them, but also in a direct social manner through their creation of forms of family life. In its early development the typical modern maroon community was populated overwhelmingly by men. But through raids on nearby plantations and estates women were acquired who subsequently produced a new generation of maroons who had never directly experienced slavery. By contrast, the Roman slave wars were too short in duration for forms of stable community life in this social aspect ever to appear—and from an aristocratic slaveowner's high-minded point of view no multitude of fugitives and brigands congregated into a single place was to be dignified with the label of a genuine community (*civitas*). But there is a little evidence to suggest that the notion of community inferable from the rebels' practical maintenance of resistance began, at least at a rudimentary level, to assume something of a recognizable social character before the wars ended.[15]

The proportion of women in the overall servile population of Sicily and Italy in the late second and early first centuries was not negligible, even if beyond precise measurement. As a probability, therefore, involvement of some female slaves in the three episodes of rebellion is to be expected: women such as those abused by Megallis at Enna had reasons as compelling as those of their male counterparts to feel hatred for and to seek revenge against their owners, as Megallis herself found out. But the record of Megallis's execution is not the only confirmation of the probability. Before the rebellions began, many male slaves must have formed unions with female slaves they regarded as their wives in marriage, women who were prepared in the event to accompany their husbands in revolt. Diodorus indeed preserves knowledge of the wife of Eunus, who became his queen when he was made a slave king, and Plutarch, it will be recalled, tells of Spartacus's wife, the prophetess, fleeing with her husband from Capua. Like Chiomara and other women who had earlier fallen into slavery, the wives of Eunus and Spartacus were remembered because of the distinctive associations attaching to them. Yet they should be taken to represent many other, less memorable, female rebels who never acquired any comparable personal notoriety, such as, for example, the two women mentioned by Plutarch when describing Crassus's operations against Castus and Gannicus. The women, who spotted advancing Roman troops while sacrificing on behalf of the insurgents, were probably slave wives like those referred to by Diodorus, together with children it should be noted, when reporting the cannibalism to which the rebels were reduced during the siege of Tauromenium in the first Sicilian rebellion.[16]

At the same time, the degree of female participation in the rebellion should not be exaggerated, and account has to be taken of the abusive treatment of women sporadically indicated in the sources. Spartacus, for example, was unable to prevent his followers from raping women and girls at Forum Antoni, so Sallust records, while Orosius mentions the suicide of a female captive who had been similarly maltreated. According to Diodorus, when Licinius Nerva captured the rebels' camp at Morgantina, "he found . . . a lot of women they had taken prisoner." Their identity is unfortunately not made clear; they could have been slaves forcibly abducted from their owners, but since they were captives, they were perhaps free women, being held either for ransom or for sexual purposes or both; it is impossible to say. Their presence in the rebel camp, however, is suggestive of the kinds of raids carried out by modern maroons to secure women from which the formation of a social community developed, and while this should not be pressed too far, Diodorus's reference, as indeed all the others concerning women, should not be dismissed out of hand.[17]

Most importantly of all, however, the promotion of resistance and the creation of a communal identity among the rebels depended primarily on the appearance of exceptional slave leaders. For no matter how strong the potential for revolt may have been among the slave populations of Sicily and Italy in the late second century and beyond, sustained rebellion was impossible without the emergence of personalities vigorous, and indeed gifted enough, to harness and direct the energies of disaffected fugitive slaves. Relatively speaking, the sources contain a considerable amount of information on the manner in which Eunus, Salvius, Athenion, and Spartacus assumed and consolidated their authority. In the case of the two Sicilian rebellions, the theme of kingship is all important. But the leadership of all three movements needs to be considered together if the monarchical elements from the Sicilian episodes are to become explicable, and in all three cases the control of the comparative evidence is to be firmly kept in mind.

As a preliminary consideration, stress has to be placed on the aura of religiosity that surrounded the leaders. First, when introducing Eunus, Diodorus calls him an *anthropos magos*, a phrase that evokes a cluster of associations offering vital clues to understanding how Eunus's authority was established. Originally the name of a priestly caste in ancient Media, the term *magi* (*magoi*) came in the Greco-Roman world to be used of all kinds of magicians and sorcerers, designating on the one hand genuine Persian or other Near Eastern priests and on the other their imitators, men whose religious claims were at times dubious if not downright fraudulent. So at Rome in A.D. 66 the Armenian king Tiridates, himself a genuine *magus* among a retinue of *magi*, visited the court of Nero and initiated the emperor into some of their rites. But earlier, in the reign of Tiberius, popular practitioners of the art of interpreting dreams and omens had become so unsavory and problematical that they were expelled from Italy or, in some cases, executed because of the evil connotations surrounding their magical powers. Cicero knew that the Persian king had to understand the lore of the *magi* in order to assume the monarchy, and in his view they were comparable to Roman augurs. But of less respectability were *magi* of the type represented by the Jew confronted in the middle of the first century A.D. in Cyprus by Paul and Barnabas: according to Paul, this *magus* was the son of a devil, and drawing on his superior Christian magic, Paul was able to strike him blind. Even so, the man had been able before the apostles' arrival to secure access to the Roman governor, a firm indication of the appeal held by itinerant seers to all social classes. Deriving from a tradition of genuine religious expression, with claims to prophecy, miracles of healing, and other wonders, those who paraded themselves as *magi* attracted followings of disciples from the witnesses of their supernatural feats throughout the Greco-Roman world and purveyed teachings, known to Plutarch, for example, of a destined time on earth of social peace, happiness, and equality. To the socially downtrodden the inherent comfort of those doctrines will obviously have been great.[18]

Against this background Eunus becomes a much more authentic figure. His reputation for magical powers and prophecy, his claims to communion with the gods through dreams and visions were of a sort all manner of people, the gullible and the educated alike, took seriously (and rural slaves especially were used to seeing magical remedies applied to sick animals), so that not all would have shared the skepticism of Diodorus and Florus when they reported the miracle-trick of the fiery nut. Indeed, something serious may lie beneath the surface here, for in Lucian's satire on the descent of Menippus into the underworld, the *magus* serving as his guide prepared a ritual meal beforehand that included nuts, and the cult of fire had always been part of the religious protocol of the *magi*: Strabo knew of their eternal fires in Cappadocia, Pausanias of their ability to effect spontaneous combustion. Antigenes, at least, was not utterly skeptical of Eunus's claims and even exploited them by having his slave entertain his guests with tales of the future. Moreover, Eunus's response to his questioners, that he would treat slaveowners moderately well once he became a king, is not out of line with the theme of social harmony Plutarch attributed to the *magi*. In the short term, Eunus's reply brought him gifts of food from his owner's guests, who are said to have asked the slave to remember their generosity once he came into his kingdom. In the sequel, they were indeed saved from the sentence of death that fell on many others.[19]

The common belief that the future was both predetermined and discoverable allowed Eunus to become the object of a large following once his credibility, like that of other *magi*, had been proven. In the second Sicilian rebellion Salvius and Athenion were likewise able to build on the same belief. Salvius enjoyed a reputation for skill in divination—that is, discovering the future from the entrails of sacrificial animals, the flight of birds, or other signs—while Athenion was highly expert in astrology, that is, discovering the future from the stars, particularly horoscopes. Both leaders were thus probably literate and well-informed in their respective spheres; they do not have to be regarded as charlatans. Divination and astrology, after all, had long been entrenched in the religious-intellectual life of the Near East and the Mediterranean, requiring of their practitioners considerable expertise in a wide body of knowledge and ritual. In the Hellenistic period astrology became a thoroughly rational pursuit, acquiring scientific and philosophical overtones, while in Republican Rome divination was a prominent feature of traditional religion. At the same time, however, astrology, in view of its eastern origins and its arrival in the Roman heartland through Greek influence, fell under some suspicion, and both astrologers and diviners not approved by Roman public religion were considered unsettling influences, inimical to the general good of society. Thus in 139 B.C. the praetor Cn. Cornelius Scipio Hispanus issued an edict banning from Rome and Italy all Chaldaeans (a term synonymous with astrologers), "since by their lies and by a false interpretation of the stars, they bewildered weak and foolish minds for their own profit." Moreover, Cato recommended among the duties of the *vilicus* in the *De Agricultura* that "he should have no desire to consult diviners, augurs, fortune-tellers or astrologers," and Columella later reiterated the injunction: "he must not let fortune-tellers or sorceresses onto the farm; both of these types of silly superstition cause unsophisticated people to spend money and result in wrongdoing." Whatever the rational or scholarly pedigree of pure astrology and divination, to disseminate purported knowledge of the future to the socially disadvantaged was to induce unrest if not dissidence; and among slaves, as the slaveowners Cato and Columella realized, it was to loosen the bonds of control masters labored to maintain. As already seen, Athenion was not the perfect *vilicus* envisioned by Cato, and both he and Salvius had the capacity, in view of their special status, to encourage the kind of resistance to authority all slaveowners feared.[20]

Spartacus is nowhere described as a seer, diviner, or prophet. But the story in Plutarch of the snake omen suggests that he too may have cast something of a spell over his followers—or sought to do so. Many politically or otherwise notorious individuals in classical antiquity came to have mysterious snake stories told about them. One relatively common notion, probably intended to connote a Herculean character, was that individuals such as Alexander, Scipio Africanus, and Augustus were sons of mothers who had been impregnated by divine snakes. Through their associations with Asclepius snakes were also believed to be agents of healing; or else they were protective forces, guarding the infant Nero, for example, against an attempt on his life, or symbols of destruction to come: Hannibal is said to have had a dream in which a monstrous, thrashing snake portended the devastation of Italy. Further, what may be especially apposite for Spartacus is that "the snake lying across the initiate's lap or bosom was a feature of the worship of Thracian Sabazius." The combined associations suggest the possibility at least that Spartacus saw himself and was seen as a mystical figure akin to Eunus, Salvius, and Athenion. All in all, therefore, there can be little doubt that the slave leaders used to advantage, like rebel leaders in later slave societies, the appeal of their religious-magical personalities to try to unify slave fugitives into bodies powerful enough to exact retribution from their oppressors once the opportunity to do so arose. At this level of understanding, many slaves may well have thought that their leaders offered a better future than continuing subjection to their masters. The mix of religion, magic, and prophecy provided the catalyst for converting potential revolt into protracted rebellion.[21]

But there was more to the slave leadership than the allure of religiosity, for in a more straightforwardly political fashion Eunus, Salvius, and Athenion all became slave kings. Eunus was elected king after the initial assault on Enna and thereupon adopted the external trappings of his new status: "he put on a diadem and decked himself out as a king in every other respect, proclaimed the woman who was living with him . . . as his queen, and made those men who seemed to be particularly intelligent his councillors." Additionally, he took the royal name of Antiochus and gave his adherents the corporate name of Syrians. His royal name ("King Antiochus") appeared on coins minted, probably, at Enna, and the whole monarchical apparatus was apparently maintained until the very end of the rebellion: in its last stages Eunus is said to have used a bodyguard of one thousand men and, when finally captured, to have had with him "four attendants—a cook, a baker, the man who massaged him in the bath and a fourth who used to entertain him when he was drinking." None of this, however, was a matter of empty display but a functional means of exercising authority; and the forcefulness of Eunus's regal status was clearly proven by Cleon's deference to him when a challenge to Eunus's leadership of the first uprising was far from out of the question.[22]

According to Diodorus, Salvius was chosen king by the rebels shortly after their defeat of M. Titinius:

> Many were deserting their masters every day. They were enjoying a quick and extraordinary increase in their numbers, so that after a couple of days there were more than six thousand of them. At this point they gathered together in a formal assembly, and when the proposal was put to them, the first thing they did was to elect someone called Salvius to be their king.

Diodorus speaks also of Salvius's self-proclamation as king after the siege of Morgantina and his adoption of the royal name of Tryphon, a name indeed that has been read on slingshots ascribed to the second Sicilian rebellion. Beyond this, "he selected sufficient men of outstanding intelligence whom he appointed as advisors and used as his council. For official audiences he also put on a purple-bordered toga and a tunic with a wide border, and he had lictors with *fasces* to walk in front of him, and had all the other things that constitute and symbolise the office of a king." As for Athenion, it was said that all Sicily was to fall to him, and he became a king five days after collecting a force of five thousand slaves in western Sicily. He took a diadem but did not hesitate to subordinate himself to Salvius in due course. Then he reappeared as king after Salvius's death, in effect "succeeding" Salvius. Florus preserves the details that he took a purple robe, a silver scepter, and a royal crown.[23]

What does all this kingly evidence mean? In many respects it plainly brings to mind the attributes and conventions of Hellenistic kingship, the institution that had dominated the political mentality of the eastern Mediterranean world since the death of Alexander and the consequent establishment of the Antigonid, Seleucid, and Ptolemaic dynasties (among others). So the slave kings' selection of councillors has to be seen as a direct imitation of the Hellenistic monarch's use of "friends" (philoi), the personally chosen favorites whose advice the king typically took in council and who themselves might be appointed as his governors, officers, and other functionaries. Specifically, Eunus's personal retinue corresponds to the Hellenistic king's elaborately specialized body of servants, which included bodyguards—if, that is, the details in Diodorus are taken literally. But they may conceal something of greater significance. In the early Hellenistic age, the king's friends were sometimes stigmatized by Greek historians and commentators as base flatterers, given the prevalent notion that those who in essence worked for the king and received gifts from him in return were engaged in a process of automatic self-denigration and so were worthy only of Greek contempt; men thus abusively described as bodyguards or jesters were in reality individuals of considerable power—generals, diplomats, and administrators. Something of this sort may lie beneath the record of Eunus's bodyguard and retinue, among the members of which, if so, may be hidden what in fact comprised the slave king's high command. The Hellenistic king's friends, sometimes bearing titles such as that of bodyguard (somatophylax, the word used by Diodorus), were expected to help the king promote and achieve his designs. Eunus's retinue therefore could well have consisted of some of the intermediary men through whom orders were channeled to and reinforced among his vast following, contributing to the creation of a hierarchical structure by which solidarity among the rebels might be promoted.[24]

Further, the election of Eunus and Salvius as kings followed what they will have judged to be successful military actions, a customary progression for any aspirant to power in the Hellenistic world. Eunus's gift to his councillor Achaeus of the house that had previously belonged to Achaeus's owners reflects also the mutually beneficial character of the relationship between Hellenistic king and friend, through which in return for sage counsel the friend frequently came to enjoy material rewards, often in land; the gift mirrors too the popular expectation of the monarch that he show himself to be a constant source of wealth, the bestowal of which upon the favored was a sign of his own continuing power. Again, Salvius's establishment of a royal headquarters at Triocala has to be understood as a direct imitation of the construction of the great royal capitals at Pella, Antioch, and Alexandria. The wearing of the diadem was the external symbol *par excellence* of monarchy in the Hellenistic age, the color purple "the most enduring status symbol of the ancient world." Eunus's royal name was one that had commonly been held by Seleucid kings, and that of Salvius was the name of a recent pretender to the Seleucid throne. Kingship in the Hellenistic world was by nature a highly personalized mode of government, relying for its effectiveness on overtly displayed ritual and ceremonial. It lies beyond all question therefore that the slave kings in Sicily believed themselves capable of bringing into existence similarly personalized regimes.[25]

None of this should be regarded as unduly exceptional if the ubiquity and longevity of Hellenistic monarchy are kept in mind, together with the fact that many of the participants in the Sicilian rebellions were first-generation slaves whose habituation to kingship in their homelands of the eastern Mediterranean will have remained with them in slavery in Sicily. Moreover, as part of the Hellenistic world Sicily itself had a long tradition of autocratic rulers, both in the form of a minor Hellenistic dynasty and of earlier tyrannical regimes. So from the political perspective the slave leaders' creation of monarchies was in every way a natural and foreseeable means of eliciting among their adherents a sense of community. In theory at least, coherence could be achieved among the slave masses by the elevated leader who deliberately exploited conventional and familiar symbols of power that demanded allegiance. Livy knew that there was an equal risk that the trappings of monarchy, if abused or conjoined with arrogance, could lead to popular alienation and hostility to the monarch. In the record as it stands, however, there is no sign that the slave kings ever forfeited the confidence of their followers, and part of the explanation of this fact must lie, as shown already, in their manipulation of the reputations they enjoyed for mediating supernatural forces as a means of legitimizing their rule. By the time of the Sicilian rebellions it had long been conventional for Hellenistic monarchs to be associated with protective deities and even to claim divine origins for themselves. Also, religious veneration of kings, the saviors and benefactors of their peoples, had long been embedded alongside the worship of the gods in the religious fabric of the Hellenistic world. Thus any man who aspired to royal authority also aspired to the godlike, and superhuman feats were essential for the realization of monarchical status. *Mutatis mutandis*, there was at root little difference between the religious persona of the slave kings and that of the kings of the established Hellenistic dynasties.[26]

In turn, the resort to kingship on the part of the slave leaders in Sicily demanded the promotion of warfare and the achievement of victory in battle. For not only did Hellenistic monarchy have its origins in warfare, but since kings had to reward their friends and sustain the loyalty of their troops if their regimes were to survive, military accomplishments and acquisitions of material spoils were also constantly needed: hence the endemic nature of warfare in the eastern Mediterranean in the previous two centuries. In the principal role expected of any Hellenistic monarch, the slave kings were undoubtedly successful and effective, their victories against Roman armies alternately validating their elevated status and justifying further engagements. The very foundation on which Hellenistic kingship was based thus impelled the rebel slaves to warfare and strengthened their will to resist. Yet there is a limit, and a very important limit, to which the slave kings in Sicily can be judged pure analogues of established Hellenistic monarchs, especially if the focus is put not so much on how, in a primitive political fashion, the slaves organized their communal resistance, but on the purpose of their organization within their immediate historical and social circumstances.[27]

In the generation following the death of Alexander in 323 B.C., various of his former generals and their descendants—the Successors—carved out from his great empire individual territorial domains. They legitimized their positions through the assumption of royal status and maintained their possessions by controlling powerful armies. The new configurations were personal modes of rule, far different in character from anything connoted by the modern concept of national states. To generate the economic resources on which they depended, the defense and, if possible, expansion of existing territories were obligatory; and despite the later emergence of what has been called the "sedentary character" of the monarchies, the notion of limitless territorial growth never disappeared from the ideology of Hellenistic kingship. Once Rome had become directly involved in the political and military affairs of the eastern Mediterranean, however, Hellenistic kingship began to lose much of its lustre, as in little more than a half-century before the first slave war in Sicily the superiority of Roman military power over that of the monarchs repeatedly demonstrated itself. Rome's defeats of Philip V and Antiochus III early in the second century paved the way both for the gradual absorption within its empire of much eastern territory and the simultaneous growth of a disproportionate influence over the affairs of the Hellenistic world at large. By 140 B.C., therefore, Hellenistic monarchy was a dubious vehicle for the achievement of political independence and the winning of land.[28]

In consequence, it is entirely implausible to imagine that Eunus, Salvius, and Athenion ever realistically thought that their kingdoms would prosper to the point at which territory in Sicily could be permanently controlled. It was not simply that Rome was the strongest military power in the Mediterranean world, with the capacity to crush any upstart ruler whenever it chose to do so: Sicily was Rome's oldest and closest province, providing valued economic dividends, and the thought of abandoning or ceding provincial land was utterly alien to the Roman mentality. Furthermore, any possible forced recognition by Rome of an aspirant to kingship such as that extorted by, say, the Macedonian pretender Andriscus in 149–48 B.C. was disqualified now by the social condition of the slave kings who, as slaves, had no legal standing or personality whatever, no matter what *éclat* their military adventures brought them in the short term. The relevance of servile status in this connection is enormous. For the legitimacy and respectability that the free adventurer might acquire from warfare and elevation to monarchy were automatically foreclosed to slave kings, whose social status by definition precluded any sort of normal entry into the contemporary framework of international politics. Admittedly, the fact that Eunus minted coins could be urged as evidence of an aspiration on his part toward a highly formalized monarchy. Equally it could be urged as evidence of a personal vanity consonant with the self-assurance of the miracle worker. But Eunus's coins (the volume of whose production, it should be noted, is unknown but which does not appear to have been great) are best understood as a mechanism to cultivate solidarity among the slave dissidents. Their depiction of Demeter is a reminder that the goddess's cult had been manipulated earlier in Sicilian history for political and even anti-Roman purposes. But it would be illogical to assume at once that a rebellion of slaves was now a rising against Rome rule. Rather, the coins' representations of natural products, grain and grapes, recall the slaves' concerns with ensuring adequate supplies of food for themselves, reestablishing as a result the importance attached to the practical aspects of resistance.[29]

The servile monarchical regimes, then, were not an end in themselves but a means to an end: the preservation of the slaves' tenuously held freedom acquired by acts of revolt and flight. The slave leaders adopted the trappings of authority most familiar to themselves and the slave fugitives who followed them because their implicit associations allowed the leaders, buoyed by an aura of religiosity, a way of melding into coherent, unified communities dissidents who otherwise were likely to reflect the character of the slave population at large and remain a heterogeneous, disorganized mass. Order and discipline were essential among the huge numbers of rebel slaves; the forms and ethos of Hellenistic monarchy created a hierarchy and structure of operations to which they could naturally respond.

This view can be corroborated by turning attention to some of the details pertinent to Spartacus's leadership. First, as with the rebels in Sicily, it is clear that discipline and military-style organization were achieved by those who allied themselves in revolt with Spartacus. Following his description of the rebels' descent from Mount Vesuvius, Plutarch states that "many of the herdsmen and shepherds who worked in the area also joined them; these were powerful and athletic types, some of whom they armed, while they used others as scouts and light troops."

Appian refers to the force of cavalry Spartacus used against Crassus, Spartacus's refusal to enlist deserters from Rome's armies, and his crucifixion of a Roman prisoner as a means of drawing from his followers their total commitment in battle. Sallust reports in the context of the campaigns against P. Varinius that it was the rebels' "habit, according to military practice, to post men on sentry and picket and other duties." The elder Pliny knew of and approved Spartacus's ban at Thurii on the slaves' possession of gold and silver, available from traders but useless for armaments. Fronto's verdict on Spartacus, therefore, a man "skilled in war and quick to strike," was one that many later observers could share. Again, like the slave kings in Sicily, Spartacus understood how to use wealth at his disposal to foster if not actually buy support, though not always to great avail. Early in the rebellion his equitable distribution of material spoils gained him many adherents, but his later gifts to the Cilician pirates he hoped would transport his followers to Sicily did not produce the desired result. He was remembered nevertheless as one who repaid kindnesses shown him. In turn, his appointment of subordinate commanders, Oenomaus and Crixus, resembles the kings' selection of friends, and the gladiatorial contest (or contests) he organized, with captive Romans fighting as gladiators and Spartacus himself in the role of *lanista*, will have made a strong impact on those he commanded. Unfortunately, there is some confusion in the sources here: Appian records that after Crixus's death, Spartacus made a funerary sacrifice of three hundred Roman prisoners; Florus appears to generalize this, and Orosius speaks of four hundred Roman prisoners being used as gladiators at the funeral of a woman who, after being raped, killed herself. But Roman soldiers were, at Spartacus's initiative, turned into sacrificial victims, perhaps in order to remind his followers of the vicissitudes of warfare, to keep revenge-seeking firmly in their minds, or, in grisly fashion, to instill discipline in them. Whether or not an ironic emulation of Roman practices was intended, the recourse to a convention that was full of religious associations and that normally lay in the gift of civic magistrates cannot but have been a strong reinforcement of Spartacus's claims to continue as the leader of rebellion.[30]

Such items of knowledge, comparable to those already noted for the slave leaders in Sicily, provide hints of how Spartacus imposed leadership on and exercised authority over the rebel slaves in Italy. Yet there is no suggestion in the sources that Spartacus ever sought kingly status for himself in the manner of Eunus, Salvius, and Athenion, even though this might have been expected of one "mighty in strength and courage." In Spartacus's Thracian homeland there were both native and Hellenistic traditions of monarchy with which Spartacus must be assumed to have been familiar. And in late antiquity the image of a kingdom (*regnum*) occurred naturally to Augustine when describing the Spartacan war, with both Spartacus and his subordinates enjoying the title of kings (*reges*). In another late tradition, moreover, Spartacus and Athenion were conjoined as rulers intolerant of noble companions, and even Cicero made the same juxtaposition for a rhetorical effect. The expectation was not fulfilled, however, and the reason lies in the effects on Spartacus of his exposure to Roman cultural and institutional forms consequent upon his service in the Roman army (presumably as an auxiliary). His appointment of Oenomaus and Crixus as subordinate officers is expressed by Appian in language that suggests that they were regarded as the equivalent of the legates (*legati*) of Roman Republican commanders, while Caesar maintained that Spartacus's followers had learned their military discipline from the Romans. If then Spartacus adopted any external appurtenances of leadership (and it should be stressed that the principal authorities, Plutarch and Appian, have virtually nothing to say about this), it is more probable that he presented himself in the role of a Roman military commander than in the guise of a Hellenistic king.[31]

Roman trappings of power were as impressive in their external aspect as those of Hellenistic kings, and an independent monarch might be expected to feel himself increased in dignity by receiving such emblems from the senate and people. So it was, for instance, with the despatch to the king Massinissa in 200 B.C. of "gold and silver vessels, a purple toga, a tunic embroidered with palm leaves together with an ivory sceptre, and a *toga praetexta*, together with a curule chair." The prestige of a triumphant Roman officeholder was visibly, even palpably, communicated to the recipient by gifts of this sort, if only in an honorific way, and Spartacus cannot have failed to know this. Accordingly, it is a reasonable inference that the ceremonial attendants (lictors) Spartacus captured from P. Varinius, along with the rods and axes (*fasces*) that signified the tenure of Roman magisterial power and right of physical coercion, were taken over by him to express symbolically the authority he commanded. Plutarch, who records the capture of the lictors, does not say that this actually happened, but Florus, generalizing the detail in Plutarch, states that Spartacus did not refuse to accept the insignia and *fasces* his followers took from Roman praetors. Frontinus provides reasonable confirmation: commenting on Crassus's victory over Castus and Gannicus, he reports that "five Roman eagles and twenty-six standards were recaptured, along with much other booty, including five sets of rods and axes." According to Roman tradition the body of twelve lictors had been created by Romulus "to increase the dignity and impressiveness of his position," and now in the age of Spartacus the "core of the lictor's task," it has been said, was "the symbolic representation of the magistrate's claim to obedience . . . expressed by a complex set of acts and rituals involving the *fasces*." The effect for Spartacus (or indeed for his subordinates) cannot have been dissimilar: obedience from the mass of rebel slaves was the desired object of a symbolic confirmation of higher status and authority.[32]

It emerges, therefore, once the slave kings and Spartacus are judged together, that like modern maroon leaders, the leaders of rebellion in antiquity turned to their advantage whatever established forms of authority and ceremonial were most appropriate or available at any point in time to enhance their own positions and further thereby the cause of rebellion. Those forms derived both from the traditions of slaves' places of birth and upbringing and from Roman traditions assimilated as a result of enslavement in the Roman heartland; in addition, there was no reason why the traditions should remain distinct from one another: in a passage from Diodorus quoted above, it was seen that Salvius actually combined Hellenistic and Roman motifs in his regal paraphernalia, adding Roman magisterial dress and (like Spartacus) the use of Roman lictors to the basic Hellenistic monarchical apparatus. So too the enigmatic T. Minucius "assumed the diadem and a purple cloak, together with lictors and the other appurtenances of office, and . . . proclaimed himself king." As long as power was achieved, maintained, and communicated to an audience, the manner in which it was visually represented was immaterial. There is thus no need to believe that the kingly apparatus of the slave leaders in Sicily was predicated on any theoretical desires to establish new kingdoms of indefinite duration and independently governed. As relatively privileged slaves, the domestics Eunus and Salvius, the overseer Athenion, and the one-time soldier Spartacus all shared the experience of having interacted closely with slaveowners in a way that many of the rural slaves who followed them in revolt did not. They used this advantage of autonomous experience to assume positions of leadership when massive, spontaneous revolt occurred, capitalized on existing modes of displaying authority, and attempted to foster thereby a sense of community and unanimity among their adherents. As modern maroon leaders expediently drew on African and colonial symbols to promote the maintenance of freedom, so too the ancient leaders looked to conventional forms for the same nonrevolutionary purpose.[33]

To characterize the Roman slave wars as episodes of maroon-style resistance is to emphasize the slave rebels' determination to extricate themselves from slavery without necessarily challenging the established order of society. But the parallels between ancient and modern servile behavior cannot be pressed too far. To a large extent, the viability of modern maroon communities depended on the availability in colonial regions of open or flexible frontiers that either rendered the sites on which maroons established themselves inaccessible to authority forces or else allowed dissidents to relocate as retaliatory pressures on them mounted. In the narratives of the Roman slave wars, details suggest that from time to time rebel slaves tried to secure control of remote natural positions for the prosecution of guerrilla-like resistance. The murderers of P. Clonius occupied and defended Mount Caprianus, so that the Roman army had to fight on inhospitable terrain; Salvius eventually based himself at the natural fortress of Triocala, which Rome was never able to take; Spartacus first sought refuge on Mount Vesuvius, later took up a position in the mountains around Thurii, and finally sought the protection of the mountains of Petelia. Moreover, the rebels' strategy of controlling certain cities as bastions of defense against authority forces can be taken in some ways as a variation on the theme of tactical withdrawal for the sake of self-preservation. To melt away into a geographical backwater was a reasonably safe option for small bands of dissident slaves, and it should be remembered that some survivors from Spartacus's uprising remained at large for more than a decade after Crassus's official termination of the war by hiding out near Thurii, perhaps again taking refuge in mountain retreats they had once shared with Spartacus himself. Sicily and the peninsula of Italy, however, were regions of comparatively dense settlement, with a multiplicity of long-established cities and towns and nonexpansionary frontiers. Lengthy retreat by large numbers of slaves into an amorphous no man's land was consequently impossible because geographical sanctuary to accommodate such numbers was not to be found. As the fugitives confronted by C. Octavius discovered in 60 B.C., once the profile of servile resistance assumed a numerically significant threshold Rome was always able to respond with devastating force. Constant movement was thus forced on the slave rebels by the size of their rebellions, counteracting the impetus toward the creation of stable slave communities that otherwise revealed itself. Their enormous scale, indeed, is a factor that cannot be underestimated in assessing the slave wars. The figures the sources provide of the numbers of disaffected slaves involved in revolt may be far from trustworthy, not least because the collection of accurate numerical information in antiquity was always difficult and at times caused historians almost to despair. But enough is known to show that their very magnitude prevented the rebels from ever achieving a coherent tactical policy.[34]

It can be assumed that the rebels were united in their desire for freedom, in their wish to end their subjection to cruelty and humiliation, in their desperate willingness to risk revolt. But what was possible once the act of revolt had been undertaken? Achaeus understood that continued acts of violence by slaves in revolt would bring retaliation against them as a matter of course. Random plundering and looting, necessary for sustaining the rebels, were nevertheless disadvantageous to their long-term safety. Negotiation was impossible. Spartacus seems to have wanted in the late stages of his rebellion to come to terms with Crassus and may have hoped

to exchange his Roman prisoners (three thousand citizens were later recovered according to Orosius) for the lives of his followers. But Tacitus
records that Spartacus was allowed no terms of surrender, and there is
no evidence that Crassus or any other Roman commander who opposed
the rebel slaves ever contemplated such action: the servile status of the
enemy forbade it. While freedom was conceded to some slaves in peaceful
contexts, it was not extorted by violence.[35]

In many ways, therefore, continuous flight was the only serious alternative by which a permanent improvement in the lives of the rebels might
be effected. Yet the kind of surreptitious long-distance travel that was
feasible for the individual fugitive was a far different proposition for easily
recognizable groups of marauders, and it is clear that none of the slave
leaders, including Spartacus, was ever able to organize a mass exodus of
slaves. In Italy the immediate attractions of violence perhaps proved too
great a diversion for many rebels, the lure of homelands insufficient to
compel unanimity of action and purpose. A crisis of leadership perhaps
adversely affected the Spartacan rebellion, while in Sicily tensions between Salvius and Athenion were constant, apparently, as long as Salvius
lived. It could be said therefore that the slave kings' authority never rose
to a level to command loyalty from which permanent benefits for the
rebels might accrue, given the kings' failure ever to become the objects
of cult in the standard Hellenistic manner. But these possible explanations
are contrived from the meager evidence of nonslave sources, and none of
them may be correct. The divisions that seem to have plagued the rebels
may just as well have been due to choices slaves purposefully made, with
various leaders in each rebellion leading disparate groups of rebels, comparable for instance to the Leeward and Windward maroons of Jamaica—
united in their opposition to their own enslavement but pursuing divergent strategies of defense and confrontation according to differences in
the forcefulness of leaders' personalities, the ethnic composition of the
groups, previous experiences in slavery, and so on. From the servile perspective, nothing dictated that all dissident slaves had to coalesce into
one unified mass under a single commander. Moreover, it is vital to recognize that the characterization of the rebellions as slave wars is a characterization derived not from the dissidents themselves but from
representatives of the social order they threatened. Thus it cannot be
assumed that slaves set out to make war, in any formal manner, against
established powers; it can only be said that slaves were prepared to use
military tactics to protect and sustain themselves in flight, to make continuous flight and the freedom it represented feasible. Almost paradoxically, however, flight could not bring permanent freedom when so many
fugitives were involved.

The numerical dimensions of the slave uprisings were therefore the
rebellions' fatal flaw. Impelled by the news of successful, but relatively

small outbursts of violent protest, vast numbers of slaves in Sicily and Italy proved themselves capable of realizing the potential for mass insurrection that lay at the heart of the Roman slavery system by striking out for freedom. But there was no program for revolution, for an inversion of society, or for fundamental alteration to the structure of society. The slaves' actions were purely individualistic, concerned with vengeance and the substitution of personal independence for slavery. As their numbers increased, the nature of the rebel communities became so multifaceted that a commonly shared long-term goal was never conceived, neither logistically nor intellectually. Through revolt, the slaves achieved their freedom, and they were prepared to defend it with tenacity and courage against the inevitable counterattack from Rome. Resistance to slavery was maintained at the practical and organizational level with some success for sustained periods of time. But without an erosion in society at large of the concept of the necessity and immanence of slavery, indeed of the naturalness of slavery—without, that is, the emergence of the kind of egalitarian ideals that led to abolitionism in the modern world but that were conceptually unknown in antiquity—resistance on a massive, violent scale could not bring about any amelioration of the lives of those slavery oppressed. The Roman slave wars were not revolutionary mass movements in any sense, but to a large extent historical accidents precipitated by a combination of circumstances that never again reappeared in the long history of slavery in the Roman world.

Epilogue

The statement that the Roman slave wars were in part historical accidents requires of course some refinement, because a cluster of factors can be identified from which the predisposition of slaves to resist their condition is eminently comprehensible: the historical determinants or precipitants of revolt, that is, are reasonably clear. Of prime importance, for instance, was the permanent state of hostility that existed between slave and master in the Roman system of slavery, a state made manifest by slaveowners' perceptions of their slaves as the enemy within when the social and political order was threatened from without. Slaveowners' fears of their slaves, though doubtless often latent, were a natural product of slaveownership, reflecting the potential for violent resistance by slaves that lay at the core of Roman society, as of any other slave society. In order to limit that potential, the individual master had to ensure that his complement of slaves remained immune from external interference, and society at large was forced to adopt devices for the better regulation of the human property. Thus before the first Sicilian war Roman slaveowners had always been able to reward certain slaves for their loyalty and to encourage compliance among others as a by-product through the practice of manumission, the history of which at Rome is very ancient indeed. In the past, slaveowners had also learned how to encourage divisiveness among their slaves by delegating authority to some set over others (as happened with Athenion) or by allowing the privilege of a quasi-marital union (as happened with Eunus and Spartacus) and the formation of families. Even Cato had recognized the utilitarian value to the slaveowner of permitting opportunities for sexual intimacy among slaves and for periodic respite from the normal regimen of work. The possibilities of servile disaffection were significantly reduced by the concession of privileges.[1]

The level of resistance represented by the slave wars, however, implies that existing modes of regulation were too haphazard or insufficiently subtle to accommodate the great increases in the servile population of the Roman heartland that followed the conquests of the middle Republican period and beyond. As changing economic patterns provided an impetus for the exploitation of large numbers of new slaves in agriculture, there can have been little opportunity for the emergence of a benign paternalistic attitude on the slaveowner's part and unquestioning deference on the slave's. The majority of slaves were never likely to see overt signs of their master's generosity or concern. If they were suddenly made plain, as when the slaveowners of Morgantina promised slaves their freedom in return for support against Salvius, they resulted in immediate compliance, whether through apprehension or trust. But otherwise nothing offset the slave's alienation from his owner or restrained his wish to free himself as best he could from the subjection of his condition. The maintenance of social harmony proved impossible when slaves could not be managed by traditional and largely unsystematic means, when methods of control had not kept pace with changes in the patterns of slave-ownership.

The point could be better understood if more evidence were available on the size of individual holdings of slaves, but unfortunately few figures exist. The *lex Fufia Caninia* of 2 B.C., which regulated testamentary manumission, assumed that holdings of more than five hundred slaves were not uncommon. C. Caecilius Isidorus, a slaveowner who flourished in the generation following the Spartacan rebellion and who was himself a former slave, had come to own 4,116 slaves at the time of his death. Isidorus was a substantial landowner, his estates comparable to those of his aristocratic contemporary L. Domitius Ahenobarbus, the consul of 54 B.C., who in 49 B.C. offered to each of the ten thousand troops (at least) serving as soldiers under him forty *iugera* of land from his own possessions. The former slave and the aristocrat may have been exceptionally wealthy men and not fully typical slaveowners in their own age or that of the slave wars. But the order of their wealth suggests in principle that the slaves who worked on their lands had virtually no chance of gaining personal knowledge of, let alone sharing any intimacy with, their owners, especially when estates were scattered over different regions of Italy or even the provinces. In the period from 140 B.C. to 70 B.C. the principle was already strong enough to preclude the development of close ties between rural slaves and their masters and to create an inducement to resistance.[2]

In addition, many of the slave rebels were individuals who enjoyed a certain freedom of movement and association in the course of their work. Their mobility gave them a taste of independence or reminded them of the freedom they had known before enslavement, weakening as a result the pressure imposed by their formal status to assume an attitude of resignation to their slavery, a pressure detectable, for example, in the owner's belief that even the slave's manner of speech should be properly circumspect and reverential in the master's presence. Account has also to be taken of such other aggravating circumstances as continuing importations of restive and disruptive first-generation slaves whose acclimatization to slavery was minimal; the lack of balance in the sexual ratio of the slave population; the consistent maltreatment of slave property by abusive owners or their underlings; and the all-embracing climate of violence in Roman society. Against such a background of material and social deprivation, the tendency of slaves to resist is explicable, and both before and after the major slave wars this mesh of interrelated factors prompted endemic flight and revolt on a localized scale. In their beginnings, therefore, the outbursts led by Eunus, Cleon, Salvius, Athenion, and Spartacus can be said to have conformed to predictable patterns of servile protest and opposition.[3]

Still further, the importance of the servile desire for freedom as a motivation for resistance cannot be overstated. In the Republican era freedom (*libertas*) was judged by Romans to be the hallmark of their civic community, connoting the rule of law and the law's availability to the community's members. Membership was marked by tenure of the Roman citizenship, which could be granted to persons brought by conquest into Rome's ambit. But the high profile given to *libertas* in Roman ideology had the inevitable corollary of pointing up its absence to those who were excluded from the civic community, and for slaves this meant a perpetual reinforcement of the reality of their rightlessness: for as a form of property subject to the dominion of their masters, slaves before the law did not exist as persons and held no rights in the civic community, in property, personal relationships, or anything else. As human agents, nonetheless, slaves had the capacity to respond to rightlessness and to compel their masters into a set of social relations required for no other form of property, one result being the creation of mechanisms for bridging the great divide between slavery and freedom. The history of manumission at Rome signifies that slaveowners had long understood the need to cater to the human agency of their slave property and the resistance to subjection it generated by absorbing within the civic community from time to time certain of the rightless. Through observation of the freedmen and freedwomen around them, all slaves could consequently see that slavery and freedom were extremes across which a path could be or might be negotiated. The conferment of freedom on some slaves of necessity encouraged its prospect in others.[4]

In the period of the slave wars, however, manumission appears to have been ill-governed and erratically practiced.[5] The tendency was for freedom to be granted to owners' personal favorites or for individuals prominent in Roman public life to engage in occasional grants of mass emancipation for political, self-serving reasons. For the majority the prospect of freedom was unrealizable, the standards required for its achievement undefined and unstated. Yet the servile response was not one of resignation or despair. Rather, the ideology of *libertas* intensified the slave's desire to acquire freedom as an act of personal will by voluntarily removing himself from the location of his servitude. In an intellectual climate and social setting where slavery and freedom were immanent, unquestioned states of being, the slave's natural objective was to escape confinement and bridge the divide by an individualistic act whose outcome was otherwise unattainable. But to become a fugitive did not mean that the slave threatened to undermine the structure of society; all that he sought was personal advancement within the contours of that structure. The rebels of the slave wars were no different in type therefore from other resisting fugitives who preceded and followed them; and that fact is reflected in the way the rebels were consistently characterized by ancient historians and commentators—not as utopian ideologues, or even aspirants to political power, but simply as fugitive slaves.

What was accidental and in no way predictable, however, was the appearance during the slave wars of a sequence of leaders who, although not at first motivated to solicit or plan massive servile resistance, were prepared, once their early outbursts had met with some success, to try to galvanize the discrete energies of vast numbers of fugitives choosing to join them in a determined effort to protect the rebels' freedom by militaristic methods. The slave leaders were charismatic figures, of visible prestige in their local social contexts, able to inspire confidence among their followers; and it was their unique contribution, in their orchestration of resistance at the practical level, that allowed normal patterns of protest to assume a new, aberrant dimension. At the same time the process of conversion was facilitated by the very naturalness of warfare in the ancient world, which created the expectation for most men that at some point in their lives they would find themselves consumed by military activities of one sort or another. Indeed, many of the first-generation slaves, like Spartacus, may previously have seen military service in the armies of Rome or of the Hellenistic kings, and for them recourse to war will not have been problematical once there were men to lead them. As slave combatants, however, they differed from other troops, seeking neither to acquire lands or material spoils for their own sake nor to impose subjection on defeated enemies but solely to preserve their release from slavery.[6]

In the most immediate sense the slave wars failed: many slaves lost not only their precarious freedom but their lives as well, in battle and, it must be imagined, to disease and starvation also. As casualties were suffered, replacements were necessary, and the leaders' sporadic efforts to deal with that contingency through recruitment are explicable without any damage to the notion that the growth of large-scale resistance was mainly spontaneous. In the end, even the most competent of the leaders were unable to cope with the scale of servile resistance their own actions had set in motion. But if only because resistance provokes reaction, the slave wars cannot have failed to make an impact on the later history of slavery at Rome. In the short term the reaction was coercive to judge from Cicero's remark that all the governors of Sicily after the time of M'. Aquillius issued orders to prevent slaves possessing arms. Other precautions may have been taken, though precisely how the Sicilian governors' edicts were enforced in practice is difficult to say. Certainly in the age from the termination of the Spartacan war until the emergence of Augustus as Rome's first emperor, slaves were frequently embroiled in the public disorders and violence that affected much of the Mediterranean world in those decades, and public figures easily harnessed the violent potential in slaves to their own political and military ambitions. But on a longer view, the advent of Empire brought a greater stability to the relationship between slaves and masters in Roman society (though that is not to say that the burdens of slavery were any easier to bear), and it is not fanciful to believe that the memory of the slave wars played a contributing role in this development, perceptible for instance in the laws controlling manumission passed under Augustus. Modifications in the regulation of slavery were made, and they were attributable in part to slaves themselves.[7]

There can of course be no explicit proof for this assessment, which is admittedly speculative. But it is undeniable that the memory of the slave leaders, kept alive for generation after generation, long reminded slave-owners of events which were not to be repeated. Until late in the Imperial age the name of Eunus remained a token of the dangers slavery posed to established Roman society, an example of how presumably at any time fate might exalt the humble slave to a position of power over the free. In the years following the second Sicilian rebellion (when, indeed, recollections of the first had not been utterly lost to the living), the name of Athenion could be used to insult a political enemy from high society without any need for the allusion to be explained: the identity and accomplishments of the king were known to all. But it was Spartacus who became the most powerful symbol of the dangers slaves posed to free society and of the need therefore for constant vigilance. Cicero conjured up his name in order to vilify the violent P. Clodius and to attack the renegade M. Antonius, while Antonius himself used the same tactic against the military adventurer C. Octavius. By the time of Horace, Spartacus had become one of Rome's canonical enemies of the past, to be numbered with Porsenna and Hannibal and assuming mythical proportions. In A.D. 22 the demands of a rebellious chieftain in Africa automatically evoked comparison with Spartacus, as did the attempt at insurrection in A.D. 64 by a band of gladiators at Praeneste. From Lucan to Claudian, Roman poets paraded his name as an emblem of danger and cruelty. No doubt these symbolic associations became increasingly platitudinous with the passage of time, and the lingering image of Spartacus was not without its positive touches: in favorable comparison with M. Antonius, for example, Pliny summoned Spartacus as an example of restraint and the avoidance of luxury, and his military reputation always stood unchallenged. But the negative characterization was far more dominant and continued, despite literary conventionality, to express fears of further massive slave unrest.[8]

Shortly after the death of Spartacus, the trial began at Rome of C. Verres, the corrupt governor of Sicily in the very years of the Spartacan rebellion. In one of his prosecuting speeches Cicero was concerned to refute Verres's claim that he had defended Sicily against threats from the rebel slaves in Italy, arguing that the island, in view of its security and disciplined administration since the second servile war, had never been under any danger from Spartacus: no attempt had been made on Sicily, and Verres therefore had no claims to military competence and expertise. In setting out the argument Cicero clearly glossed over the effort Spartacus had actually made to invade Sicily, and by referring to Verres's schemes to extort money from Sicilian slaveowners through allegations of local servile unrest and conspiracies, he unintentionally revealed the constant possibilities of insurrection among agricultural slaves that existed in the late seventies B.C. Nor was it just a question of Sicily. Cicero hinted, without making too much of it, that M. Crassus's victory over Spartacus had not eliminated all servile resistance in southern Italy, and as already seen, it was to take another decade for the record on the Spartacan war to be closed. His allusions to the "fugitives' war in Italy," a "particularly great and terrible war," were contrived to damn Verres by reminding his audience of threats recently averted; the effect was to emphasize the dangers that still existed as long as government was lax and complaisant.[9]

Yet the threats and dangers never again revealed themselves in the form of major slave rebellions; instead, slaves continued to resist subjection through flight, minor revolts, and other means. Perhaps it was the case that individuals of the same caliber as Eunus and his successors never again emerged to try to lead violent resistance on the grand scale. Certainly fragmentation of the Roman slave population remained a constant obstacle to the concept of mass rebellion, as it had proved an insuperable hindrance to servile cohesion and unanimity of purpose in the rebellions that have been surveyed here. Without class awareness, common cause was impossible to achieve. But it is likely too that as a result of the events in Sicily and Italy of the period from 140 B.C. to 70 B.C., slaves of all descriptions learned the futility of even contemplating mass revolt: their protests were better made along safer avenues of resistance that did not attract the might of the Roman military machine. Beyond this, however, the sense of an improved stability in the master-slave relationship of the Imperial age implies that established society came eventually to perceive the need for making social adjustments that would go some way toward accommodating the interests of certain elements within the overall slave population. In part, the result was an adjustment of the means of social control. To the extent, therefore, that servile interests came to be recognized, the slave wars were not perhaps a complete failure.

Appendix I.
The Literary Sources for
the Slave Wars

The principal accounts of the slave wars are provided by the Greek authors Diodorus Siculus, Plutarch, and Appian. All three wrote long after the events concerned and thus, in the standard manner of ancient historians and biographers, drew on predecessors' works as their own source material. The extant narratives of the slave wars, therefore, are all derivative in nature.

The Sicilian wars were recounted by Diodorus, a native of Agyrium in Sicily, in Books 34–36 of his *Bibliotheca Historica*, a universal history designed to set on record the histories and traditions of the various peoples Rome had brought under its rule by the time Diodorus wrote. Born *circa* 90 B.C. and surviving into the early years of the Augustan regime, from *circa* 60 B.C. Diodorus spent some thirty years on the composition of his work, with the city of Rome itself as his chief center of operations. He was not a man of any great intellectual originality, and it is generally agreed that his method of composing history was to follow very closely one main authority for whatever period he was concerned with, taking over even his sources' attitudes as well as their factual material; to this he occasionally added information from supplementary sources and appropriate personal comments. As one attracted by Stoic teachings, Diodorus could be expected to have found the slave wars an appealing subject, because of the sensitivity to servile conditions Stoicism sometimes encouraged, and his Sicilian origins may well have increased his interest in the subject.

Scholars agree that the source Diodorus followed for the slave wars was Posidonius of Apamea, a figure from the previous generation (his probable dates are *circa* 135 B.C.–51 B.C.) best known for his achievements as a Stoic philosopher but also the author of another universal history. Apart from a number of fragments, none of which is datable later than 86 B.C., Posidonius's history is no longer extant. But it began in 145 B.C. where Polybius had left off, and there is reason to think it may have gone down into the sixties (possibly therefore incorporating the Spartacan war). The suggestion has been made from what can be recovered of the work that Posidonius had a special, and innovative, interest in social issues. And even more than Diodorus, his Stoic cosmopolitanism is likely to have promoted a certain sympathy toward slaves that would have been apparent in his account of the wars in Sicily. The following passage from Diodorus (34/35.2.33 Loeb) is commonly understood to illustrate this tendency:

> Not only in the exercise of political power should men of prominence be considerate towards those of low estate, but so also in private life they should—if they are sensible—treat their slaves gently. For heavy-handed arrogance leads states into civil strife and factionalism between citizens, and in individual households it paves the way for plots of slaves against masters and for terrible uprisings in concert against the whole state. The more power is perverted to cruelty and lawlessness, the more the character of those subject to that power is brutalized to the point of desperation. Anyone whom fortune has set in low estate willingly yields place to his superiors in point of gentility and esteem, but if he is deprived of due consideration, he comes to regard those who harshly lord it over him with bitter enmity.

Nonetheless, Posidonius was not a mature contemporary of all the slave wars, and his account in turn relied on sources no longer available and not even positively identifiable. Moreover, it has been thought that his narrative of the Sicilian wars was colored by the history of Spartacus's rebellion. Still, if the generally high opinion of Posidonius's history held by classical scholars were considered valid and if Diodorus followed his usual methodological procedures when using it, the latter's account of the slave wars could be assumed to be reasonably accurate, reliable, and comprehensive.

In the text above, Diodorus is cited as an authority for the slave wars in Sicily in fully conventional style, though with the necessary implication that the material referred to is authentic Diodorus. But the implication is false: for the relevant Diodoran books survive today only in excerpted form, and this is why it is impossible to produce a detailed and uncontroversial narrative of the wars. The excerpts fall into two categories. The first consists of items from a work now usually called the *Bibliotheca* of Photius, a ninth-century Byzantine scholar and civil servant who was also twice Patriarch of Constantinople. Composed *circa* 845 A.D., the *Bibliotheca* is a private collection of summaries of all the books Photius (*circa* 810 A.D.–893 A.D.) had read when, about to leave Constantinople on a diplomatic mission, he responded to his brother's request for a distillation of his reading. It combines abridgements and paraphrases with notes from Photius's reading made long before the *Bibliotheca* was ever conceived; and although it can be regarded as a product of the ninth-century revival of Byzantine learning, its accuracy is open to question. The second category of excerpts is even later in date. Responding to the perception that the number of books was too enormous for readers to handle, the tenth-century Byzantine emperor Constantine

Porphyrogenitus (913 A.D.–959 A.D.) ordered the redaction of an encyclo-
pedia to contain morally edifying extracts from earlier writers arranged
under topical headings. The compilation his scribes made does not now
exist in its entirety. But the portions that are extant suggest that the
scribes combined direct quotations with paraphrases of their authors,
their selection being arbitrary and the final product uneven in quality.

The account of "Diodorus," therefore, is in reality the work of much
later men, who were under no compulsion at all to give a faithful reflec-
tion of the original narrative they read. This means that the correct sequence of the surviving excerpts is strictly indeterminable. Moreover, the
material first used by Posidonius has gone through any number of intermediate transmissions before reaching its present state.

If faced with a comparable situation, historians of modern slave societies would probably despair, with some justification. The more so if they
were to learn that a separate history of the slave wars written by a certain
Caecilius of Caleacte had once existed but has now vanished. But for the
ancient historian the situation is not all that unusual. The fact remains
that some Diodoran material exists, and the attempt has to be made to
make some sense of it. That can best be done through placing it, as here,
in a sequence of historical contexts, not the least important of which is
the comparative one.

It should be pointed out perhaps that classical scholars devoted to the
occupation of source criticism have detected in Diodorus's account of the
Sicilian wars more than just one source. The following statement appears
in the description of the background to the first Sicilian war (Diodorus
34/35.2.3 Loeb):

> For most of the landowners were Roman knights [equites], and since it was
> the knights who acted as judges when charges arising from provincial affairs
> were brought against the governors, the magistrates stood in awe of them.

Yet the statement is anachronistic, referring in reality to a development
in the history of the Roman courts firmly datable to 122 B.C. Some scholars accordingly see a source different from Posidonius here, since Posidonius is thought to have been unlikely to make such a chronological
mistake. Ultimately, however, such theories must always remain un-
proven, even if inherently plausible, unless new texts are discovered.
Suspicion has also fallen on what are conventionally called "doublets"
in the Diodoran narratives of the wars (for example, the parallel separate
risings of Cleon and Athenion): it is as though some elements were almost
artificially contrived. Again this is an issue incapable of final resolution—
though a detailed case sufficient to render unlikely any notion of invented
doublets was argued long ago—and the historian can only state a position.
Given the history of the transmission of the Posidonian-Diodoran ma-

terial, together with the historical context of the wars in Sicily, the position adopted here is that it requires too great an act of faith to believe that the excerpts now extant preserve evidence of literary ingenuity there is no good reason to presume.

The most convenient text of the Diodoran excerpts currently available is in volume twelve of the Loeb Classical Library edition of Diodorus Siculus, the work of Francis R. Walton (Cambridge, Mass., and London, 1967), which contains an English translation. A somewhat livelier translation of some of the excerpts, not always preserving the same order as Walton, appears in Wiedemann (1981), 200–15. Walton's sequence in turn varies in some places from the older standard text of Felix Jacoby, *Die Fragmente der Griechischen Historiker II* (reprint, Leiden, 1961), no. 87 ("Poseidonios von Apamea"), F 108. The following bibliographical items can be consulted for further information pertinent to Diodorus Siculus and his evidence: Brunt (1980); Càssola (1982); Farrington (1937); Hornblower (1981), 18–39; Malitz (1983), 134–69; Manganaro (1967); Nock (1959); Pareti (1927); Rizzo (1976); Strasburger (1965); Treadgold (1980); Verbrugghe (1975); Wilson (1983), 89–119, 143–45.

The earliest extant narrative of Spartacus's rebellion consists of four sections (8–11) of the biography of the triumvir M. Licinius Crassus, one of the great sequence of *Parallel Lives* composed by Plutarch of Chaeronea (*circa* 45 A.D.–120 A.D.) in the last two decades or so of his life. The collection as a whole is didactic and ethical in purpose, for Plutarch intended his portrayals of character to allow his readers to achieve virtue through imitating or avoiding (as appropriate) the moral conduct of the great public figures of the past. But because moral biography of an improving kind, with its concentration of focus on a single individual's personality, encouraged a selective mode of writing rather than full historical analysis, and because information was drawn from vast reading and transmitted in part through reliance on memory, the modern historian cannot expect from Plutarch total accuracy and comprehensiveness of detail on Spartacus, who was after all only incidental to Crassus from Plutarch's point of view.

The *Crassus* is a very imbalanced biography, more than half its contents comprising an account of the campaign against the Parthians in which Crassus lost his life. His grisly demise, which Plutarch elaborates with a dramatic description of the delivery of Crassus's head to the Parthian king, depended on an excess of ambition, one of Crassus's two serious failings, the other being avarice. Crassus was clearly not for Plutarch a figure to emulate. Still, Plutarch has a grudging sympathy for Crassus, evident in the comparison made with his Greek counterpart Nicias: Crassus at least aimed high, and his death was not that of a coward; poor judgment was the immediate cause of his downfall. The portion of the *Crassus* that deals with Spartacus is, however, fuller than might have been expected. The first two sections offer a summary of the rebellion before Crassus was appointed to the command against Spartacus, and they illustrate Plutarch's occasional tendency to digress irrelevantly (but here fortunately) from his main theme. The material is introduced abruptly, but because of Cn. Pompeius's final intervention, the account as a whole eventually provides a variation on the topic of rivalry between Crassus and Pompeius. The early details may simply be due to Plutarch's recollection of what he had read about Spartacus. But in a sense the relatively abundant treatment of the Spartacan war foreshadows the even more detailed account of the Parthian campaign. These were the two most important military undertakings of Crassus's career, and Plutarch's view of the dangers of ambition is made the more tellingly when the reader understands that the success of the first led directly to the catastrophe of the second in Crassus's desperate struggle to keep pace with Pompeius (and Caesar).

Is it possible to say precisely where Plutarch found his material on Spartacus? On the basis of a list of possible parallels between Plutarch and the fragments of Sallust's *Histories*, it has been argued that Sallust was Plutarch's sole source. The *Crassus* is one of six Roman biographies that are dominated by a now lost historical work by the Augustan consular C. Asinius Pollio, again so it has been maintained, but since this work only began with the year 60 B.C., it cannot have given information on Spartacus. Thus Sallust might well have filled the gap. But Livy is also a possibility, and the influence of Posidonius has been detected as well. In reality, positive identification of the sources of Plutarch's material on Spartacus is impossible to achieve, especially when the biographer's individuality in shaping his work is taken into account. His text thus has to be accepted as the most accurate version of which he was capable when the *Crassus* was composed.

For further information on Plutarch, the nature of his biographies, his methods of writing, and his sources for Spartacus, the following items can be consulted: Flacelière and Chambry (1972), 187–203; Hamilton (1969), xiii–xlix; Jones (1971), 80–109, 135–137; Pelling (1979, 1980); Russell (1973), 100–16, 133–34, Scardigli (1979), 107–13, 192; Wardman (1974), 18–37, 42–43, 175. English translations of Plutarch on Spartacus are available in volume three of the Loeb Classical Library edition of Plutarch's Lives (Cambridge, Mass., and London, 1916), the work of Bernadotte Perrin; in the Penguin volume, *Plutarch: Fall of the Roman Republic* (Harmondsworth, 1972); and in Wiedemann (1981), 215–20.

The second of the main narratives on Spartacus is provided by Appian of Alexandria, who was writing a generation or so after Plutarch. It consists of five sections of the first book of the *Civil Wars* (1.116–120), a work that ran from the tribunate of Ti. Gracchus in 133 B.C. to the age of Augustus and that was intended to show how the disciplined concord of the Roman imperial system of the second century A.D. had evolved from the chaos of the first century B.C. With Appian's version of events there is no need to take account of an author's concentration on one specific figure. But again his record depends on much earlier writings no longer available. It has been maintained that Asinius Pollio's history had a very large influence on Appian's account of the late Republic and that Appian used supplementary sources when Pollio was inadequate for his purposes. As in the case of Plutarch, therefore, Appian will probably have used a supplementary source for Spartacus, which some have identified as a Latin work that went back to Sallust. Once more, however, there are obvious limits to which searches of this kind can be made, and their common failure to allow that authors whose works do survive might have been capable of independent opinion and judgment is particularly wearisome. The following can be consulted for discussion of the problem: Gabba (1956); (1967), 316–33; and Levi (1972b), attempting to distinguish between favorable and unfavorable portrayals of Spartacus in the sources and their conceptions of the rebellion as either a slave revolt or a broader movement including other discontented elements. The results are dubious. Stampacchia (1976) discusses the whole literary tradition on Spartacus. English translations of Appian on Spartacus can be found in volume three of the Loeb Classical Library edition of Appian's *Roman History* (Cambridge, Mass., and London, 1913), by Horace White; and in Wiedemann (1981), 220–22.

Additional material on the slave wars comes from a number of fragmentary or minor historical sources, beginning with the allusions contained in Cicero's writings and continuing through to Orosius in late antiquity. Purely incidental references in other forms of literature (such as those to Spartacus in Roman poetry) add little of substance.

From what has been said already of Plutarch and Appian, it is obvious that the loss of the *Histories* of Sallust (*circa* 86 B.C.–35 B.C.), the first Roman historian to write of Spartacus, is severe. The work occupied Sallust's last years but was never completed; it is known, however, that it began with the year 78 B.C. and that the rebellion of Spartacus was included. Of the fragments still extant, those dealing with Spartacus have considerable value. But in view of the weaknesses Sallust's monographs contain—errors of chronology and geography, for instance, not to mention a jaundiced political attitude—his account of Spartacus is not likely to have been unimpeachable, even if written fairly close in time to the events themselves. The loss of the books which dealt with the slave wars in the history of Livy (*circa* 64 B.C.–A.D. 12) is another tragedy. Some notion of what they contained can be gleaned from the so-called *Periochae*, summaries of Livy's books made later in antiquity, and from the brief reports of Florus, Eutropius, and Orosius, who all drew on Livy. The *Periochae* are commonly assumed by scholars to belong to the fourth century A.D.

and to be based on an intermediate abridgement of Livy. A condensed version of Livy was certainly in existence in the first century A.D., but whether this was a work now lost or, in fact, the *Periochae* themselves is indeterminable. At any rate, the *Periochae* as a whole are of very poor quality. It can at least be said that Livy's record of the Spartacan war will have been independent of that of Sallust, for whom Livy held a certain distaste.

This bleak picture scarcely improves with the summary history of Rome of Velleius Paterculus, published in A.D. 30. It contains nothing on the wars in Sicily and just a few lines on Spartacus. Velleius was influenced by both Sallust and Livy, but since his accuracy at large has been seriously impugned, little profit derives from trying to disentangle the sources he used for Spartacus. Equally open to criticism is the epitome of Roman history (to the time of Augustus) written in the second century by Florus, although in this case material on all three rebellions is available. Florus's work lacks all objectivity, his point being, as far as the slave wars are concerned, to illustrate the extent of Rome's disgrace in having to fight slaves at all. Although dependent on Livy, the work is careless and inaccurate. The compendium of Roman history (to A.D. 364) written *circa* A.D. 370 by Eutropius, by contrast, has a greater reputation for reliability. But for present purposes it has only a very small amount of information. More detail appears in Orosius, the Christian historian whose *History against the Pagans*, undertaken early in the fifth century at the instigation of Augustine, was designed to refute the charge that Christians were responsible for current misfortunes by pointing to the disasters of pre-Christian history. As a repository of Livian material, Orosius's account of the slave wars is important, but his bias is unmistakable.

For fuller details on the Latin historical tradition see Begbie (1967); Bessone (1982); den Boer (1972), 1–18, 114–72; Cels (1972); Jal (1963), 19–42, 380; Reynolds (1983), 159–62, 164–66; Syme (1964), 178–213; (1978).

At first blush the literary sources for the slave wars appear to be copious and rich. But on appraisal they turn out to be full of defects and subject to various sorts of distortion. However, the inadequacies and limitations of the sources lend emphasis to an important fact, namely, the general lack of interest the slave population commanded among the literary elite of Roman society. For whatever mitigating impact Stoicism may have had in raising sensitivities to the hardships of slavery, men of letters did not find the history of slavery a subject worthy of their talents unless it impinged on the affairs of the socially prominent or led to exceptional developments. This indifference at once mirrors the unquestioned and unquestionable place of slavery in the social structure of Rome and the impossibility of altering that structure without profound intellectual and mental realignments.

Appendix II.
The Beginning of the
First Slave War in Sicily

The year in which the first slave war began (and hence the length of the war) is unknown and cannot be fixed precisely. But for the sake of convenience a summary of the evidence is in order.

Diodorus 34/35.2.1 seems to place the beginning of the war in 141 B.C.: counting from the end of the second Carthaginian war (201 B.C.), he prefaces his remarks on the origins of the slave war with the statement that Sicily had been at peace for sixty years previously; but it is unclear whether the number sixty is exact or merely an approximation. Livy, *Periocha* 56 seems to put the beginning of the war in 134 B.C., with the appointment against the rebels of the consul C. Fulvius Flaccus; but this text also recognizes that an unspecified number of unnamed praetors had previously failed against the slaves. The item is thus confused. Orosius 5.6.3 dates the outbreak of the war to 135 B.C.; but little confidence can be placed in the information, since Orosius's summary of the early war is very vague. Obsequens 27 has the war begin in 134 B.C., but that is plainly wrong and probably influenced by the appointment in that year of the first consular commander against the rebels. If the four praetors named at Florus 2.7.7 (see chapter 3, note 2) each held office in annual succession (the order cannot be independently determined, of course), the outbreak of the war would fall in 138 B.C., since Florus refers to the capture of their camps after referring to Eunus's uprising. But Florus's list does not necessarily include all the praetors who preceded the consuls (134 B.C.–132 B.C.); and it is just possible that in the years before 134 B.C. two praetors served in Sicily simultaneously, or two in some years and one in others. So altogether the range of possibilities for the initial year of the war extends from 141 B.C. to 136 B.C.

The only safe point that can be made on the duration of the war is that it covered at least the years 136 B.C.–132 B.C. and perhaps a little longer: especially so if Valerius Maximus 3.7.3, on the high price of grain at Rome in 138 B.C., is associated with the war; this, however, cannot be certain. But the war's duration over a minimal period of five years, although an imprecise piece of information, helps point up the lack of balance in the extant literary source material (relatively full for the beginning and end, lacunose in between) and helps draw attention to the rebels' success in maintaining their resistance over a substantial interval of time. The length of the war cannot be understood without the presumption of carefully sustained organization after the revolt at Enna. See further among recent works Green (1961), 28–29; Astin (1967), 135 n.5; Verbrugghe (1973), 27–29.

Appendix III.
The Duration of the Spartacan War

Chronological precision is notable by its absence in the sources for the war of Spartacus, and the details provided are hardly consistent with each other. The phases of the war are thus perhaps best understood from concentrating on the identities of the magistrates Rome sent to oppose the rebel slaves. As seen above, the sources are confused on these individuals, but modern rationalization of the evidence produces a time-span for the rebellion of 73 B.C.–71 B.C. The appropriate entries in *MRR*, referred to in the notes to chapter 5, offer the best assessment of the available material, while a full presentation of all the chronological indicators on the Spartacan war appears in Stampacchia (1976), 90–107. The following chart, drawing on this information, is intended as an approximate guide to the course of the war.

Summer 73 (?)	1. Gladiators' escape from Capua.
	2. Occupation of Mount Vesuvius.
	3. Repulse of Capuan troops?
Autumn 73	4. Siege of Mount Vesuvius by C. Claudius Glaber.
	5. Defeat of C. Claudius Glaber.
	6. Appointment of P. Varinius.
	7. Defeats of P. Varinius's subordinates.
	8. Defeats of P. Varinius.
Winter 73	9. Rebels' migration into Lucania.
Spring 72	10. Appointment of L. Gellius and Cn. Cornelius Lentulus.
	11. Death of Crixus in Apulia.
	12. Rebels' northward migration.
	13. Defeats of consuls and of C. Cassius Longinus.
	14. Rebels' southward migration.
Autumn 72	15. Appointment of M. Licinius Crassus.
	16. Rebels' withdrawal to Bruttium.
Winter 72	17. Siege of Rhegium.
	18. Defeat of Castus and Gannicus?
	19. Spartacus's escape from siege.
Spring 71	20. Defeat of Spartacus in Lucania.

It should be noted that Sallust, *Histories* 3.96, 98, fixes the campaigns of P. Varinius to the autumn of 73 B.C.; and that Appian, *Civil Wars* 1.21 specifies Crassus's termination of the war in six months (though despite *MRR* III, p. 120, *CIL* 10.8070.3 [*ILLRP* 1013] does not prove that the rebellion was over by April 1, 71 B.C.).

Notes

In the notes that follow, the appearance of a modern name immediately after the citation of an ancient source will usually indicate the translation used in the main text. An exception is the name of Shackleton Bailey, which will indicate either the edition of Cicero's correspondence drawn on or the translation followed or both. The translations given are for the most part those of the easily accessible Loeb Classical Library or Penguin Classics series, but many have been taken or slightly adapted from the valuable collection of Wiedemann (1981) and a few from other authors easily traceable. Ancient authors and their works, sometimes referred to by English titles, sometimes by ancient titles as seemed most suitable, are cited in full for the benefit of those unfamiliar with the rather arcane reference system generally used by ancient historians and classicists. References to Sallust's *Histories* are from the edition of B. Maurenbrecher.

The following abbreviations are used in either the Notes or Bibliographical References:

AE	*L'année épigraphique*
ANRW	H. Temporini, ed., *Aufstieg und Niedergang der römischen Welt*
CAH	*Cambridge Ancient History*
CIL	*Corpus Inscriptionum Latinarum*
IG	*Inscriptiones Graecae*
ILLRP	A. Degrassi, ed., *Inscriptiones Latinae Liberae Rei Publicae*
ILS	H. Dessau, ed., *Inscriptiones Latinae Selectae*
MRR	T. R. S. Broughton, *The Magistrates of the Roman Republic*
PECS	*The Princeton Encyclopedia of Classical Sites*
RE	*Paulys Realencyclopädie der classischen Altertumswissenschaft*
SRPS	Andrea Giardina and Aldo Schiavone, eds., *Società romana e produzione schiavistica*

Prologue

1. The secondary literature on the slave wars is vast, and a detailed doxography of the various ways in which they have previously been regarded would serve little useful purpose. For recent summaries of opinion, however, see Vogt (1975), 83–85; Guarino (1979), 13–20; Doi (1985); Wiedemann (1987), 47–48; and for access to material cf. also Vogt and Brockmeyer (1971), 149–57; Brockmeyer (1979), 172–77, 331–35. For the view that the wars were not principally slave wars, see especially in recent times Manganaro (1967) (cf. Manganaro [1964], 424–25; [1982]; [1983]), arguing for "nationalist" uprisings in Sicily against Roman rule; Rubinsohn (1971); Verbrugghe (1974); Guarino (1979), advocating the notion of a peasant revolt for the rebellion led by Spartacus and that of autonomous revolts in Sicily; Rubinsohn (1982). A presentist connection between ancient and modern liberation movements forms a constant theme in the work of Doi; see, for example, Doi (1978). For a summary of views on the belief that the rebels in Sicily set out to found slave kingdoms, with some theoretical objections, see

Bradley (1983), 436–40. For the utopian element, see Farrington (1937), 24–35, speaking of the slaves looking "to establish a permanent society under their own control" (p. 24) and their "conscious effort to set up a new society" (p. 25). For the notion that the slave wars are of no historical importance, see Badian (1981), 50.

2. Note that in the Christmas Rebellion of 1831–1832 in Jamaica, a number of free blacks joined in the largest of the slave revolts of the British West Indies; and that Denmark Vesey, the leader of an abortive rising of slaves in 1822 in Charleston, South Carolina, was an ex-slave who had bought his freedom; see Craton (1982a), 316; Genovese (1972), 411; note also Geggus (1982), 10, on St. Domingue. For assessment of the primary sources of information on the slave wars, see Appendix 1. Biezunska-Malowist (1981) rather underestimates the significance of the servile condition in antiquity at large.

3. On universal degradation in the master-slave relationship and universal resistance to slavery, see Patterson (1982), 11, 77–101, 173, 207.

I. Slave Resistance in the New World

1. No special expertise is claimed in the area of New World slavery of course, and I confine myself to description alone, making no apology for the amount of quoted material. On the all-pervasiveness of slavery in antiquity, with interesting remarks on its effect on the free (notably a fear of enslavement), see Biezunska-Malowist (1981). Torture: see *Digest* 48.18, with Robinson (1981) for a useful survey of the criminal penalties to which slaves in the Imperial period were subject. Quotation on Antigua: Gaspar (1985), 29. For recent emphasis on the brutality of slavery in the Roman world, see Hopkins (1978), 118–23; Finley (1980), 93–97; and on the general theme of violence in Roman society, see Wiseman (1985), 5–10.

2. For summaries of modern work on slavery in the New World, see Davis (1974); Elkins (1976), 223–302; Stampp (1980), 39–102; Rose (1982), 150–176; Craton (1982b); Shapiro (1984); Kolchin (1986). For flight in eighteenth-century Virginia and the nineteenth-century South and Cuba, see respectively Mullin (1972); Stampp (1956), 109–24; Knight (1970), 79; and for illustrations of notices of flight from Brazil, see Conrad (1983), 113–15; 362–66; cf. Schwartz (1985), 469–72. Quotations: Conrad (1983), 114–15; Mullin (1972), 40.

3. Stampp (1956), 123.

4. For the general features of maroon societies, see Price (1979a), 1–30; Kopytoff (1978); Genovese (1979), 52–54, 77–79; Craton (1982a), 61–66; Higman (1984), 386–93; Gaspar (1985), 171–84; Klein (1986), 198–205. Price (1979a), 1 n.1, gives the following etymology of the term "maroon": "the English word 'maroon,' like the French *marron*, derives from Spanish *cimarrón*. As used in the New World, *cimarrón* originally referred to domestic cattle that had taken to the hills in Hispaniola . . . and soon after to Indian slaves who had escaped from the Spaniards as well. . . . By the end of the 1530s, it was already beginning to refer primarily to Afro-American runaways . . . and had strong connotations of 'fierceness,' of being 'wild' and 'unbroken.' " For the distinction between *petit marronage* and *grand marronage*, cf. Craton (1982a), 61: "what distinguished true maroons from those engaged in what the French termed *petit marronage*—running away by an individual or for only a short term—was the organization of an effective band with an ability to defend, feed, and demographically sustain itself either by new recruits or, ultimately, through natural increase."

5. On Palmares, see Kent (1979); Genovese (1979), 60–66; Conrad (1983), 366–

79. Letter: quoted from Conrad (1983), 380. The description of the Buraco do Tatú is derived from Schwartz (1979), 218–23. On other Brazilian *quilombos*, see Bastide (1979); Russell-Wood (1982), 41–42, 124–26, 179–80, 190–93.

6. On the maroons of Surinam, see Price (1976); (1983a); (1983b). Creutz and Hentschel quoted from Price (1983a), 20, 39, 116, 117, 119.

7. Creutz and the modern Saramaka tradition quoted from Price (1983a), 20–21. Kwasi: quotation from ibid., 32–34; see also Price (1979b).

8. Factors: see Price (1976), 22; Schwartz (1979), 201–206.

9. On the maroons of Jamaica, see Patterson (1967), 260–83; (1979); Kopytoff (1976a); (1976b); (1978); Genovese (1979), 35–36, 51–57, 65–82; Craton (1982a), 67–96, 211–23. Quotations from Craton (1982a), 77–78. On the connection between marronage and general conspiracy, see also Gaspar (1985), 176.

10. Quotation on Jamaican geography: Kopytoff (1978), 290; see also Craton (1982a), 67. Note the decline of maroon activities in eighteenth-century Antigua as more and more of the island was cleared for settlement and sugar cultivation: Gaspar (1985), 185–214. James Knight: quoted in Kopytoff (1978), 297. R. C. Dallas: quoted in Price (1979a), 8–9. On the Jamaican maroon leaders in general, see Patterson (1979), 261–62; Kopytoff (1978), 297–300. On the religion of the Jamaican maroons, which allowed leaders such as Cudjoe, Nanny, and Accompong to become part of the spirit world after their deaths, see Kopytoff (1987), who comments: "In warfare during the pre-treaty times, the world of the spirits was very important to the Maroons, as it was to other Maroons elsewhere in the hemisphere. It was used to prepare the warriors for battle, making them invulnerable to enemy attack, and to help estimate risks and devise strategies. The supernatural advantage the Maroons believed their religion gave them in warfare against the English is remembered today in Maroon song, dance and ritual" (p. 468).

11. On forms of maroon leadership in general, see Price (1979a), 20. Ganga Zumba: see especially Kent (1979), 179–80. Brazilian Indians: see Schwartz (1985), 47–50. For the Jamaican maroons' loss of independence, see Kopytoff (1976a). On Cudjoe and freedom, see Craton (1982a), 82.

12. On revolts before marronage, see especially Kopytoff (1978), 292–93. Typology: Patterson (1967), 266–67. Tacky's Rebellion: see Craton (1982a), 127, citing the account of Edward Long.

13. Alternative schema: Craton (1982a).

14. Summary: Genovese (1979), 85. For the Haitian Revolution in full, see James (1963); and for the economic impact of the Haitian Revolution on the slave societies of the Caribbean and South America, see Klein (1986), 89–137. On restorationist and revolutionary revolts, see Genovese (1979) (quotation, p. 83). For the counterview, see Craton (1982a), (quotation, p. 331).

15. Tailors' Revolt: see Schwartz (1985), 476–77. Antigua: see Gaspar (1985) (quotation from the judges' General Report on the conspiracy, p. 3). United States: see Kilson (1964), 175–76.

16. Quotation on Brazil: Schwartz (1985), 473; cf. also Kent (1969–1970) on the religious element in the revolt of 1835 in Bahia. On St. Domingue see Geggus (1982), 33–45 (quotation, p. 39), 290–325.

17. See respectively Patterson (1979), 288, and Genovese (1979), 11–12; cf. also Klein (1986), 205, 208.

18. Suggestion: Patterson (1979), 279. Note in Patterson (1967), 274–75, 278, the brief allusion to the first Roman slave rebellion in Sicily.

19. Information and quotations on the Zanj Rebellion from Davis (1984), 5–8.

20. On the essential continuity of slave history from antiquity to the modern era, see Phillips (1985); Klein (1986), 1–20. On modes of comparative history, their

strengths and weaknesses, see Skocpol and Somers (1980); cf. Higman (1984), 1–3; Degler (1971), x–xi. For the relevance of ancient slave revolts to the modern comparative perspective, see Genovese (1979), 165–66; Craton (1982b), 418.

II. Slavery and Slave Resistance at Rome

1. On Rome and Italy, see Sherwin-White (1973), 134–49; Gabba (1976), 70–130; Salmon (1982), 73–142. On the growth of Roman power overseas, see Badian (1958), 33–153; Nicolet (1978); Harris (1979), 131–254; Gruen (1984). For the theme of Polybius' history, see Polybius 1.1.5 with Walbank (1957), 40.

2. On empire and the rise of wealth among the Roman elite, see Harris (1979), 54–104; Gruen (1984), 288–315. Political competitiveness: see Millar (1984) on the political character of Rome in the first half of the second century. For the traditional view of the economic transformation of Italy and the growth of slavery, see Hopkins (1978), 8–56; for the alternative, see Rathbone (1981), relying on the agrarian history of a specific region of southern Etruria; cf. the summary of Rich (1983), 296–99, and see also Potter (1987), 94–124. On ranching in Italy and Sicily, see Frayn (1984), 110–26.

3. On defining slave society, see Hopkins (1978), 99–100; but cf. Finley (1980), 67–92; see also Ste. Croix (1981), 209; Gruen (1984), 296–97. On the number of slaves in Italy in 225 B.C., see Brunt (1971), 121. Population proportions can never be more than estimated, and conjectures do not always coincide: the servile population of Italy at the end of the first century has been calculated at two million out of a total population of six million (Hopkins [1978], 102), and three million out of a total of seven and a half million (Brunt [1971], 124). For the scope of the problem of measurement, see Nicolet (1977), 209–11. On the qualitative evaluation of Rome as a slave society, see Bradley (1985a); cf. De Martino (1974); Crawford (1985), 24 n.34. Indications: under a provision of the Twelve Tables, the first codified body of Roman law dating to the middle of the fifth century, the law regarded the physically injured slave as a human being; but under the terms of the *lex Aquilia*, the traditional date of which is 287 B.C., the killing of a slave was deemed tantamount to the killing of an animal; see Watson (1987), 46, 54–58.

4. Legal statement: *Digest* 1.5.4.2–3 (Wiedemann); cf. Patterson (1982), 5: "Archetypically, slavery was a substitute for death in war." For details on mass enslavements in the middle Republic, see Westermann (1955), 60–61; Volkmann (1961); Toynbee (1965), II, 171–73; Staerman (1969), 43–44; Harris (1979), 58–63. The following examples can be noted in particular: 262 B.C., 25,000, Agrigentum (Diodorus Siculus 23.9.1); 256 B.C., 20,000, North Africa (Polybius 1.29.7); 254 B.C., 13,000, Panormus (Diodorus Siculus 23.18.5; cf. Polybius 1.38.9–10); 241 B.C., 10,000, Lilybaeum (Polybius 1.61.8); 218 B.C., 2,000, Lilybaeum (Livy 21.51.2); 215 B.C., 5,000 Hirpini (Livy 23.37.12); 214 B.C., 3,000, Munda (Livy 24.42.4); 213 B.C., 7,000, Atrinum (Livy 24.47.14); 209 B.C., 4,000, Manduria (Livy 27.15.4); 209 B.C., 30,000, Tarentum (Livy 27.16.7); 204 B.C., 8,000, North Africa (Livy 29.29.3); 197 B.C., 5,000, Macedonia (Livy 33.10.7; 11.2); 177 B.C., 5,632, Mutila and Faveria (Livy 41.11.8); 171 B.C., 2,500, Haliartus (Livy 42.63.11); 167 B.C., 150,000, Epirus (Livy 45.34.5); 146 B.C., 55,000 Carthaginians (Orosius 4.23.3); 142 B.C., 9,500, Lusitania (Appian, *Iberica* 68). Scipio Aemilianus: Valerius Maximus 6.2.3; *De Viris Illustribus* 58.8; cf. Velleius Paterculus 2.4.4; Astin (1967), 234. Cicero: *Tusculan Disputations* 3.53 (Loeb). The material assembled in Bang (1910), 225–29 remains a useful indicator of the enormous regional diversity of the Roman slave supply under the Republic.

5. Scipio Aemilianus: Appian, *Iberica* 98; and for commanders sending slaves to Rome, see also Livy 30.16.1; 17.1.11. Alesia: Caesar, *Gallic Wars* 7.89; cf. Westermann (1955), 70. Quaestor: see Walbank (1967a), 217, and cf. n.15 below. Corbio: Livy 39.42.1. Istrian towns: Livy 41.11.7–8. Epirotes: Livy 45.34.5; Strabo 7.7.3 = Polybius 30.15 (16); Plutarch, *Aemilius* 29.3; see recently Ziolkowski (1986), arguing that the enslavement was dictated by a severe shortage of slaves in Italy caused by the effects of plague in 175 B.C.–174 B.C. For legitimate purchase in this context, see Varro, *Res Rusticae* 2.10.4. Pindenissum: Cicero, *Letters to Atticus* 113.5 (Shackleton Bailey). Quotation on peddlers: Finley (1969), 169; cf. Harris (1980), 125. Perceptible convention: Polybius 14.7.3; Livy 10.17.6.

6. Delos: Strabo 14.5.2. (on piracy, see chapter 4 below). On Gallic slaves and Italian wine, see Tchernia (1983), conjoining the archaeological evidence with the essential texts, Diodorus Siculus 5.26.3, Cicero, *Pro Quinctio* 24, and Afranius 236–237 (Daviault); cf. Middleton (1983), but for some doubts see Crawford (1985), 168–71. On Danubian slaves see Crawford (1977a); (1985), 226–35, 348. On the major centers of slave trading, see Gordon (1924), 93–96; Harris (1980), 125–28. Guarino (1979), 36–37, gives proper emphasis to the importance of the slave trade; cf. Kolendo (1978), 30. For signs of slave trading in Republican Capua, see Frederiksen (1984), 302. On slave dealers, see Harris (1980), 129–32; cf. also Bradley (1984), 61–62, 114–16. Note that the term *mango* (slave dealer) appears as early as Lucilius 29.900. Cicero: *Orator* 232. Own slaves: *Digest* 14.4.1.1; cf. 14.3.17 pr.-1. Lucius Publicius: Cicero, *Pro Quinctio* 24. A. Kapreilius Timotheus: *AE* 1946. 229, on which see Finley (1969), 162–76; cf. Kolendo (1978); Finley (1983), 167–75; Duchêne (1986). It should be noted that even men of high social status did not remain averse to the profits of slave dealing: C. Sallustius Crispus Passienus, twice consul and briefly the stepfather of the emperor Nero, is known to have had connections with the dealers of Ephesus: *AE* 1924.72; cf. Harris (1980), 130; D'Arms (1981), 156.

7. Shackles: eight shackled slaves are depicted on the stele of A. Kapreilius Timotheus (above n.6); see also the relief from Mainz of two Gallic captives chained at the neck described by Ducrey (1968), 223 (plate IX), with his references (p. 224) to Plautus, *Captivi* 110–114, and Polybius 20.10.7–8. On forced migration, note Cicero's casual remark (*Letters to Atticus* 89.7 [Shackleton Bailey]; cf. 92.5) that Caesar's presence in Britain would at least put captives on the market, and Varro's bland references (*Res Rusticae* 2.10.4) to acquiring slaves from Spain or Gaul for use in Italy (cf. 1.17.5, Epirotes). Cf. Bradley (1984), 59–60, for later evidence. From the comparative point of view, for contemporary descriptions of the severe conditions of the Atlantic sea passage to Brazil (in particular), including slave sources, see Conrad (1983), 5–52; and in general Klein (1978). Much must have been similar in antiquity. Mass suicide: Appian, *Civil Wars* 4.64; cf. 4.80.

8. Minimal importance: for various statements of this view, see Brunt (1971), 707–708; Hopkins (1978), 102; Harris (1980), 121–22; Ste. Croix (1981), 228, 234–36; cf. also Brunt (1958), 166; White (1970), 368–70; Nicolet (1977), 214; De Martino (1979), 76–78, 108, 263–91. Staerman (1969), 36–70, on the other hand, has placed a greater emphasis on breeding; but her view that Rome's captives in warfare were mainly already slaves is questionable; cf. Crawford (1977b), 49. Most scholars of course would allow that breeding was well in evidence at the end of the Republic, on the basis, for example, of such texts as Cornelius Nepos, *Life of Atticus* 13.3; Horace, *Epodes* 2.65. For the difficulties of defining the term "breeding," see Bradley (1987), 54–58. For the question of slaves as an object of policy, see Harris (1979), 83–85; Gruen (1984), 295–99; cf. Nicolet (1977), 212–13. Illustrations of Rome not enslaving defeated enemies: Polybius 10.17.6–16; Livy 27.19.2. For a collection of legal references to *partus ancillae*, see Jonkers (1933),

112–14; and for an analysis of inscriptions recording *vernae*, see Rawson (1986). The earliest *verna* inscription, *ILLRP* 1218, belongs in fact to the third century B.C. Cf. Treggiari (1969), 248, for freed *vernae*. It should be observed that the role of warfare as a supplier of slaves under the Empire has traditionally been underestimated; see Harris (1980), 122; Whittaker (1987), 97–98.

9. Manumission in the Twelve Tables: Ulpian, *Tituli* 2.4, 29.1; Gaius, *Institutes* 1.165, 3.51. Matralia: Ovid, *Fasti* 6.551–558; Plutarch, *Camillus* 5.2; *Roman Questions* 16–17; see Ogilvie (1965), 680–81; Scullard (1981), 150–51; Thomsen (1980), 267–68; Dumézil (1980); cf. Bradley (1985a), 2–3. *Feriae ancillarum*: Plutarch, *Camillus* 33; *Romulus* 29; Macrobius, *Saturnalia* 1.11.36; (cf. Ovid, *Ars Amatoria* 2.257–258); see Latte (1970), 106; Dumézil (1980), 241–56; Scullard (1981), 161–62. That the festival has a much older background is clear: see Robertson (1987), arguing that rain magic lies behind the historical celebration. Female captives expected: Livy 30.14.3. Anticyra in Phocis: Polybius 9.39.2–3. L. Mummius: Pausanias 7.16.8. Carthage: Orosius 4.23: cf. Appian, *Libyca* 130; Florus 1.31.16. Capsa: Sallust, *Jugurthine War* 91.7. Colenda: Appian, *Iberica* 99. Capua: Livy 26.34.2–3. In accounts that do not specify the gender of captives it is implausible to assume exclusive male enslavement: in 189 B.C. Same of Cephallenia was besieged by M. Fulvius Nobilior; Livy states (38.29.11) that when the city was captured all who surrendered were sold as slaves; since women and children are specifically said to have taken refuge in the city the day before it fell, the presumption must be strong that women and children were indeed enslaved. Cf. similarly Livy 42.63.12; Appian, *Iberica* 68. Observe the unauthenticated statement of Finley (1980), 128: "Rome's eastern conquests threw hundreds of thousands of men, women and children on to the slave market while the conquests were proceeding."

10. Tenable statement: Gordon (1924), 103. Scipio Africanus: Livy 26.50. Ti. Sempronius Gracchus: Livy 40.49.4–6. Chiomara: Plutarch, *Moralia* 258E; cf. Livy 38.24, 23.9, 21.14. For another celebrated former *ancillula*, the *scortum* Hispala Faecenia, see Livy 39.9.5. Cato: Plutarch, *Cato* 21.2. Licinia: Plutarch, *Cato* 20.3. For the argument from the agricultural writers, see Brunt (1971), 707 (but contrast Brunt [1971], 131, 144–45, which paradoxically seems to give relative importance to breeding in the late Republic); Ste. Croix (1981), 233, 235; cf. De Martino (1979), 76–78. For the differences between their works, see the comments of White (1970), 19–20, 26–28; and on the selective nature of Cato's work especially, see Astin (1978), 189, 242–43. For the objection, cf. also Finley (1976), 4, not convincingly dealt with by Ste. Croix (1981), 588. See further Bradley (1987), 61 n.34.

11. See in turn Cato, *De Agricultura* 5.5; 10.5; 11.3–4; 13.1; 14.1; 56; 57; 4; 143.1; 156.6; 157.5; 157.10–11; 127.2; cf. Saint-Denis (1980), 845–48. For domestic roles, see especially *Digest* 33.7.12.5, and for Cato's ownership of domestic slaves, Astin (1978), 261; cf. Sicard (1957). Columella: *Res Rusticae* 12.3.6; cf. Ste. Croix (1981), 234; and see also the legal texts cited by Brunt (1971), 707.

12. Appian: *Civil Wars* 1.7, for rejection of which, see Ste. Croix (1981), 235; cf. Frank (1933), 111–12; Gabba (1967), 17–18; Harris (1979), 84 n.2; Finley (1980), 130, suspending judgment. Cicero's reference: *De Finibus* 1.12; cf. Frier (1985), 164. Note also Frederiksen (1984), 301, on slave breeding at Capua under the Republic.

13. On slave jobs in the late Republic and early Empire, see Maxey (1938); White (1970), 368–83; Treggiari (1975); (1976). Quotation on agriculture: Rathbone (1983), 167, summarizing Carandini (1981). Concessions: Rathbone (1983), 162.

14. On the date of composition of Cato's book, see Astin (1978), 190–91. For Cato's information described here, see *De Agricultura* 2.1; 2.2; 2.4; 4; 5.1; 5.4;

5.5; 10.1; 10.5; 11.1; 11.3; 11.4; 13.1; 14.1; 25; 56; 57; 58; 59; 66.1; 83; 134; 136; 141; 142; 143; 144.3; 145.1; 145.2; 149.2; 155.1.

15. See Plautus, *Asinaria* 540; *Miles* 1183; *Rudens* Arg. 1; *Vidularia* 21; 24; 25; 47; *Mostellaria* 780; *Captivi* 661; *Mostellaria* 35; 19 (cf. *Captivi* 944); *Casina* 52; 99; 103; 105; 109; 117–131; 255–259; 418; *Asinaria* 215–26; *Miles* 955; *Stichus* 102; *Trinummus* 408; *Miles* 193; *Truculentus* 107. The basic discussion of slaves in Plautus is Spranger (1960), perhaps unduly conservative on the realistic element. The purchase of slaves provided by warfare from the quaestor, given at Plautus, *Captivi* 34; 110–111, 454, is one authentic detail of particular relevance here.

16. See Plautus, *Captivi* 889; *Miles* 1008; *Stichus* 433; *Amphitruo* 365; *Rudens* 218; *Miles* 698; and the references from *Casina* in n.15 above. Cf. in general Spranger (1960), 74–84. The comment of Patterson (1982), 40, that "we learn . . . from the comedies of Plautus and Terence that the slave was one who recognized no father and no fatherland," is not really true.

17. See Plautus, *Amphitruo* 1049; 1081; *Casina* 254–256; 632; *Epidicus* 43; 130; 210–211; *Mercator* 201; 211; 261; 350; 390; 415; 975; *Poenulus* 1124–1126; 1130; *Rudens* 706–779; *Trinummus* 250–252; 799; *Truculentus* 770–771; 895; *Aulularia* 488–503; *Casina* 261; 709; *Curculio* 616; *Menaechmi* 120; 801; *Persa* 472; *Truculentus* 401; 530–533; *Amphitruo* 1102–1104; *Asinaria* 183–184; 804; 868; *Curculio* 580; 643; *Menaechmi* 797; *Mercator* 396–398; *Miles* 910; 960; *Poenulus* 222–223; *Truculentus* 901–908; *Mercator* 414–416; 509; *Mostellaria* 756; 758; 908.

18. See Plautus, *Trinummus* 251–252; 405; 772; *Captivi* 629; *Truculentus* 131; *Mercator* Arg. I 4; II 5; *Curculio* 76; *Aulularia* 691; 807; 815; *Curculio* 643; *Miles* 698; *Poenulus* Arg. 4; *Prol.* 28–31; 84–86; 88; 898; 1105; 1111–1112; 1124–1126; *Truculentus* 901–908. Cf. Spranger (1960), 80–81, and on the later role of the *nutrix*, see Bradley (1986a). Entertainers (cf. Livy 39.6.8) and prostitutes are of course standard in Plautus.

19. See Plautus, *Trinummus* 251–252; *Aulularia* 488–502; *Casina* 462; *Asinaria* 85–86; *Poenulus* Prol. 41; 1283; *Captivi* 895; *Miles* 824; 1009; *Mercator* 123; 852; *Bacchides* 162; *Pseudolus* 148; 157–158; 161–164; 776. Cf. Spranger (1960) 75; 81–83. On the cook in Plautus, see Lowe (1985). It can be added that the diversity of the Roman *familia* in the late Republic and early Empire did not derive from the influences of Greek comedy.

20. On child labor, see Bradley (1985b); cf. Burford (1972), 87–91; Bradley (1986b), 50–51; add *Digest* 14.3.5.10, apprentice launderers; *Digest* 14.3.8, boys and girls commonly working as shopkeepers. Cato's speech: Polybius 31.25.5a. Luxury tax: Livy 39.44.3. Plutarch: *Cato* 21.7 (Loeb); cf. Astin (1978), 261–62.

21. Quotation on Antigua: Gaspar (1985), 93. Will of Dasumius: *CIL* 6.10229, supplemented by *AE* 1976. 77. The identity of the testator is in doubt: long thought to be L. Dasumius Hadrianus (cos. suff. A.D. 93), he might in actuality have been Cn. Domitius Tullus (cos. suff. A.D. 98; cf. Pliny, *Epistles* 8.18), if not a complete *ignotus* (see Eck [1978]; Syme [1985]; cf. Champlin [1986], 251–55). The following list of members of the *familia* is that given by Mommsen in the commentary to *CIL* 6.10229 (the numerals refer to the line numbers of the text):

Achilles lib. 63.100.	Cym[aeus?] 100.
Anatellon lib. 61.107.	Diadumenus cubicularius 68.
Arrus piscator 36.	Diadumenus notarius 43.
Ca. . . . 48.	Encolpius actor 86.
[C]olonus lib. 47.	Epaphro[ditus] 72.
C[r]ammicus c. . . . . .42.	Eros vestiarius 50.

Eurota lib. 49.131.
Eutyches cubicularius maior (?) 78.
Faustus sutor 70.
Heliopaes lib. 48.63.100.
Hymnus 92.
Menecrates 80.
My . . . 40.
Paederos 80.
Philocyrius 73.
Pho[ebus?] 51.
Sabinus notarius 40.
Stephanus dropacator 69.
Dasumia Syche nutrix 13? 35.47.

Syn(?) . . . 13.*
[Te]rpnus lib. 63.
Thal[l]us ornator 59.
Thaumastus lib. 61.107.
Venugus piscator 36.
. . . . .cocus 42.
. . . . .[cu]rsor 86.
. . . . .[d]ispensator 77.
. . . . .tus medicus 72.
. . . . . .medicus 129.
. . . . [paeda]gogus 51.
. . . . sumptuarius 44.

(*Note that *AE* 1976. 77 now gives in line 13 "Syneros servos"). Since the will is so fragmentary, the reasons governing the appearance of these people in it are not always clear. Some of the slaves were to be set free when the will was implemented (e.g. Diadumenus the *notarius*, Eros the *vestiarius*); others were bequeathed to the testator's aunt (e.g., Faustus the *sutor*, Encolpius the *actor*; cf. Syme [1985], 57, but contrast Champlin [1986], 252); and the two *piscatores* seem to have been left to the *nutrix* Dasumia Syche, the only female on the list and perhaps not a freedwoman of the testator himself. At the same time, several individuals were to receive gifts (e.g., Eurota, Heliopaes), and a ban was apparently imposed on the future manumission of some slaves (Menecrates, Paederos, and perhaps Hymnus). But while these matters are reasonably certain, other factors remain obscure. For the evidence on the household of Augustus's wife Livia, see Treggiari (1975); but, as she makes clear, the material extends over long stretches of time and will not allow an inventory at any specific moment to emerge.

22. Varro: *Res Rusticae* 1.17.5 (Wiedemann); cf. Plutarch, *Cato* 21.4 (quoted below). Quotation on Brazil: Schwartz (1985), 252. Class consciousness: see Levi (1972a); Guarino (1979), 96–97; Runciman (1983). Though, as the example of Bahia makes clear (cf. Schwartz [1985], 132–59), it does not follow that slavery in and of itself could not prompt violent resistance, separate from other discontents elsewhere in society. Dumont (1967), 96, finds evidence of servile class consciousness in the *Captivi* of Plautus.

23. Cicero, *Letters to His Friends* 212 (Shackleton Bailey). For flight in the Republic generally, see Staerman (1969), 240–43, and under the Empire, Bellen (1971). P. Sulpicius Rufus: *MRR* II, 299.

24. For a view of Cicero as a "humane master" and "generous manumitter," perhaps at odds with the case of Dionysius, see Treggiari (1969), 252. Note the cynical attitude of Cicero, *Letters to Quintus* 1.17 (Shackleton Bailey).

25. Rural slave dishonesty: Columella, *Res Rusticae* 1.7.6–7; cf. Bradley (1984), 27–28. Petty sabotage in modern slave societies: Stampp (1956), 97–108; Genovese (1972), 597–621. Military action in Dalmatia: Wilkes (1969), 35, who suggests (p. 42) that Dionysius ran away "probably when Cicero was in the Pompeian camp two years before" (i.e., Illyricum in 49 B.C.); there is no evidence for this view.

26. P. Vatinius: *MRR* II, 310. His correspondence with Cicero: Cicero, *Letters to His Friends* 255; 257 (quoted); 259 (Shackleton Bailey).

27. Q. Tullius Cicero: *MRR* II, 191. Quoted letter: Cicero, *Letters to Quintus* 2.14 (Shackleton Bailey). Clodius Aesopus: Treggiari (1969), 139.

28. Cicero in Cilicia: *MRR* II, 243, 251–52. The correspondence: Cicero, *Letters to Atticus* 108.3; 115.13 (Shackleton Bailey). *Vernae*: Cornelius Nepos, *Life of Atticus* 13.3.

29. See Plautus, *Poenulus* 832; *Captivi Arg.* 7–10; 17–20; 207–209; *Casina* 397; *Pseudolus* 365; *Menaechmi* 79–86 (Loeb). Cf. Dumont (1967), 97.

30. *Vilicus:* Cato, *De Agricultura* 2.2. Quotation: Plautus, *Captivi* 207–209 (Loeb). Lucilius: 29.917–918. 210 B.C.: Livy 26.27.1–9. Diplomacy: see, for example, Livy 30.16.10; 30.37.3; 34.35.4; 38.11.4; 38.38.7; Polybius 21.32.5; 21.42.10; Appian, *Mithridatica* 22; 55; 61; Caesar, *Gallic Wars* 1.27; cf. Walbank (1979), 133; Gruen (1984), 640. First century: see Bradley (1978) on the year 63 B.C. Unknown senator: *ILS* 23 = *ILLRP* 454; various suggestions on his identity have been made, but certainty is impossible; see Wiseman (1964); Verbrugghe (1973); *MRR* III, 16–17; 56; 169.

31. Intermittent dimensions: Gruen (1974), 407 n.4. Legal definition: *Digest* 21.1.17 pr. (Watson). For slavecatchers, see Daube (1952). The term *fugitivarius* first appears, metaphorically, in Varro, *Res Rusticae* 3.14.2. Aedilician edict: Aulus Gellius 4.2.1. Ulpian: *Digest* 21.1.10.1. Daube (1956), 95–97, conjectures that "it was Cato himself who, when aedile in 199, prompted the publication of the earliest edict on the sale of slaves."

32. Refuge: see *Digest* 47.12.3.11 for tombs inhabited by slaves; Asconius 37 Clark for a slave sleeping in a shop arrested as a fugitive. Praetor: above n.30. Q. Sertorius: Livy 91.

33. On first-generation slaves, see *Digest* 21.1.37. Aulus Gellius: 11.18.14.

34. Athenaeus 265d-266e (Wiedemann). For analysis, see Fuks (1968); Vogt (1973); Finley (1980), 113–14; cf. Cartledge (1985), 38–39, 45–46.

35. C. Octavius: Suetonius, *Augustus* 3.1 (Loeb); cf. 7.1; see Carter (1982), 92–93.

36. On the lack of revolts in the United States, see Genovese (1972), 587. For full sources and analysis of the Republican revolts before the major insurrections, see Capozza (1966) with, however, the critical comments of Dumont (1967) and Bosworth (1968); cf. also Ogilvie (1965), 423–24. 259 B.C.: Orosius 4.7.11, with Capozza (1966), 75–92, for the Carthaginian explanation. 419 B.C.: Livy 4.45.1–2; Dionysius of Halicarnassus 12 fr. 6.6. Betrayal: see Livy 22.33.2 for betrayal by a slave informant of the conspiracy of 217 B.C. Contemporary anxieties: the phrase *terror servilis* at Livy 3.16.3 seems far more apposite for contemporary than historical conditions.

37. 198 B.C.: Livy 32.26.4–18; cf. Briscoe (1973), 216–18; Toynbee (1965) II, 318–19. Contravention: on the hostages, see the comments of Walbank (1967), 470–71.

38. 196 B.C.: Livy 33.36.1–3; cf. Briscoe (1973), 317–18; Toynbee (1965) II, 319–20; cf. Baldwin (1966–1967), 294, on the speed of Rome's response to revolt. Quotation: Harris (1971), 142. 185 B.C.: Livy 39.29.8–10 (Loeb); Toynbee (1965) II, 320–21, who, following Frank (1927), regards the insurgents as connected with the cult of Dionysus, thus minimizing Livy's reference to brigandage. Pastoral farming: see Brunt (1971), 283–84.

39. L. Aemilius Paullus: *ILLRP* 514; cf. *MRR* I, 362; III, 9–10. Slave family: see Bradley (1984), 47–80, for the Imperial period. Already in the second century Plautus's *Casina* implies that owners had the capacity to arrange their slaves' marriages. Minturnae: *ILLRP* 724–726. Plutarch: *Cato* 21. 1–4 (Wiedemann).

III. The First Slave War in Sicily

1. On Enna in general, see *PECS*, s.v. "Enna"; Manni (1981), 168–69; Coarelli and Torelli (1984), 170–71. "Navel of Sicily": Cicero, *Verrines* 2.4.106; Diodorus

Siculus 5.3.2. Myths: Cicero, *Verrines* 2.4.106–107; 111; Diodorus 5.3.1–5.5.3; see Martorana (1982–1983a) in particular on Persephone at Enna. Special sanctuary: Cicero, *Verrines* 2.4.111. Cicero: *Verrines* 2.4.107 (Loeb); Livy: 24.39.8; 24.37.2 (Loeb); cf. Strabo 6.2.6. Enna was underpopulated by Strabo's time. Communication: it appears from Cicero, *Verrines* 2.3.192 that any point on the coasts of Sicily could be reached from Enna in one day. 258 B.C.: Livy 23.9.4–5; Polybius 1.24.12. 214 B.C.: Livy 24.37.1–24.39.10; Frontinus, *Stratagems* 4.7.22.

2. On Rome's annexation of Sicily and the sequel in general, see Finley (1979), 109–21. M. Valerius Laevinus: Livy 27.5.2–5; cf. 26.40.15–18; see Capozza (1956–1957), 80–81; Manganaro (1980), 415–22; Mazza (1981), 27–30. Soubriquet: Cicero, *Verrines* 2.2.5.

3. On Sicily as a supplier of grain to Rome in general, see Rickman (1980), 104–106. Florus: 2.7.3 (Loeb), but use of the term *latifundia* is probably anachronistic; see Mazza (1981), 42. Diodorus: 34/35.2.1–2; 27–30. Strabo: 6.2.6.

4. On the economy of Sicily in general, see Mazza (1981), emphasizing especially the mixed nature of agriculture; Manganaro (1980), 428–37, emphasizing the wide extent of smallholdings in Sicily; cf. Coarelli (1981), 2–8; Capozza (1956–1957), 87–88 (exaggerating the importance of *latifundia*). On agriculture leading to an increase in slavery, note Appian, *Civil Wars* 1.9, with Gabba (1967), 25. Accuracy of Diodorus: Verbrugghe (1972), offset by Coarelli (1981), 8–18; Mazza (1981), 35–38. Reputation: Scramuzza (1937), 278–281. Cleon: Diodorus 34/35.2.43. Diodorus: 34/35.2.2; 27 (cf. 32). Cicero's evidence (pastoral and mixed farming): *Verrines* 2.2.188; 2.3.57; 2.5.7; 2.5.15; 2.5.17; 2.5.20; cf. Mazza (1981), 44–47. Damophilus: Diodorus 34/35.2.34; 36; cf. Toynbee (1965) II, 323. For the assumption that the inmates of *ergastula* were nonpastoral slaves, see Capozza (1956–1957), 87.

5. Cicero, *Verrines* 2.5.29; 2.3.57; 2.5.15–17 (on Matrinius, see Fraschetti [1981], 67–68); 2.5.10; 2.5.7 (on L. Domitius Ahenobarbus, cf. *MRR* II, 7); 2.2.35–36; 2.2.46 (cf. 2.2.47); 2.2.63; 2.2.140; *In Caecilium* 55–57.

6. Damophilus's domestics: Diodorus 34/35.2.34–35 (Wiedemann); 38. Traders: Cicero, *Verrines* 2.5.146. First-generation slaves: Diodorus 34/35.2.36 especially; Green (1961), 11, 12–13, posits a slave population in Sicily made up of Italian fugitives, local Sicilians, Chaldaeans and Jews, refugees from the Viriathic war in Spain, Cilicians and Syrians; cf. also Capozza (1956–1957), 86: the slave population of Sicily grew as a result of Rome's wars in Spain, Macedonia, Greece, Africa, and Asia. But the evidence for all these groups is not specific. The enslavement of the surviving population of Agrigentum in 210 B.C. (Livy 26.40.13) may have contributed to the later production of homeborn slaves. Eunus and his companion: Diodorus 34/35.2.5; 16; Livy, *Periocha* 56; Florus 2.7.4. Cleon and Comanus: Diodorus 34/35.2.17; 20; 43; Valerius Maximus 9.12 ext. 1. Megallis: Diodorus 34/35.2.15; 37.

7. Scale of slaveowning: see Mazza (1981), 23. Settlers: on the emigration of Romans and Italians to Sicily, see Wilson (1966), 55–64; Fraschetti (1981), 53–61 (stressing landownership); cf. also Frank (1935); De Laet (1949), 65–70; Brunt (1971), 211; Nicolet (1974), 292–94. Little detailed evidence is available before Cicero's *Verrines*, when, "apart from the merchants and traders, whom Cicero indicates as temporary residents rather than settlers, the Sicilian Romans fell into three main classes, the *aratores* and *pecuarii*, the *negotiatores*, and men connected with the collection of the *decumae*, the *scriptura*, or the *portoria*; some may have combined these various pursuits" (Wilson [1966], 56). But the picture given by the *Verrines* cannot be unique to the period of Verres's governorship. In this respect, the possible early career of P. Rupilius, cos. 132 B.C. (on whom, see further

below), is instructive: "he was said to have worked collecting *portoria* for a Roman *societas*, then to have been employed by Sicilians who had secured the local collection of *decumae*" (Wilson [1966], 58, with reference to Valerius Maximus 6.9.8; cf. also Toynbee [1965] II, 327; Badian [1972], 49). Diodorus: 34/35.2.27; 34. 205 B.C.: Livy 29.1.15–18. 199 B.C.: Livy 32.1.6 (but note Brunt [1971], 211 n.1). 193 B.C.: *ILS* 864 (cf. *MRR* I, 347). Q. Caecilius Niger: see Wiseman (1971), 22. On the peaceful development of Sicily after the Roman reconquest in general, see Manganaro (1980), 422–28.

8. Diodorus: 34/35.2.38; 1–2; 27; 32. Westermann (1945), 8, regarded Diodorus 34/35.2.1–2 as "a brilliant analysis of the neglect of definite slave expectations, generally granted under the Greek, and so under the Sicilian, slave system." To understand that slaves reacted to maltreatment by revolt is essentially correct. But because first-generation slaves were particularly involved in the rebellion, it cannot be true that they "had been torn away ruthlessly from their customary work, whereby they earned money for their owners, and so obtained their own living and support." The slaves in Sicily did not respond to a change in conventionally accepted modes of treatment, but first to servitude itself and then to harsh living conditions.

9. On the physical abuse of slaves in general, see Hopkins (1978), 118–23; Bradley (1984), 113–37; for a collection of evidence on sexual exploitation, mainly from the Imperial period, see Kolendo (1981). P. Vedius Pollio: Seneca, *On Anger* 3.40.2; *On Mercy* 1.18.2; Pliny, *Natural History* 9.77; Cassius Dio 54.23.1–4. Larcius Macedo: Pliny, *Epistles* 3.14. Recourse: see Watson (1987), 116–20; contrast the occasional right of slaves in colonial Brazil to denounce cruel slaveowners: Schwartz (1985), 134. Plautus: e.g., *Amphitruo* 291–462; *Mostellaria* 859–884. Cato: above, chapter 2, and Plutarch, *Cato* 4.5. On violence as a fundamental element of the master-slave relationship, see Patterson (1982), 3–4; Wiedemann (1987), 25.

10. Cato: *De Agricultura* 5.2; 59. Plautus: *Casina* 495. Legal source: *Digest* 34.2.23.2. For other evidence, see Columella, *Res Rusticae* 1.8.9; Palladius 1.43.4, with White (1970), 364; Frayn (1984), 84–88, and the iconographic material to which they refer. Animal skins: Diodorus 34/35.2.29. Anecdotes: Livy 30.4.1; Tacitus, *Annals* 13.25; *Histories* 2.29; 3.73; 4.36; Appian, *Civil Wars* 2.33; 4.39; 4.44; 4.48; 4.49; see also items referred to by Frayn (1984), 66–68. For sumptuously dressed domestics, see Appian, *Civil Wars* 2.120 (clearly rhetorical). The implication of Seneca, *On Mercy* 1.24.1, that the dress of slave and free was indistinguishable can at most refer only to urban domestics in wealthy households. For slave dress as stigmatic, see Patterson (1982), 58.

11. Cato: *De Agricultura* 56–58; 5.2; cf. Isidore, *Etymologies* 20.2.15; for discussion of the adequacy of Cato's rations, see Etienne (1981). On daily bread supplies to shackled slaves, see Oates (1934); Rowland (1970). Legionary soldier: Polybius 6.39.3; cf. Walbank (1957), 722. *Plebs frumentaria*: see Brunt (1971), 382; Rickman (1980), 10. Seneca: *Moral Epistles* 80.7 (see also Sallust, *Histories* 3.48.19 [cf. 1.55.11]; but note Donatus, Terence, *Phormio* 1.1.9.7: four *modii* a month). Quotation: Duncan-Jones (1974), 147. Minimal needs: see Rowland (1970); White (1970), 361; Brunt (1971), 382; Rickman (1980), 10. Milk and meat: Diodorus 34/35.2.30.

12. Cato: *De Agricultura* 14.2. Varro: *Res Rusticae* 1.13.1–2. Columella: *Res Rusticae* 1.6.3; 1.6.7–8.

13. For a survey of current information on the variety of villas known in Italy, see Potter (1987), 94–124; cf. Potter (1979), 120–37. Settefinestre (also going back approximately to the second quarter of the first century): see Carandini (1985) I,

158, 177; II, 153–56, 171–81. Southern Campania: see Carrington (1931), 122, 128; cf. 126–27, 129; White (1970), 437; cf. 422–23, 428; Rossiter (1978), 40–48. Posto: see Cotton (1979), 18, 20. San Rocco: see Cotton and Métraux (1985), xxv, 55, 57–58, 82. Villa Sambuco: see White (1970), 419; Potter (1979), 123. Stocks: Rossiter (1978), 43, questioning older identifications of the rooms in which they were found as *ergastula*. It should be noted that the phenomenon of voluntary slavery was not unknown at Rome; see Ramin and Veyne (1981) for discussion of the evidence (mainly legal). But it does not follow, as some might assume, that Roman slavery was, by definition, mild: if people chose to enslave themselves to gain money for food or to acquire access to jobs they hoped would lead to material advancement (as Ramin and Veyne [1981] argue), they either exchanged one form of misery for another or exposed themselves to complete rightlessness—hardly enviable situations. However, the incidence of the phenomenon is beyond measurement.

14. Diodorus: 34/35.2.2–3; 27–31. On the importance of dogs to *pastores*, see Varro, *Res Rusticae* 2.9.

15. On the economic link between Sicily and Italy, see Mazza (1981), and on brigandage in general, see Pelham (1911). Wiseman (1964) 34–36; Brunt (1971), 551–57; Frayn (1984), 76–77. Southern Italy: see Brunt (1971), 370–75. Livy: 28.12.8. Fugitive slaves: Diodorus 16.15.1–2; Strabo 6.1.4. L. Sergius Catilina: Sallust, *Conspiracy of Catiline* 42.1–2; 46.3; Cicero, *Pro Sestio* 12; cf. Bradley (1978). Cn. Pompeius: Caesar, *Civil Wars* 1.24. *Ergastula*: Caesar, *Civil Wars* 3.21–22. Quotation: Stockton (1971), 19; on the *Pro Tullio* and the legal procedure that led to the outbreak of violence, see Frier (1985), 79–80. A.D. 24: Tacitus, *Annals* 4.27; *ILS* 961. A.D. 54: Tacitus, *Annals* 12.65. See also Cicero, *Pro Cluentio* 161; Asconius 87 Clark.

16. "Chronic brigandage": Wiseman (1964), 35. Lawlessness: see also Strabo 6.2.6, making clear that brigandage still existed in Sicily in Strabo's age; and for the late third century B.C., see, confirming Diodorus (above, n.14), Livy 26.40.15–18; Polybius 9.27.11 (cf. Walbank [1967a], 161–62. "Class apart": Frayn (1984), 69, on sheep farmers. Varro: *Res Rusticae* 2.10.1; 2.10.3; 1.16.1–2; 2.1.6; 2.2.9; cf. Toynbee (1965) II, 319 n.1. Transhumance: see Frayn (1984), 45–65. Axes, sickles, javelins: Livy 1.40.5; 1.40.7; 9.36.6. Saepinum: *CIL* 9.2438; see Corbier (1983), 126–27; Frayn (1984), 176–79. The havoc slave bandits caused might well have been of the kind suffered by Thomas Woodyatt in Antigua in 1737. Woodyatt reported that

> as he was coming from St. Johns about Ten O'Clock at Night, about Three or four Hundred yards to the Eastward of Judge Watkins's Windmill formerly Monteyro's he met four Negroe Men all Armed with Cutlasses, One of them having a Pistol beside; that they came up . . . and told him, that they were Lynch's Negroes, that they must have that Something he had got there; that they held up their Cutlasses . . . and Swore they would kill him Dead if he did not Deliver what he had got, and all the money he had[.] That . . . being unarm'd, but on the Horseback, they took from him Six yards of Ozenbriggs, and a New Pair of Shoes which he had bot in Town, and one of them Thrust his hand into [his] Pocket with such Violence that he broke out the Bottom of the Pocket and Drove the Keys down to the Knees of his Britches and took one Pistole and an half . . . the same Person Saying at the same time, let us kill him . . . [Woodyatt] told them he belonged to Col. Morris, they said God Damn Col. Morris we will have his hearts blood out by and by. One of them Clapp'd the Pistol to [Woodyatt's] breast, while another took

the Mony out of his Pocket, and another Cut the Knee of his Britches with his Cutlass, they Pulld [him] three times Off his Horse, as Oft as he got up, between the Place they first met him and Pearn's Gut, Over Which they followed him when he Rid as fast as he Could up to Doc. Dunbar's; they tore [his] Shirt all to Pieces, and Threatned Several times they would have Col. Morris's heart blood; and . . . if he had not been on Horseback, . . . they wou'd have Murder'd him. (See Gaspar [1985], 192–93.)

17. Eunus: see references in n.6 above. Natural slaves: Cicero, *De Provinciis Consularibus* 10; Livy 35.49.8; 36.17.5; cf. Plautus, *Trinummus* 542; 546, Syrians renowned for their *patientia*. *Ergastula*: Ammianus Marcellinus 14.11.33, *ergastularius servus*: this may simply be an offhand way of referring to Eunus. Diodorus: 34/35.2.5–7 (Wiedemann).

18. Florus: 2.7.5. Lucian: *Alexander the False Prophet*. Asclepius: see Kee (1983), 78–104. Asclepiades: Pliny, *Natural History* 26.14–15. Apollonius: Philostratus, *Life of Apollonius* 4.45; see Smith (1978), 84–87. MacMullen (1967), 95–127, shows how all-pervasive belief was in the Mediterranean world of the Roman Imperial period; the situation is not likely to have been vastly different in earlier times, and the Roman tradition of antimagic legislation, which began with the Twelve Tables, is to be noted.

19. Lucian: *Syrian Goddess* 50–51 (Attridge and Oden). Apuleius: *Metamorphoses* 8.27–28. Hymn: Isidorus 1 (Vanderlip). It can be assumed that Eunus's devotion to the Syrian Goddess was shared by other slaves in Sicily from the East. For undated epigraphical evidence of the cult at Syracuse, see Sfameni Gasparro (1973), 162–64, 295. On the Syrian Goddess, cf. Bömer (1961), 84–85. Despite Brisson (1959), 61–64, there is no evidence that Stoicism had any impact on the first slave war.

20. For modern accounts of the first slave war in general, see Brisson (1959), 55–77, 104–10; Green (1961); Toynbee (1965) II, 322–28; Finley (1979), 139–44; Manganaro (1980), 435–40. Diodorus: 34/35.2.4; 10; 24b (on the textual difficulties, see Forrest and Stinton [1962], 89; but the distinction between general discussion of revolt among the slaves of Sicily and the specific action of those belonging to Damophilus can still be maintained); see also Livy, *Periocha* 56; Florus 2.7.6.

21. Diodorus 34/35.2.11–14; 24b; 39; cf. 40. At the time of the attack on Enna, Damophilus and Megallis were in an orchard, according to Diodorus 34/35.2.13, which should probably mean one of their extra-urban estates, for which, see Diodorus 34/35.2.35. 214 B.C.: Livy 24.39.1–7. Toussaint: Geggus (1982), 41.

22. Diodorus 34/35.2.14–16; 41–42. Eunus's regal status is also attested by the coins he minted during the war; see below, chapter 6. There is no evidence that Hermeias and Zeuxis were members of Eunus's council, despite Green (1961), 14.

23. Diodorus: 34/35.2.16. On the chronology of the war, see Appendix 2.

24. Diodorus 34/35.2.17; 43; Livy, *Periocha* 56; Orosius 5.6.4. For Cilicia as a source of slaves, Strabo 14.5.2. Green (1961), 16, maintains that Eunus and Cleon were in contact before the revolt at Enna and that Cleon attacked Agrigentum according to a previously arranged plan. There is no evidence for this view.

25. Rhetorical claims: Diodorus 34/35.2.25 (cf. Florus 2.7.2: Sicily suffered more from the slave war than from the war against Carthage). Bases: Diodorus 34/35.2.20 (Tauromenium); Strabo 6.2.6 (Enna, Catina, Tauromenium, and other unspecified places); Florus 2.7.8 (Tauromenium); Orosius 5.9.6 (Morgantina = Mamertium); 5.9.7 (Enna and Tauromenium). Agrigentum: for its defenses, see Polybius 9.27.1–9. Messana: Orosius 5.6.4. Syracuse: Diodorus 34/35.9 (Wiede-

mann); 5.3.5–6 (Loeb). Atargatis: see Glueck (1965), 391–92. From an apparent change in their status between *circa* 175 B.C. and 70 B.C., Manganaro (1964), 423–25 (cf. Manganaro [1967], 216–19) has inferred that C. Rupilius, cos. 132 B.C., punished certain cities not named in the literary sources for their support of Eunus. But doubts must persist, and not simply because of the "nationalistic" character he ascribes to the rebellion: the theory will not explain why Tauromenium was not reduced in status, and there is of course no direct evidence for the actions putatively claimed for Rupilius. C. Fulvius Flaccus: see *MRR* I, 490. Florus: 2.7.7; for the identities of the praetors, see *MRR* I, 482–83, 484, 485, 486; III, 159. Witticism: Frontinus, *Stratagems* 3.5.3. Diodorus: 34/35.2.18.

26. Supply of grain: Valerius Maximus 3.7.3 indicates a rise in the price of grain at Rome apparently as early as 138 B.C.; it does not necessarily follow that Rome was then already experiencing shortages attributable to the slave war, as maintained by Verbrugghe (1973), 28 (cf. also Forrest and Stinton [1962], 91); but for the possibility that interrupted supplies influenced the proposal of C. Gracchus in 123–122 B.C. to sell grain to Roman citizens at a subsidized price, see Garnsey and Rathbone (1985). L. Calpurnius Piso Frugi: *MRR* I, 492. Reputation: Valerius Maximus 4.3.10. C. Titius: Valerius Maximus 2.7.9; Frontinus, *Stratagems* 4.1.26. Piso's son: Valerius Maximus 4.3.10. Morgantina: Orosius 5.9.6. Slingshots: *ILLRP* 1088.

27. P. Rupilius: *MRR* I, 497–98; Orosius 5.9.7; Rupilius may have known Sicily particularly well: see above n.7. Cannibalism: Diodorus 34/35.2.20. Comanus: Diodorus 34/35.2.20; Valerius Maximus 9.12 ext. 1. Betrayal and captives: Diodorus 34/35.2.21. Q. Fabius: Valerius Maximus 2.7.3; in the view of Green (1961), 16, this text refers to the original fall of Tauromenium to the rebels, which may be correct; but it is difficult to believe that Fabius had been kept in Sicily for three years (on Green's chronology), and it is better to place the loss of the citadel with Rupilius's siege in 132 B.C., when Fabius was perhaps quaestor (*MRR* I, 498).

28. Florus: 2.7.8; M. Perperna: *MRR* I, 498. Cleon: Diodorus 34/35.2.21. Simultaneous fronts: *MRR* I, 499 n.2; III, 155; cf. Green (1961), 18. Enna: Diodorus 34/35.2.21. Ti. Gracchus: Cicero, *Verrines* 2.4.108; see Le Bonniec (1958), 283–89, 367–69, referring also to Valerius Maximus 1.1.1; Lactantius, *Divine Institutes* 2.4.29–30. There is no evidential basis to support the suggestion that the embassy of priests was "designed to counteract Eunus' use of the cult in the Sicilian struggle against Rome" (Verbrugghe [1974], 55), nor any reason to suppose Cicero inaccurate in his explanation of the mission; White (1964), 278, is perhaps overconfident here (cf. similarly Manganaro [1967], 216).

29. Diodorus 34/35.2.22–23; Plutarch, *Sulla* 36.6. Scabies: Keaveney and Madden (1982).

30. Motivation: Diodorus 34/35.2.4; 10; 37; 40 (cf. Florus 2.7.4, *ad libertatem et arma*). Achaeus: Diodorus 34/35.2.42.

31. Morgantina: see *PECS*, s.v. "Morgantina"; Erim (1958); Coarelli and Torelli (1984), 188–201. 211 B.C.: Livy 26.21.12–14; 17. 214 B.C.: Livy 24.36.10; cf. 24.38.3. Tauromenium: see *PECS*, s.v. "Tauromenium"; Manni (1981), 234–35; Coarelli and Torelli (1984), 354–64. 36 B.C.: Appian, *Civil Wars* 5.109; 116. Supplies: Cicero, *Verrines* 2.3.47; 2.3.56; 2.3.100 (cf. 2.3.192; Livy 27.8.19; Strabo 6.2.7); Cato, *De Agricultura* 6.4 (cf. Pliny, *Natural History* 14.46); Strabo 5.4.8 (cf. 6.2.3); Pliny, *Natural History* 14.25; 14.35. Leontini: Cicero, *Verrines* 2.3.47; 2.3.109 (see also 2.3.148); *Pro Scauro* 25; cf. Rickman (1980), 104.

32. Quotation: Finley (1979), 133. Servile proportion: Hopkins (1978), 101.

33. L. Hypsaeus: Diodorus 34/35.2.18 (for the force of two hundred soldiers kept permanently at the temple of Venus at Eryx, see Diodorus 4.83.7; *ILLRP* 446; *IG* 14.282; 335; see Appian, *Sicelica* 5 for the general absence of troops at

Tauromenium). Difficulties of recruitment: Astin (1967), 167–68. Military dispositions: Brunt (1971), 426–29, 432–33. Roman legion: see Brunt (1971), 671–76. Allied complement: see Brunt (1971), 677–86.

IV. The Second Slave War in Sicily

1. On Halicyae in general, see Manni (1981), 177–78. First war against Carthage: Diodorus 23.5. Status: Cicero, Verrines 2.3.13; cf. 2.3.91, with Scramuzza (1937), 231; Badian (1958), 37 (cf. also Capozza [1956–1957], 81–82); and, in contrast, Sherwin-White (1973), 176 n.5; Gruen (1984), 145 n.78 (cf. also Finley [1979], 124). Eumenides: Cicero, Verrines 2.5.15. To place the first episode of revolt at Halicyae is to follow the widely accepted emendation at Diodorus 36.3.4 of ᾿Αγκυλίων to ᾿Αλικυαίων.

2. Diodorus 36.3.4–6. Varius: Diodorus 36.3.4 gives the name as ᾿Οάριος, which is commonly understood to be a Greek transliteration of the Latin form; cf. Manganaro (1980), 440. P. Licinius Nerva: MRR I, 559. Local militias: see Brunt (1971), 104; Scramuzza (1937), 315–16.

3. Diodorus 36.3.1–3; cf. Cassius Dio 27.93.1–3. On the site of the shrine of the Palici, see PECS, s.v. "Paliké"; Manni (1981), 213. On the importance of manumission prospects, see Schwartz (1985), 157.

4. Quotations on Palici: Croon (1952), 126. It is clear that the cult was ancient, but its "national" character is not proven by the actions of the rebel slaves as Croon (1952), 118, 127, maintains. Asylum, not the cult's ancient or indigenous features, was the key factor here. Diodorus Siculus: 11:89.6–8 (Loeb); cf. 11.89.1–5; his knowledge probably depends on autopsy; see Drews (1962), 392 n.30; cf. Macrobius, Saturnalia 5.19.15–31; Strabo 6.2.9.

5. P. Rupilius: MRR I, 498; Marshall (1972), 672, suggests an ovation. Florus: 2.7.8. For the triumphal celebrations, see Degrassi (1954), 105–107, and MRR I, 504, 509, 514, 518, 521, 524, 529, 531, 541, 544, 552, 554, 558. For the Gallic campaigns of the late 120s, see Ebel (1976), 64–74; and for the campaigns in Illyria, see Wilkes (1969), 32–34. For the assumption of continuing mass enslavements, cf. Harris (1979), 272. Scipio Aemilianus: Appian, Iberica 98. C. Marius: Sallust, Jugurthine War 91.6. C. Sextius Calvinus: Diodorus 34/35.23. Himerus: Diodorus 34/35.21; cf. Justinus 42.1.3, and see Debevoise (1938), 38. Dealers and pirates: for the view that the slave trade from East to West maintained slave numbers in Sicily after the first war, see Coarelli (1981), 11.

6. On piracy in general, see Ormerod (1924), 190–247; Davies (1984), 285–90; and on Cilicia in particular, see Sherwin-White (1983), 97–101. Strabo: 14.5.2; cf. 14.3.2 for the use of Side in Pamphylia by Cilician pirates for the sale of slaves. For the possibility that the so-called Agora of the Italians at Delos was a slave market, built as a result of the first slave war, see Coarelli (1982); note, however, the spirited denial of Bruneau (1985). Clear evidence: see Ormerod (1924), 205; Garlan (1987), 9. For the role of the Hellenistic naval powers in restraining piracy in the second century, see Sherwin-White (1976), 3–4; and on the increase in its scale see Magie (1950), 278–84. Scipio Aemilianus: Strabo 14.5.2; see Astin (1967), 127, 138–39; Gruen (1984), 243, 280, 714–15; on the date of the tour, see most recently Mattingly (1986). 133 B.C.: see Sherwin-White (1976), 3–4. M. Antonius: MRR I, 568. For the so-called "piracy law," which was probably passed late in 101 B.C., see Hassall, Crawford, and Reynolds (1974); Sherwin-White (1976); Sherk (1984), no. 55.

7. Quotation: Sherwin-White (1983), 98. Own defenses: see Scramuzza (1937), 315–16. Athenion: Diodorus 36.5.1; Florus 2.7.9.

8. On the economic structure of Sicily, see Mazza (1981), 39–47, against any notion that Rupilius was responsible for a massive lurch in farming practices; cf. Manganaro (1980), 439, and contrast Scramuzza (1937), 246–48; Toynbee (1965) II, 327. *Lex Rupilia*: see *RE* XII, 2 col. 2413; cf. Manganaro (1980), 439–40. Heraclea: Cicero, *Verrines* 2.2.125; there is no evidence that the colonization was due to the city having been destroyed in the first war, as stated by P. Orlandini, *PECS*, s.v. "Herakleia Minoa," and Guido (1970), 104; but its population might have suffered from the ravages of Cleon; cf. Coarelli and Torelli (1984), 108.

9. C. Titinius Gadaeus: Diodorus 36.3.5–6; cf. *RE* VI A, 2 col. 1551. Is the *cognomen* to be associated with *Gaditanus*, indicating a Spanish origin? Gorgus of Morgantina: Diodorus 34/35.11. On brigandage cf. also Cassius Dio 27.93.3.

10. Minturnae: Orosius 5.9.4. Sinuessa: Orosius 5.9.4. Rome: Diodorus 34/35.2.19. Cn. Servilius Caepio and Q. Metellus: Orosius 5.9.4; see *RE* II, A 2 col. 1781; *MRR* I, 471, 477; Toynbee (1965) II, 317 n.2. Attica: Diodorus 34/35.2.19; Orosius 5.9.5. Delos: Diodorus 34/35.2.19; Orosius 5.9.5. Other places: Diodorus 34/35.2.19; Obsequens 27 (134 B.C.) reports a conspiracy in Italy, apparently before the first slave war began, that was crushed; Obsequens 27b (132 B.C.) reports the deaths of many thousands of slaves who had conspired in Italy, perhaps referring to events at Minturnae and Sinuessa. Nuceria: Diodorus 36.2.1; 2a. Capua: Diodorus 36.2.1; 2a. Attica: Athenaeus 6.272e–f, but this may be a reduplication of the earlier revolt (see Toynbee [1965] II, 317 n.2). T. Minucius: Diodorus 36.2.2–6; 2a. L. Licinius Lucullus: *MRR* I, 559.

11. Diodorus: 36.2.1; 34/35.2.19. Orosius: 5.9.5. On the lack of coordination, see Guarino (1979), 51–52. On working conditions in the Attic mines, see Burford (1972), 74–75. Delos: Strabo 14.5.2. Capua: see below, chapter 5.

12. Diodorus 36.4.1–4. Diodorus has Licinius cross a river Alba before reaching Mount Caprianus (36.4.2), the name of which may be connected with that of the town of Allava on the south coast, between Agrigentum and Lilybaeum; see *RE* I, 2 col. 1584; Manni (1981), 141. Mount Caprianus: see Manni (1981), 83. P. Clonius: Fraschetti (1981), 54, 67, plausibly regards him as an *arator* domiciled in southwest Sicily (cf. Nicolet [1974], 839–40 on the obscurity of the name); Manganaro (1972), 451–52, regards him as an example of an increase in Italian emigration to Sicily encouraged by the *lex Rupilia* (cf. Manganaro [1980], 440); but observe Nicolet (1974), 840: "on pourrait songer à un grec romanisé." Drinking cup: the object was found in 1942 in the river Meuse near Stevensweert in Holland; it contains on the underside of its base the inscription, *M. Titini*. Roes and Vollgraf (1952), 65–67 (cf. *AE* 1953. 156; *MRR* III, 206) proposed that the name is that of the man defeated by the slave rebels and that the cup was stolen from a temple of Zeus in Sicily where it had been dedicated. According to critics examining the cup's stylistic history and epigraphical features, however, the true date of the cup may be too late for the attribution to stand firm; see Bivar (1964), with bibliography. Doubt must remain. For modern accounts of the second slave war in general, see Brisson (1959), 153–76; Toynbee (1965) II, 327–31; Finley (1979), 144–46; Manganaro (1980), 440–41.

13. Diodorus 36.4.4–5.

14. Diodorus 36.4.5–8. Slingshots: *IG* 14.2407.

15. Later writers: see, for example, Cicero, *Verrines* 2.3.66; 125; Florus 2.7.9–12; Appian, *Mithridatica* 59.

16. Florus: 2.7.9. Diodorus: 36.5.1 (οἰκονόμος = *vilicus*). Cato: *De Agricultura* 5.1–5. Varro: *Res Rusticae* 2.1.23; 2.2.20 (cf. 2.10.5, responsibility expected of the *magister pecoris*; 1.2.14, the *magister pecoris* equated with the *vilicus* in arable farming). On slave managers as symbols of upward social mobility, see Schwartz

(1985), 156; contrast Maróti (1976), 124. Italian villas: see Rossiter (1978), 43; Cotton and Métraux (1985), 54; above, chapter 2.

17. Diodorus 36.5.2–4; Florus 2.7.10. For Lilybaeum and its impregnability in former times, see *PECS*, s.v. "Lilybaion"; Guido (1977), 84; cf. Manni (1981), 195–96.

18. Diodorus 36.7.1–4. Palici: Manganaro (1980), 441, believes that Salvius made contact with the slaves who had taken refuge at the shrine after their denial of manumission at Syracuse. Slingshots: see above n.14. Triocala: the site has not been safely identified, though the general location is clear enough; see *RE* VII, A 1 cols. 166–68; Finley (1979), 145; Manni (1981), 238–39.

19. Diodorus: 36.6; 36.11.1–3.

20. Diodorus 36.8.1–5. L. Licinius Lucullus: *MRR* I, 564. For the location of Scirthaea, see Manni (1981), 222. On Lucullus' victory, observe the comment of Gruen (1968), 176: "Lucullus had inherited the character of his father, the consul of 151, who had shown no respect for treaty or human life in the Spanish wars of that era."

21. Florus: 2.7.11. Diodorus: 36.9.2. C. Servilius: Diodorus 36.9.1; *MRR* I, 568; his quaestor was probably a certain L. Philo (cf. *MRR* I, 569; III, 156, perhaps a Veturius), whose role in the war is unknown. The sequel: Lucullus was convicted at Rome of *peculatus*, probably in 102 B.C.; for his trial and its political context, see Gruen (1968), 176–78: his prosecutor was a Servilius, but probably not his successor in Sicily so much as a relative of that man; however, C. Servilius was himself also convicted after his return from Sicily in 101 B.C., probably on a charge of *repetundae*.

22. Florus: 2.7.11. Diodorus: 36.9.1. Cassius Dio: 27.93.4; cf. Manganaro (1980), 441. On Macella and its proximity to Messana, see Manni (1981), 198–99. Slingshots: see above, n.14. For Salvius's death, see Diodorus 36.9.1.

23. M'. Aquillius: Diodorus 36.10.1 (cf. Livy, *Periocha* 69; Obsequens 45; Cicero, *Verrines* 2.3.125; 2.5.5); *MRR* I, 571, 577. For the date of his return to Rome, see *MRR* II, 2–3, 4 n.10; Badian (1958), 205 n.2; cf. Brunt (1971), 104. For the lending of grain, see Cicero, *De Lege Agraria* 2.83. Plutarch: *Quaestiones Convivales* 2.3.3; cf. Manganaro (1980), 441.

24. Diodorus 36.10.1–3; Florus 2.7.11 (according to Florus 2.7.12, Athenion was captured alive and torn to pieces by a crowd of his captors; this conflicts with the version of Diodorus [36.10.1] and is to be rejected). Peculation: For Aquillius's trial and its political context, see Gruen (1968), 194–95. At the trial Aquillius's defense counsel, M. Antonius, displayed Aquillius's battle scars as part of the strategy to secure an acquittal (he was successful, despite Aquillius's obvious guilt; cf. Cicero, *Pro Flacco* 98): note Cicero, *Verrines* 2.5.3 (Loeb): "[Antonius] tore open [Aquillius's] shirt and exposed his breast, that his countrymen might see the scars that he bore on the front of his body; and dwelling at the same time on the wound he had received in his head from the enemy's leader [i.e., Athenion], reduced those with whom the decision lay to a state of trembling agitation." Badian (1964), 45–46, dates the trial to about 95 B.C., Gruen to about 97 B.C. The trials of Aquillius, Servilius, and Lucullus do not shed a great deal of light on the slave war: military failure could obviously be exploited by political opponents, but even success was no guarantee against attack in the courts if grounds for charges of provincial misgovernment seemed available. Rebels' numbers: according to Athenaeus 6.272f, more than a million slaves died in the course of the second slave war; this is a clear exaggeration (cf. Westermann [1943], 457).

25. Discussions of revolt: Diodorus 36.3.3, at the shrine of the Palici; cf. the general comment on servile discontent at Diodorus 36.3.4.

26. For Roman legionary dispositions in the period of the second slave war,

see Brunt (1971), 430–33; and for the assumption of one legion in Sicily under Lucullus and Servilius and two legions under Aquillius, see Brunt (1971), 104.

V. The Slave War of Spartacus

1. On Capua in the second Carthaginian war and following, see Salmon (1982), 79–80, 82, 175; Frederiksen (1984), 238–63; cf. Sherwin-White (1973), 43–46. Polybius: 3.91.6 (Penguin). Prosperity: note Livy 4.37.1–2, 7.30.6, 7.30.16, 7.31.1, 7.38.5–7, 22.14.1, 23.2.1, 23.18.10–16 (Hannibal's army corrupted by the easy living of Capua), 26.16.7. On the economic structure of Capua in the late Republic and early Empire, see Frederiksen (1984), 285–318.

2. On the servile population of Capua, see Frederiksen (1984), 281–84 (magistri lists; cf. also Flambard [1983]), 286, 301–303. On local slaves, note Livy 26.4.1.

3. Small-scale episodes: see above, chapter 2.

4. Sociological perspective: see Hopkins (1983), 1–30. Twenty-five exhibitions: Ville (1981), 57–72. Millar (1984), 10, exaggerates the frequency of early gladiatorial displays. On schools in the late Republic and permanent institutions, see Ville (1981), 281–83, 296; Sabbatini Tumolesi (1980), 147–48: 105 B.C. may be the earliest date for an attested ludus at Capua. Friedländer (1908–1913) II, 53, believed that there was a gladiatorial school at Rome as early as 63 B.C. on the basis of Cicero, Catilinarians 2.9, but the text is not decisive. Observe, however, that according to Livy 41.20.13 (175 B.C.), Antiochus Epiphanes acquired gladiators from Rome. On the origins of gladiatorial games, see Ville (1981), 1–8; cf. Hopkins (1983), 3–4. For their funerary associations in the late Republic, see Veyne (1976), 417–19. 63 B.C.: Sallust, Conspiracy of Catiline 30.7. C. Marcellus: Cicero, Pro Sestio 9. 49 B.C.: Cicero, Letters to Atticus 138.2 (Shackleton Bailey); cf. 152.1; Caesar, Civil Wars 1.14. For Campania's gladiatorial associations in general, see Strabo 5.4.13; Livy 9.40.17.

5. Cn. Lentulus Batiatus: Plutarch, Crassus 8.1; Florus 2.8.3; Orosius 5.24.1. Low esteem: Sabbatini Tumolesi (1980), 128–29; Ville (1981), 343, 464. Martial: 11.66; cf. Juvenal 3.158; Seneca, Controversiae 10.4.11, 10.4.18. Senatorial decree: text given by Levick (1983), 98: ex histrione aut gladiatore aut lanista aut lenone (line 16); cf. Talbert (1984), 439. Table of Heraclea: ILS 6085 (line 123), on which see Brunt (1971), 519–23; Yavetz (1983), 117–22. For epigraphical attestations of individual lanistae, see Sabbatini Tumolesi (1980), 128–29; Ville (1981), 245, 272–76.

6. Spartacus: Plutarch, Crassus 8.2–3; Appian, Civil Wars 1.116; Florus 2.8.8; Orosius 5.24.1. His followers: Plutarch, Crassus 8.1 (cf. 9.5): Gauls and Thracians; 9.6: Germans; Livy, Periocha 97: Gauls and Germans; Orosius 5.24.1: Gauls (Crixus and Oenomaus); Sallust, Histories 3.96: Gauls and Germans. The servile status of Spartacus seems to be confirmed by Digest 41.2.3.10 (see Tomulescu [1979], 102–105), but the relevant words ut fecit Spartacus may be a gloss (see Guarino [1980]). The question of Spartacus' geographical origin is complicated by Plutarch's phrase, θρᾷξ τοῦ νομαδικοῦ γένους, which should perhaps be amended to θρᾷξ τοῦ Μαιδικοῦ γένους; see Ziegler (1955), arguing that Spartacus was a prisoner from the Maedi of the central Strymon valley, acquired in Rome's campaigns of either 86 B.C. or 76 B.C. For a clear statement of the possible origins of Spartacus and his followers, see Deman and Raepsaet-Charlier (1981–1982), 83–90: they conclude that the Thracians, Gauls, and Germans were all from the Balkans,

recently brought to Italy as prisoners of war. However, this view underestimates the role of trade in providing slaves to Italy from Gaul itself, while the evidence of Caesar, *Gallic Wars* 1.40.5, seems decisive in its implication that some of Spartacus's followers were originally from Gaul. On the importance of Rome's wars against the savage tribes of Thrace as a source of slaves, see Walbank (1981). Cicero's generic description: *Tusculan Disputations* 2.41. Cicero: *Pro Sestio* 134. Livy: 28.21.2 (206 B.C., a gladiatorial display at New Carthage). Sepulchral inscriptions: *ILS* 5085, 5088 (cf. 5089, 4117), 5104, 5096, 5098, 5095; see Ville (1981), 264–67. Guarino (1979), 68, believes that some of the gladiators accompanying Spartacus were not slaves.

7. William Smith: quoted in Dillard (1972), 73–74. For the expectation of a difference in accent between rural and urban residents, note Livy 10.4.9–10; cf. Frayn (1984), 68–69, Explanation: Ste. Croix (1981), 146; (1984), 98. Pidgin and creole languages: Dillard (1972); and see also Gaspar (1985), 37, 131; Klein (1986), 163.

8. Beryllus: *ILS* 5095; Paeragrinus: *ILS* 5100; Urbicus: *ILS* 5115; see Ville (1981), 329–32. Spartacus's wife: Plutarch, *Crassus* 8.3. For the effects of sale on slave families, see Bradley (1984), 52–63. 56 B.C.: Cicero, *Letters to Atticus* 78.2 (Shackleton Bailey; cf. 79.2). For descriptions of the gladiatorial barracks, of early Imperial date, at Pompeii, see Mau (1907), 157–64; cf. Friedländer (1908–1913) II, 55; Ville (1981), 298–99: Ville estimates that one hundred and forty gladiators could be housed here; according to Plutarch, *Crassus* 8.2, some two hundred gladiators at Capua were planning their escape before the Spartacan revolt actually began. Slave quarters: see Carrington (1931), 122. Woman: Mau (1907), 163; Ville (1981), 303; Hopkins (1983), 23, referring to Juvenal 6.103–112. Newborn infant: Mau (1907), 164; Ville (1981), 303. On rewards for gladiators under the Empire, see Ville (1981), 426; cf. Levick (1983), 108, and note Livy 44.31.15 (168 B.C.): ten talents, hardly a gladiator's fee. Cell units: Ville (1981), 299. Kitchen: Mau (1907), 161; Ville (1981), 298.

9. Quotation on accumulation: S. W. Mintz in Gaspar (1985), 146. Urban indigent: see Scobie (1986), 427. Ostia and Rome: see Frier (1977); quotation: Brunt (1974), 86. Outlays of cash: Pliny, *Natural History* 33.53; Cicero, *Letters to Quintus* 9.3 (Shackleton Bailey). A.D. 6: Suetonius, *Augustus* 42; Cassius Dio 55.26.1; cf. Livy 4.12.10: slaves' daily rations reduced in the emergency of a famine in the middle of the fifth century. Literary references: Propertius 4.8.25 implies that gladiators' food was plentiful but plain, and Juvenal 11.20 that the mess rations were not usually very good; see also Tacitus, *Histories* 2.88. Elder Pliny: *Natural History* 18.72. Nutritional value of barley: see Rickman (1980), 5. Sallust: *Histories* 1.55.11. Strabo: 5.1.7. On the feeding of gladiators in general, see Ville (1981), 301–303.

10. Prison: Mau (1907), 163; Ville (1981), 298. 57 B.C.: Cassius Dio 39.7.1–3. 44 B.C.: Nicolaus of Damascus, *Life of Augustus* 25, 26a; Cassius Dio 44.16.2; cf. Appian, *Civil Wars* 2.118; 120. Personal security forces: see Lintott (1968), 83–85. 65 B.C.: Suetonius, *Caesar* 10.2. 22 B.C.: Cassius Dio 54.2.4; for later restrictions, see also Tacitus, *Annals* 13.49; Richmond and Stevens (1942), 68; Talbert (1984), 385, 419. Observe the conclusion of Scobie (1986), 433: "High density living in insanitary urban dwellings and surroundings can have only one major consequence in a preindustrial society which lacks effective and cheap medical care: a short, often violent, life."

11. 49 B.C.: Caesar, *Civil Wars* 1.14. For gladiators in the civil wars of A.D. 69–70, see Tacitus, *Histories* 2.11, 2.23, 2.34, 2.36, 2.88, 3.76. Seneca: *Moral Epistles* 70.20–21, 23. Symmachus: *Epistles* 2.46.2. Cf. Bradley (1986b).

12. A.D. 21: Tacitus, *Annals* 3.43. A.D. 64: Tacitus, *Annals* 15.46. Cicero's

rationalization: *Tusculan Disputations* 2.41 (note especially *crudele gladiatorum spectaculum et inhumanum non nullis videri solet*; on the essential cruelty of gladiatorial games, see also Seneca, *Moral Epistles* 7.3–5 [cf. Griffin (1976), 178]; Tertullian, *Spectacles* 12).

13. Ti. Gracchus: Appian, *Civil Wars* 1.9. 85 B.C.: Appian, *Mithridatica* 59. 90 B.C.: Appian, *Civil Wars* 1.42. 87 B.C.: Appian, *Civil Wars* 1.74. On slaves' participation in the political violence of the late Republic in general, see Kühne (1962); Rouland (1977); Welwei (1981).

14. On the Roman tradition of self-help, see Lintott (1968), 22–24, 34, 66, 175–76, 204. 138 B.C.: Cicero, *Brutus* 85. 83 B.C.: Cicero, *Pro Quinctio* 28, 83. 76 B.C.: Cicero, *Pro Tullio* 7–12; cf. Lintott (1968), 28–29, 129; Frier (1985), 52. Cicero quotation: *Pro Tullio* 8 (Lintott). On the *lex Lutatia*, establishing a permanent court (and the *lex Plautia* which replaced it, probably in 70 B.C.), see Lintott (1968), 110–11, 123; Gruen (1974), 224–27. For the dates of the *Pro Tullio* and *Pro Caecina*, see Frier (1985) 45–46, 52 n.39.

15. Q. Servilius Caepio: Appian *Civil Wars* 1.44. M. Aemilius Scaurus: Pliny, *Natural History* 7.128; cf. Suetonius, *Grammarians* 3. Q. Sertorius: Plutarch, *Sertorius* 3.5; Orosius 5.23.7. C. Flavius Fimbria: Diodorus Siculus 38/39.8.1. Sulla: Appian, *Mithridatica* 38; 61. Zenobius: Appian, *Mithridatica* 47.

16. Cicero: *Pro Roscio Amerino* 154 (Loeb), for the date of which, 74 B.C., see Frier (1985), 126 n.95. On the sources for the Spartacan war, see Appendix 1.

17. Plutarch: *Crassus* 8.2 (Wiedemann); cf. above n.6. Florus: 2.8.1. Diodorus Siculus: 38/39.21. Anecdote: Plutarch, *Crassus* 8.3 (Wiedemann); cf. Baldwin (1966–1967), 290.

18. Plutarch, *Crassus* 8.1–2; Florus 2.8.3–4; Appian, *Civil Wars* 1.116; Livy, *Periocha* 95; Velleius Paterculus 2.30.5; Eutropius 6.7.2; Orosius 5.24.1. For modern accounts of the Spartacan war, see particularly Brisson (1959), 200–42; Guarino (1979). Summer of 73 B.C.: see Appendix 3. The number of slaves who broke out of Capua is variously reported: Cicero, *Letters to Atticus* 116.8 (Shackleton Bailey): less than fifty (taken at face value); Sallust, *Histories* 3.90: seventy-four; Livy, *Periocha* 95: seventy-four; Velleius Paterculus 2.30.5: sixty-four; Plutarch, *Crassus* 8.2: seventy-eight; Florus 2.8.3: thirty plus; Appian, *Civil Wars* 1.116: about seventy; Eutropius 6.7.2: seventy-four; Augustine, *City of God* 3.26: less than seventy; Orosius 5.24.1: seventy-four. The important point is the sources' agreement that the beginnings of the rebellion involved only a relatively small number of individuals. According to Plutarch (*Crassus* 8.2), the outbreak was preceded by a plan to escape made by two hundred gladiators (perhaps the full complement of Batiatus's school; cf. above, n.8); when the plan was betrayed, seventy-eight gladiators left at once. But no other source refers to prior planning. Plutarch does not introduce Spartacus until the occupation of Mount Vesuvius, where the slaves chose three leaders, Spartacus being one of them, and indeed the most important (πρῶτος; cf. Sallust, *Histories* 3.90, *princeps gladiatorum*); the other two were Crixus and Oenomaus, Gauls according to Orosius 5.24.1. Florus (2.8.3) has Crixus and Oenomaus escaping with Spartacus from the school; whereas Appian (*Civil Wars* 1.116), while agreeing that they were gladiators, shows them emerging as Spartacus's subordinates once pillaging from Mount Vesuvius was in progress. However, Livy, *Periocha* 95, suggests that Crixus and Spartacus were co-leaders (Oenomaus is not mentioned here), while Orosius (5.24.1) suggests that all three were more or less equal leaders when Vesuvius was occupied.

19. Florus: 2.8.3. Claudius Glaber: the sources are confused over his name and position. Plutarch (*Crassus* 9.1) simply calls him Clodius. Frontinus (*Stratagems* 1.5.21) and Orosius (5.24.1) refer to the praetor Clodius, while Florus (2.8.4) speaks

of Clodius Glaber. Appian (*Civil Wars* 1.116) has Varinius Glaber, and Livy, *Periocha* 95, refers to the *legatus* Claudius Pulcher. Despite the confusion, it is certain that the sources here are referring to the same individual, and the confusion indeed can be dispelled to some extent: the Livian *Periocha* errs in calling him Pulcher and in using the term *legatus*, and Appian has combined his name with that of his successor; Claudius Glaber can then safely be admitted as praetor in 73 B.C.: *MRR* II, 109, 115 n.1; III, 54. According to Plutarch (*Crassus* 9.1), the gladiators first repelled troops sent against them from Capua, but no other source has this detail; but for a local garrison at Capua, see Livy 23.46.11. Army of three thousand: Plutarch, *Crassus* 9.1; cf. Brunt (1971), 450.

20. Plutarch, *Crassus* 9.2–3; Florus 2.8.4; Frontinus, *Stratagems* 1.5.21; Orosius 5.24.1. In effecting the vine-ladder descent, Spartacus may have used only a portion of the forces available to him, who were joined by other rebels once the attack on the Roman position began.

21. Varro, *Res Rusticae* 2.10.1–6 (Wiedemann; for the date of the work, see White [1970], 22); cf. Deman and Raepsaet-Charlier (1981–1982), 91–94, concluding, "Le texte de Varron . . . procure une documentation précieuse sur ce que Spartacus pouvait trouver dans les régions rurales adonnées à l'élevage: des esclaves, hommes et femmes, armés et aguerris, parmi eux, certains sachant lire et écrire, et capables de mettre sur pied une organisation permettant à des hommes et à des bêtes de survivre, la plupart aussi de même origine ethnico-géographique que les compagnons gaulois de Spartacus." T. Pomponius Veientanus: Livy 25.1.4 (Penguin).

22. Plutarch, *Crassus* 9.4–5; Appian, *Civil Wars* 1.116; Sallust, *Histories* 3.94–96; Livy, *Periocha* 95; Florus 2.8.5–7; Frontinus, *Stratagems* 1.5.22. Salinae: cf. *RE* I A, 2 col. 1900. P. Varinius: the second Roman commander is also variously identified by the sources. Plutarch (*Crassus* 9.4) calls him the praetor P. Varinius, a name also given by Frontinus (*Stratagems* 1.5.22), but with the title of proconsul. Livy, *Periocha* 95, has P. Varenus, praetor, and Florus (2.8.5) refers to the "Varenian camp." Appian (*Civil Wars* 1.116) has Varinius Glaber (cf. above, n.19). P. Varinius is the accepted correct name, and 73 B.C. the year of his praetorship: *MRR* II, 109. The discrepancy between Plutarch and Frontinus on Varinius's office can be explained by assuming that Varinius's operations extended through the winter of 73–72 B.C., making a promagisterial appointment necessary when Varinius's praetorship expired at the end of 73 B.C.: *MRR* II, 115 n.1, 119. Furius: *MRR* II, 112. L. Cossinius, perhaps praetor in 73 B.C.: *MRR* II, 110; III, 77. C. Toranius: *MRR* II, 110, 115 n.4. P. Valerius: *MRR* II, 110.

23. Appian, *Civil Wars* 1.116; Florus 2.8.5–7; Sallust, *Histories* 3.97–99 (*in agro Lucano*). Winter of 73–72 B.C.: see Appendix 3. On depopulation in the south and its economy, see Brunt (1971), 359–75. For the prosperity of the Campanian cities, see Frederiksen (1984), *passim*. Metapontum: see *PECS*, s.v. "Metapontion"; Brunt (1971), 363; Metapontum as a grain-producing region: Livy 24.20.15. Thurii: see *PECS*, s.v. "Thurii"; Strabo 6.1.13–14; Brunt (1971), 359–60; Cosentia: Strabo 6.1.5; Brunt (1971), 50, 360, 362.

24. The consuls of 72 B.C.: Plutarch (*Crassus* 9.7) simply calls them Gellius and Lentulus; Florus (2.8.10) names Lentulus alone; Livy, *Periocha* 96, has Cn. Lentulus and L. Gellius; Orosius (5.24.4) Gellius and Lentulus; Appian (*Civil Wars* 1.116) gives no names at all. Their full names were L. Gellius Publicola and Cn. Cornelius Lentulus Clodianus: *MRR* II, 116; cf. III, 67. Cn. Manlius: Livy, *Periocha* 96; *MRR* II, 116; III, 135. Q. Arrius: he is called praetor by Livy, *Periocha* 96, but was probably a promagistrate, subordinate to L. Gellius: *MRR* II, 117; cf. III, 25. On the legions, see Brunt (1971), 450; and on Gellius's age, see Badian (1970), 7 n.3. Crixus: Appian, *Civil Wars* 1.117. Plutarch, *Crassus* 9.7; Livy, *Periocha* 96;

Orosius 5.24.4; Sallust, *Histories* 3.104–105; on the unreliability of the recorded numbers of casualties in the Spartacan war, see Kamienik (1970). Plutarch: *Cato the Younger* 8.1–2; cf. *MRR* III, 194. C. Cassius Longinus: Plutarch, *Crassus* 9.7; Appian, *Civil Wars*, 1.117; Livy, *Periocha* 96; Florus 2.8.10; Orosius 5.24.4; he was killed in battle; cf. *MRR* II, 117. The plan to leave Italy: Plutarch (*Crassus* 9.5–6) reports an unsuccessfully implemented plan on Spartacus's part to lead his followers north, so that they could disperse to Thrace and Gaul, before the intervention of the consuls of 72 B.C. Appian (*Civil Wars* 1. 117), however, reserves this point until the consuls have already begun to fight the rebels. Plutarch's implication that the northern move was completely rejected cannot be entirely correct, for he subsequently (*Crassus* 9.7) has Spartacus making for the Alps once the consuls have become involved. On Spartacus's lack of a coherent policy and the endemic disunity among his forces, see Guarino (1979), 61, 72–73, perhaps overstated. The assault on Rome is referred to by Appian, *Civil Wars* 1.117, after defeats of both consuls by Spartacus and a further victory in Picenum (cf. Sallust, *Histories* 3.106); and by Florus (2.8.10), after a rebel victory against Lentulus in the Apennines. For the defeat of the consuls, and of Q. Arrius and Cn. Manlius in 72 B.C., see also Livy, *Periocha* 96; Orosius 5.24.4.

25. Plutarch, *Crassus* 10.1–3; Appian, *Civil Wars* 1.118; Livy, *Periocha* 96; 97; Sallust, *Histories* 4.21–22; Florus 2.8.12; Frontinus, *Stratagems* 2.5.34; Eutropius 6.7.2; Orosius 5.24.5–6. Probably late in the year: see Appendix 3; cf. Guarino (1979), 80. M. Licinius Crassus: there is no ambiguity over the identity of Rome's final commander against Spartacus, but there is confusion in the sources over his status. Plutarch (*Crassus* 10.1), Florus (2.8.12), and Orosius (5.24.5) give him no title at all. Livy, *Periochae* 96, 97, describes him as praetor. Appian (*Civil Wars* 1.118) seems to suggest that Crassus became praetor at the election of 72 B.C. Eutropius (6.7.2) refers to him as proconsul. The modern consensus is that Crassus held the praetorship in 73 B.C., and in 72 B.C. was given an extraordinary command against Spartacus. See on this, and for limitless speculation on the political background, Badian (1964), 153 n.12; Shatzman (1968), 347–50; Badian (1970), 6–8; Marshall (1972), 670–71; (1973); cf. *MRR* II, 118, 121 n.2, 123; III, 120. Mummius: *MRR* II, 119. Military balance: Appian (*Civil Wars* 1.118) has it that Crassus first defeated some ten thousand rebels encamped apart from Spartacus himself, killing two-thirds of them, and then attacked and defeated Spartacus before pursuing him to the sea. Florus (2.8.12) simply says that the rebels, having been defeated by Crassus, took refuge in southern Italy. Livy, *Periocha* 97, specifies Crassus's killing of thirty-five thousand Gauls and Germans, including their leaders, Castus and Gannicus. Orosius (5.24.6) knew of the same encounter, though his total of the defeated is thirty thousand. He records also that Crassus previously killed six thousand rebels and captured nine hundred. Frontinus (*Stratagems* 2.4.7; 2.5.34) refers to the operations against the detached Gauls and Germans, with the total of thirty-five thousand dead; he has the encounter begin from a position near Mount Cantenna (2.5.34) and near Camalatrum (2.4.7), a site to be placed in Lucania (cf. *RE* Supp. VI, col. 20). Q. Marcius Rufus: *MRR* II, 125. C. Pomptinus: *MRR* II, 125; III, 167. See also n.26.

26. Plutarch, *Crassus* 10.3–5; 11.4–7; *Pompeius* 21.1–2; Appian, *Civil Wars* 1.118–20; Florus 2.8.13–14; Sallust, *Histories* 4.30–31, 34, 41; Frontinus, *Stratagems* 2.5.34; Livy, *Periocha* 97; Orosius 5.24.6–8. Winter of 72–71 B.C.: see Appendix 3; cf. Guarino (1979), 81. Castus and Gannicus: although Livy, *Periocha* 97, and Orosius 5.24.6 refer to Crassus's action against the separate Gauls and Germans (above, n.25), they do not mention the siege at Rhegium at all. On the other hand, Plutarch places their demise after the siege was well under way: Spartacus, he maintains, evacuated a third of his army across Crassus's ditch on

a snowy, stormy night (*Crassus* 10.6; cf. Sallust, *Histories* 4.35, *frigida nocte*), and saved the destruction by Crassus of a splinter group of rebels near a lake in Lucania (*Crassus* 11.1). There followed Crassus's action against Castus and Gannicus, with Crassus killing twelve thousand three hundred of the rebels (*Crassus* 11.2–3), and in response Spartacus's retreat toward the mountains of Petelia on the opposite coast of Bruttium (*Crassus* 11.4). Appian's version is rather different: he has Crassus foil an attempt by Spartacus to break through the siege ranks, with two losses of six thousand rebels on the same day, though Spartacus was still able to keep up harrying attacks on the Romans afterwards (*Civil Wars* 1.119). Then Spartacus, having made an offer to come to terms, which Crassus refused, burst through the siege with the aid of cavalry reinforcements and made for Brundisium, with Crassus in pursuit (*Civil Wars* 1.120). Petelia: see Strabo 6.1.3; Brunt (1971), 50, 126–27, 360, 362; Petelia was a prosperous but small center; again it will have been its hinterland rather than the town itself that drew Spartacus. L. Quinctius: *MRR* II, 125; cf. III, 180. Cn. Tremellius Scrofa: *MRR* II, 122; III, 208. M. Terentius Varro Lucullus: *MRR* II, 124; cf. III, 204. The decisive encounter: Plutarch and Appian again have the fullest accounts of the final stages of the war, but there is little more than general agreement between them. According to Plutarch (*Crassus* 11.4–7), after the defeat of Crassus's subordinate officers on the retreat to Petelia, the overconfident rebels persuaded Spartacus to face Crassus, who encamped, started to build a trench, and found the rebels attacking it; a major battle ensued, in which Spartacus himself was killed, while five thousand fugitives were encountered by Cn. Pompeius and cut down. Appian (*Civil Wars* 1.120) has Spartacus engage Crassus for the final battle in desperation, having learned of Lucullus's arrival at Brundisium; after Spartacus's death, Crassus pursued the fugitives to the mountains, wiping them all out except for the six thousand who were crucified. Orosius (5.24.7–8) reports sixty thousand rebel dead, and six thousand captured, with many fugitives killed by pursuing Roman generals. Ovation: in the celebration, Crassus wore a crown of laurel rather than the customary myrtle, which may have been regarded as a special distinction; Cicero, *In Pisonem* 58; Pliny, *Natural History* 15.125; Aulus Gellius 5.6.23; see Marshall (1972), 672–73.

27. Pompeius: Plutarch, *Crassus* 11.4–7; *Pompeius* 21.1–2; *Comparison of Crassus and Nicias* 3.2; Appian, *Civil Wars* 1.120; Cicero, *De Lege Manilia* 30; cf. *MRR* II, 124. Six months: see Appendix 3.

28. Plutarch: *Crassus* 8.1–2 (Wiedemann). Appian: *Civil Wars* 1.116 (Wiedemann). Florus: 2.8.3.

29. Quotation: Augustine, *City of God* 3.26 (Loeb). Rural slaves: see Oliva (1965), 77–79. Sallust: *Histories* 3.98. Hints: Florus 2.8.3; Livy, *Periocha* 95; Athenaeus 6.292f. Eutropius 6.7.2; Orosius 5.24.2; Augustine, *City of God* 4.5; the hints are all vague on the manner in which recruitment was to be undertaken and do not offset the view that the proliferation of slave numbers was largely accidental. Appian: *Civil Wars* 1.116–117 (Wiedemann), which Rubinsohn (1971) uses to argue that the Spartacan war embraced remnants of "nationalistic," anti-Roman sentiment from the Social War (cf. Levi [1972a]); had this been the case, some impact on the source tradition might reasonably have been expected. Peasant revolt: thus Guarino (1979), 71–72, 99, 116–17; see, however, the discussion of Stampacchia (1980). *Coloni*: Sallust, *Histories* 3.98. Veteran soldiers: see Brunt (1971), 300–12. Catilina: see Bradley (1978).

30. Plutarch: *Crassus* 9.5–6 (Wiedemann); 10.3–4. Free Italians: Guarino (1979), 77; Bodor (1981), 88–91; evidence for a rebellion of slaves and nonslaves against "un padronato ottuso e aspro" (Guarino [1979], 99) is not to be found. Florus: 2.8.13 (Loeb); cf. Sallust, *Histories* 4.30–31. C. Verres: Cicero, *Verrines*

2.5.5; Sallust, *Histories* 4.32; cf. Stampacchia (1980), 109. According to Cicero, *Verrines* 2.5.158–170, Verres executed the Roman citizen P. Gavius of Consa (Compsa? cf. *RE* VII, 1 col. 866) on the charge of having been a spy (*speculator*) sent to Sicily by the *duces fugitivorum*. Rubinsohn (1971), 291, views this as symptomatic of involvement in the Spartacan war of a free element in the Italian population (above, n.29). Cicero (*Verrines* 2.5.161) is adamant that the charge against Gavius was baseless. But even if Verres were given the benefit of the doubt, the character of the slave war would hardly be put in jeopardy. Nothing further of Gavius is known. Logistical difficulties: to explain the rebels' change of direction after Mutina and the failure of their effort to reach Sicily, Kamienik (1972) points to the limitations imposed by adverse geographical factors and the conditions of winter.

31. Sallust: *Histories* 3.96 (Carter); Plutarch: *Crassus* 9.7, 11.1 (cf. Sallust, *Histories* 4.37), 11.2 (cf. Sallust, *Histories* 4.38; Orosius 5.24.6), 11.5 (cf. 9.6), 11.4. Appian: *Civil Wars* 1.118.

VI. The Maintenance of Rebellion

1. Seneca, *Moral Epistles* 47; *On Benefits* 3.18–28. For the many other references to slavery in Seneca's writings, see Griffin (1976), 256–85; Reekmans (1981).

2. Bradley (1986c).

3. "Revolutionary" phrases: Vogt (1975), 46, 85, followed by Patterson (1982), 97; cf. also Green (1961), 24; Verbrugghe (1974), 51–52. Farrington (1937), 15–18, saw a "revolutionary complexion" in Stoicism's "championship of the slave" from the outset and wrote of the Stoics' "rejection of slavery." A distinction nonetheless has to be observed between a theoretical ideal and efforts to achieve its implementation. On the absence of revolutions in Greek and Roman history at large, see Finley (1986a). Modern abolitionism: see Davis (1984). Nexus: see Astin (1967), 161–74. Ti. Gracchus: Plutarch, *Tiberius Gracchus* 8.4; Appian, *Civil Wars* 1.9; see Harris (1971), 203–204; and Nagle (1976), maintaining that the anecdote about Gracchus and Etruria does not provide evidence for the disappearance there of small farmers. Quotation: Astin (1967), 196. For a catalogue of the attempts made at agrarian reform in the late Republic, see Brunt (1962), 69, with the conclusion (p. 84): "The Roman revolution may then have effected no permanent changes in the agrarian society of Italy."

4. Engenho Santana: see Schwartz (1985), 158–59. Quotation on Roman politics: Millar (1986), 7–8.

5. Diodorus Siculus 34/35.2.11 (cf. 24b), 16 (Loeb), 14; 36.4.2; Plutarch, *Crassus* 8.2; Appian, *Civil Wars* 1.116 (Wiedemann); Velleius Paterculus 2.30.5; Frontinus, *Stratagems* 1.7.6; cf. Sallust, *Histories* 3.102–103; Florus 2.8.6 (Loeb); Diodorus 34/35.2.29 (Wiedemann).

6. Diodorus 34/35.2.15; 36.4.4–5; Appian, *Civil Wars* 1.116; 1.117 (Wiedemann); Sallust, *Histories* 3.96 (Carter).

7. Diodorus 36.4.3, 7 (Wiedemann); Plutarch, *Crassus* 9.1, 9.3, 9.7, 10.2; cf. Appian, *Civil Wars* 1.117.

8. Polybius 6.21.6–25.10, with Walbank (1957), 701–708; for the date of composition, see Walbank (1972), 134. The text, it should be recognized, raises a number of difficulties, for discussion of which see Rawson (1971), 13–23. But the point remains that it offers a guide to the type of equipment captured by the rebel slaves. On Roman arms in general, see Harmand (1967), 55–98. Modifications: see Bell (1965); Keppie (1984), 63–67.

9. Appian, *Civil Wars* 1.117.
10. Diodorus 34/35.2.11 (cf. 24b); 34/35.8; 34/35.2.43; 36.4.2; Plutarch, *Crassus* 8.2; Frontinus, *Stratagems* 1.5.21, 1.5.22; Sallust, *Histories* 3.96; Plutarch, *Crassus* 10.5; Frontinus, *Stratagems* 1.5.20; Diodorus 34/35.2.46 (Wiedemann).
11. Diodorus 34/35.2.16; 36.4.4–5; Appian, *Civil Wars* 1.116; Diodorus 36.4.3; 34/35.2.18; 36.4.7, 8.2–4, 10.1; Plutarch, *Crassus* 11.5–7; Appian, *Civil Wars* 1.120.
12. Diodorus 36.9.1, 4.8, 5.3; 34/35.2.20, 21; 36.8.5, 4.4–5. On siege warfare in general, see Lévêque (1968), 271–73; Préaux (1978), 323–31; Meiggs (1982), 157–72; Garlan (1984), 353–62. Numantia: Appian, *Iberica* 90–98; see Astin (1967), 135–36; Keppie (1984), 46–51. Tauromenium: Diodorus 34/35.2.20 (Wiedemann). Garnsey (1988), 29 n.16, cautions against "tales of cannibalism" in siege contexts, but they cannot be simply dismissed. Spartacus: Sallust, *Histories* 3.93; Plutarch, *Crassus* 10.6. Axiom: Livy 37.53.16 (Penguin).
13. Diodorus 34/35.2.30; Appian, *Civil Wars* 1.116; Horace, *Odes* 3.14.19; Diodorus 36.4.5; Sallust, *Histories* 3.96, cf. 4.20; Diodorus 34/35.9; 2.48; 36.5.2, 3.
14. Baggage trains: see Harmand (1967), 151–63. Polybius: 6.31.13; 6.40; 6.39.12–15; cf. Walbank (1957), 722; Brunt (1971), 411. Spain: Appian, *Iberica* 85; cf. Frontinus, *Stratagems* 4.1.1. Africa: Sallust, *Jugurthine War* 44.5 (Penguin). C. Marius: Frontinus, *Stratagems* 4.1.7; Plutarch, *Marius* 13.1. "Stocks of armour": Sallust, *Jugurthine War* 43.3 (Penguin). Appian: *Civil Wars* 1.116. Plutarch: *Crassus* 9.5.
15. Label: Cicero, *Stoic Paradoxes* 27.
16. Megallis: Diodorus 34/35.2.10, 13, 15, 37. Wife of Eunus: Diodorus 34/35.2.16. Spartacus's wife: Plutarch, *Crassus* 8.3. Two women: Plutarch, *Crassus* 11.3. Cannibalism: Diodorus 34/35.2.20.
17. Sallust: *Histories* 3.98. Orosius: 5.24.3. Diodorus: 36.4.6 (Wiedemann).
18. Diodorus: 34/35.2.5. On *magi* in general, see Nock (1933); Smith (1978), 71–74. Tiridates: Pliny, *Natural History* 30.14–17; cf. Suetonius, *Nero* 13, 30.2, 34.4. Tiberius: Tacitus, *Annals* 2.32. Cicero: *On Divination* 1.90. Paul and Barnabas: *Acts of the Apostles* 13.6–12. Plutarch: *On Isis and Osiris* 46–47, on which see Griffiths (1970), 470-82.
19. Magical remedies: Frayn (1984), 104–105. Lucian: *Menippus* 7. Strabo: 15.3.14–15. Pausanias: 5.27.6; cf. Dio Chrysostom 36.38–48. Eunus: Diodorus 34/35.2.8–9. On Eunus as a mystical figure, see Brisson (1959), 64–67; Bömer (1961), 96–101; and on the importance of religiosity to the slave leadership at large, see Oliva (1965), 83–84.
20. Salvius: Diodorus 36.4.4. Athenion: Diodorus 36.5.1. On the history of astrology, see Cramer (1954), 3–60, recognizing the slave leaders' "reputation as prophets" as the ultimate basis of their authority. On Roman divination, see Liebeschuetz (1979), 7–29. 139 B.C.: Valerius Maximus 1.3.3 (quoted); Livy, *Oxyrhynchus Epitome* 54. Cato: *De Agricultura* 5.4 (Wiedemann). Columella: *Res Rusticae* 1.8.6 (Wiedemann).
21. Impregnated: see Walbank (1967b), 54–69. Asclepius: see Kee (1983), 81–83. Nero: Suetonius, *Nero* 6.4. Hannibal: Livy 21.22.8–9; cf. 1.56.4; 25.16.1–4; 28.11.2; 43.14.4 for snakes as omens. Quotation on Sabazius: MacMullen (1967), 118; note also the reference there to "the popularity of these several snake cults in northern Asia Minor."
22. Diodorus 34/35.2.14 (cf. 41), 16 (Wiedemann), 24, 22 (Wiedemann). Coins: Robinson (1920); Manganaro (1982); (1983). Pareti (1927), 51, thought that Antiochus may have been Eunus's name before he became a slave.
23. Diodorus 36.4.4 (Wiedemann); 7.1; 7.4 (Wiedemann); 5.1–2; 10.1; Florus 2.7.10. Slingshots: Manganaro (1982); (1983).

24. On *philoi* and servants, see Préaux (1978), 200; Herman (1980–1981); Walbank (1984), 68–70; Austin (1986), 462–63. Greek contempt: see Herman (1980–1981), 117–24.

25. Customary progression: Austin (1986), 457. Eunus's gift: Diodorus 34/35.2.42. Beneficial character: Walbank (1984), 70, 84; Austin (1986), 459–60, 463. Triocala: Diodorus 36.7.2–3. Diadem: Walbank (1984), 67 with Polybius 30.2.4. Quotation on purple: Reinhold (1970), 71. Recent pretender: see Gruen (1984), 668–69; cf. Vogt (1975), 58. Ritual and ceremonial: Lévêque (1968), 276–79; Walbank (1984), 67; Austin (1986), 458.

26. Autocratic rulers: the long history of tyrannical and monarchical rule in Sicily, from the archaic age onward, is conveniently accessible in Finley (1979). It cannot be said that the slave leaders will have been overly conscious of the Sicilian tyrants' regimes. But the rule of the tyrants easily merged into the rule of Hellenistic kings (Dionysius, Timoleon, Agathocles), so it is not necessary to look to the eastern Mediterranean alone for models on which the servile regimes could be based: they were already independently present in Sicily. A personalized slave regime was a very natural development of the Sicilian historical tradition, no matter how many "Syrians" may have been used to monarchy elsewhere. Livy: 24.5.3–5. Protective deities: Walbank (1984), 85. Religious veneration: Préaux (1978), 238–71; Walbank (1984), 87–99. The argument does not require that any of the slave leaders purposefully sought worship of himself as a god; at least there is no direct evidence to suggest so. Nor can it be altogether true, as maintained by Guarino (1979), 51, that the slaves of the first Sicilian rebellion sought domination of the whole of Sicily, comparable to the Seleucids' domination of Syria, "con l'ascendenza divina della monarchia."

27. On warfare and Hellenistic kingship, see Lévêque (1968), 261–62; 276–79; Préaux (1978), 295–319; Walbank (1984), 66–67, 81–82; Austin (1986).

28. "Sedentary character": Austin (1986), 456. On Philip V and Antiochus III, see Préaux (1978), 150–63; Gruen (1984), 382–98; 612–43.

29. Andriscus: see Préaux (1978), 174–75. See above n. 22 for references to Eunus's coins. On Demeter and Sicilian politics, see White (1964). For the predominant association of Demeter with the grain harvest in Sicily, see Martorana (1982–1983b).

30. Plutarch, *Crassus* 9.3 (Wiedemann); Appian, *Civil Wars* 1.119, 1.120 (cf. Florus 2.8.7), 1.117; Sallust, *Histories* 3.96 (Carter); Pliny, *Natural History* 33.49; Fronto, *Letters* 2, pp. 146–47 (Loeb); cf. pp. 214-17. Appian, *Civil Wars* 1.116; Plutarch, *Crassus* 10.4; Diodorus 38/39.21; Appian, *Civil Wars* 1.117; Florus 2.8.9; Orosius 5.24.3. Kamienik (1976) emphasizes that Spartacus may have followed a Thracian custom in giving gladiatorial games in honor of the dead; cf. also Ville (1981), 229.

31. Quotation: Sallust, *Histories* 3.91. Augustine: *City of God* 4.5. Late tradition: *Historia Augusta, Maximinus* 9.6. Cicero: *De Haruspicum Responsis* 26. Appian: *Civil Wars* 1.116; cf. Mason (1974), 154–55. Caesar: *Gallic Wars* 1.40.5. On the involvement of Thracian mercenaries in Hellenistic warfare, see Préaux (1978), 316.

32. Massinissa (only nominally independent of course): Livy 31.11.11 (Penguin); cf. Briscoe (1973), 85, and Rawson (1975), 155, for other examples. Plutarch: *Crassus* 9.5 (for ῥαβδοῦχος = *lictor*, see Mason [1974], 82–83). Florus: 2.8.7–8. Frontinus: *Stratagems* 2.5.34 (Loeb). Tradition: Livy 1.8.1–2 (Penguin). Quotation on lictors: Nippel (1984), 23.

33. T. Minucius: Diodorus 36.2.4 (Loeb; note again ῥαβδούχους, cf. above n.32 and Pareti [1927], 52). For the regal perceptions of Roman conquerors, see Rawson (1975).

34. Mount Caprianus: Diodorus 36.4.2. Triocala: Diodorus 36.8.5. Mount Vesuvius: Appian, *Civil Wars* 1.116; Plutarch, *Crassus* 9.1. Thurii: Appian, *Civil Wars* 1.117. Petelia: Plutarch, *Crassus* 11.4. C. Octavius: above, chapter 2, note 35; cf. also Cicero *Verrines* 2.5.39. On Spartacus as essentially a guerrilla leader, not a brilliant general or strategist, see Guarino (1979), 60–61; cf. 75, 103. But the view that his image was deliberately aggrandized by Roman propagandists seems unduly conspiratorial. Despair: see, for example, Livy 29.25.1–3 (204 B.C.): "The actual size of the army which sailed to Africa varies considerably in the accounts of different authors. In one I find an estimate of 10,000 foot and 2,200 horse; in another 16,000 foot and 1,600 horse; yet another account gives the numbers at more than double—mentioning the embarkation of 35,000 foot and horse combined. Some writers have made no statement of numbers, and since the question cannot be clearly determined I should prefer to follow their example" (Penguin).

35. Achaeus: Diodorus 34/35.2.42. Terms: Appian, *Civil Wars* 1.120. Orosius: 5.24.7. Tacitus: *Annals* 3.73.

Epilogue

1. Enemy within: Livy 3.16.3. External interference: Livy 5.3.8. Cato: Plutarch, *Cato* 21.2; Cato, *De Agricultura* 2.4, 132.1, 140.

2. *Lex Fufia Caninia*: Gaius, *Institutes* 1.43 (cf. also Tacitus, *Annals* 14.43). C. Caecilius Isidorus: Pliny, *Natural History* 33.134. L. Domitius Ahenobarbus: Caesar, *Civil Wars* 1.17.3. Isidorus and Ahenobarbus are discussed in detail by Brunt (1975).

3. Manner of speech: Livy 39.37.9; cf. 39.26.8. Predictable patterns: recognizing that flight was a prevalent mode of slave resistance, Brisson (1959), 175–76, maintained that this was impossible in Sicily because of the island's compact size. But the issue is one of scale: the history of marronage in the Caribbean proves the viability of flight in small islands as long as numbers did not grow large enough to attract military retaliation from the slaveocracy.

4. On the character of Republican *libertas*, see Wirszubski (1950), 1–30.

5. On modes of manumission and its practice in the late Republic, see Treggiari (1969), 1–36.

6. Naturalness of warfare: Finley (1986b), 68, 75.

7. Cicero's remark: *Verrines* 2.5.7. On relationships between slaves and masters in the Imperial period, see Bradley (1984).

8. Eunus: Ammianus Marcellinus 14.11.33; cf. Athenaeus 6.273g. Athenion: Cicero, *De Haruspicum Responsis* 26. Spartacus: Cicero, *Stoic Paradoxes* 29, 31; *De Haruspicum Responsis* 26; *Philippics* 4.15, 13.22, 3.21; Horace, *Epodes* 16.1–10; cf. *Odes* 3.14.19; Tacitus, *Annals* 3.73, 15.46; Lucan, *Pharsalia* 2.552–554; Claudian, *In Rufinum* 1.255–256; *De Bello Gothico* 154–164; cf. Sidonius Apollinaris, *Carmina* 2.235–239; *Epistulae* 13.10; Pliny, *Natural History* 33.49. On Spartacus as a later symbol, see Oliva (1965), 87.

9. Cicero, *Verrines* 2.5.1–42, in which it is of some significance that Cicero never actually refers to Spartacus by name. Verres's trial began on August 5, 70 B.C. The fifth oration of the *actio secunda* was never delivered by Cicero because Verres abandoned his defense and went into voluntary exile. The speech, with others, was subsequently made public by Cicero.

Bibliographical References

Astin (1967). A. E. Astin, *Scipio Aemilianus* (Oxford).
Astin (1978). Alan E. Astin, *Cato the Censor* (Oxford).
Austin (1986). M. M. Austin, "Hellenistic Kings, War, and the Economy" *Classical Quarterly* 36: 450–66.
Badian (1958). E. Badian, *Foreign Clientelae (264–70 B.C.)*(Oxford).
Badian (1964). E. Badian, *Studies in Greek and Roman History* (Oxford).
Badian (1970). E. Badian, "Additional Notes on Roman Magistrates" *Athenaeum* 48: 3–14.
Badian (1972). E. Badian, *Publicans and Sinners: Private Enterprise in the Service of the Roman Republic* (Oxford).
Badian (1981). E. Badian, "The Bitter History of Slave History" *New York Review of Books*, 22 October 1981, 49–53.
Baldwin (1966–1967). Barry Baldwin, "Two Aspects of the Spartacus Slave Revolt" *Classical Journal* 62: 289–94.
Bang (1910). M. Bang, "Die Herkunft der roemischen Sklaven" *Mitteilungen des Kaiserlich Deutschen Archaeologischen Instituts, Roemische Abteilung* 25: 223–51.
Bastide (1979). Roger Bastide, "The Other *Quilombos*" in Price (1979a), 191–201.
Begbie (1967). Cynthia M. Begbie, "The Epitome of Livy" *Classical Quarterly* 61: 332–38.
Bell (1965). M. J. V. Bell, "Tactical Reform in the Roman Republican Army" *Historia* 14: 404–22.
Bellen (1971). H. Bellen, *Studien zur Sklavenflucht im römischen Kaiserreich* (Wiesbaden).
Bessone (1982). Luigi Bessone, "La tradizione epitomaria liviana in età imperiale" *ANRW* II, 30.2: 1230–1263.
Biezunska-Malowist (1981). Iza Biezunska-Malowist, "Les hommes libres face à l'esclavage" *Index* 10: 3–10.
Bivar (1964). A. D. H. Bivar, "The Stevensweert Kantharos: Its Metrology and Eastern Connections" *Journal of the Warburg and Courtauld Institutes* 27: 307–11.
Bodor (1981). A. Bodor, "The Ethnic and Social Composition of the Participants in the Slave Uprising Led by Spartacus" in Chr. M. Danov and Al. Fol, eds., *Spartacus: Symposium Rebus Spartaci Gestis Dedicatum 2050A* (Sofia), 85–94.
Bömer (1961). F. Bömer, *Untersuchungen über die Religion der Sklaven in Griechenland und Rom III* (Wiesbaden).
Bosworth (1968). A. B. Bosworth, review of Capozza (1966), *Journal of Roman Studies* 58: 272–74.
Bradley (1978). K. R. Bradley, "Slaves and the Conspiracy of Catiline" *Classical Philology* 73: 329–36.
Bradley (1983). K. R. Bradley, "Slave Kingdoms and Slave Rebellions in Ancient Sicily" *Historical Reflections/Réflexions Historiques* 10: 435–51.

Bradley (1984).   K. R. Bradley, *Slaves and Masters in the Roman Empire: A Study in Social Control* (Brussels [New York and Oxford, 1987]).

Bradley (1985a). K. R. Bradley, "The Early Development of Slavery at Rome" *Historical Reflections/Réflexions Historiques* 12: 1–8.

Bradley (1985b). K. R. Bradley, "Child Labour in the Roman World" *Historical Reflections/Réflexions Historiques* 12: 311–30.

Bradley (1986a). K. R. Bradley, "Wet-nursing at Rome: A Study in Social Relations," in Beryl Rawson, ed., *The Family in Ancient Rome: New Perspectives* (London and Sydney), 201–29.

Bradley (1986b). K. R. Bradley, "Social Aspects of the Roman Slave Trade" *Münstersche Beiträge zur Antiken Handelsgeschichte* 5: 49–58.

Bradley (1986c). K. R. Bradley, "Seneca and Slavery" *Classica et Mediaevalia* 37: 161–72.

Bradley (1987).   K. R. Bradley, "On the Roman Slave Supply and Slavebreeding" *Slavery and Abolition* 8: 42–64 = M. I. Finley, ed., *Classical Slavery* (London), 42–64.

Briscoe (1973).   John Briscoe, *A Commentary on Livy, Books XXXI–XXXIII* (Oxford).

Brisson (1959).   Jean-Paul Brisson, *Spartacus* (Paris).

Brockmeyer (1979).   Norbert Brockmeyer, *Antike Sklaverei* (Darmstadt).

Bruneau (1985).   Philippe Bruneau, "Deliaca V" *Bulletin de correspondance hellénique* 109: 545–67.

Brunt (1958).   P. A. Brunt, review of Westermann (1955), *Journal of Roman Studies* 48: 164–70.

Brunt (1962).   P. A. Brunt, "The Army and the Land in the Roman Revolution" *Journal of Roman Studies* 52: 69–86.

Brunt (1971).   P. A. Brunt, *Italian Manpower, 225 B.C.–A.D. 14* (Oxford).

Brunt (1974).   P. A. Brunt, "The Roman Mob," in M. I. Finley, ed., *Studies in Ancient Society* (London), 74–102.

Brunt (1975).   P. A. Brunt, "Two Great Roman Landowners" *Latomus* 34: 619–35.

Brunt (1980).   P. A. Brunt, "On Historical Fragments and Epitomes" *Classical Quarterly* 30: 477–94.

Burford (1972).   Alison Burford, *Craftsmen in Greek and Roman Society* (Ithaca).

Capozza (1956–1957).   Maria Capozza, "Le rivolte servili di Sicilia nel quadro della politica agraria romana" *Atti dell'Istituto Veneto di scienze, lettere ed arti, Classe di scienze morali e lettere* 115: 79–98.

Capozza (1966).   Maria Capozza, *Movimenti servili nel mondo romano in età repubblicana I* (Rome).

Carandini (1981).   Andrea Carandini, "Sviluppo e crisi delle manifatture rurali e urbane" *SRPS* II, 249–60.

Carandini (1985).   Andrea Carandini, ed., *Settefinestre: Una villa schiavistica nell'Etruria romana* (Modena).

Carrington (1931).   R. C. Carrington, "Studies in the Campanian Villae Rusticae" *Journal of Roman Studies* 21: 110–30.

Carter (1982).   John M. Carter, *Suetonius: Divus Augustus* (Bristol).

Cartledge (1985).   Paul Cartledge, "Rebels & Sambos in Classical Greece: A Comparative View," in P. A. Cartlege and F. D. Harvey, eds., *Crux: Essays Presented to G. E. M. de Ste. Croix on His 75th Birthday* (London), 16–46.

Càssola (1982). Filippo Càssola, "Diodoro e la storia romana" *ANRW* II, 30.1: 724–73.

Cels (1972). Denis Cels, "Les esclaves dans les 'Verrines' " *Actes du colloque 1971 sur l'esclavage,* (Paris), 175–92.

Champlin (1986). Edward Champlin, "Miscellanea Testamentaria" *Zeitschrift für Papyrologie und Epigraphik* 62: 247–55.

Coarelli (1981). Filippo Coarelli, "La Sicilia tra la fine della guerra annibalica e Cicerone" *SRPS* I, 1–18.

Coarelli (1982). Filippo Coarelli "L' 'Agora des italiens' a Delo: il mercato degli schiavi," in F. Coarelli, D. Musti, and H. Solin, eds., *Delo e l'Italia* (Rome), 119–145.

Coarelli and Torelli (1984). Filippo Coarelli and Mario Torelli, *Sicilia: Guide archeologiche Laterza* 13 (Bari).

Conrad (1983). Robert Edgar Conrad, *Children of God's Fire: A Documentary History of Black Slavery in Brazil* (Princeton).

Corbier (1983). Mireille Corbier, "Fiscus and Patrimonium: The Saepinum Inscription and Transhumance in the Abruzzi" *Journal of Roman Studies* 73: 126–31.

Cotton (1979). M. Aylwin Cotton, *The Late Republican Villa at Posto, Francolise* (London).

Cotton and Métraux (1985). M. Aylwin Cotton and Guy P. Métraux, *The San Rocco Villa at Francolise* (London).

Cramer (1954). Frederick H. Cramer, *Astrology in Roman Law and Politics* (Philadelphia).

Craton (1982a). Michael Craton, *Testing the Chains: Resistance to Slavery in the British West Indies* (Ithaca).

Craton (1982b). Michael Craton, "A Cresting Wave? Recent Trends in the Historiography of Slavery, with Special Reference to the British Caribbean" *Historical Reflections/Réflexions Historiques* 9: 403–19.

Crawford (1977a). Michael H. Crawford, "Republican Denarii in Romania: The Suppression of Piracy and the Slave-Trade" *Journal of Roman Studies* 67: 117–24.

Crawford (1977b). Michael H. Crawford, "Rome and the Greek World: Economic Relationships" *Economic History Review* 30: 42–52.

Crawford (1985). Michael H. Crawford, *Coinage and Money under the Roman Republic: Italy and the Mediterranean Economy* (London).

Croon (1952). J. H. Croon, "The Palici: An Autochthonous Cult in Ancient Sicily" *Mnemosyne* 5: 116–29.

D'Arms (1981). John H. D'Arms, *Commerce and Social Standing in Ancient Rome* (Cambridge, Mass.).

Daube (1952). David Daube, "Slave-Catching" *Juridical Review* 64: 12–28.

Daube (1956). David Daube, *Forms of Roman Legislation* (Oxford).

Davies (1984). J. K. Davies, "Cultural, Social and Economic Features of the Hellenistic World" *CAH*, 2d edn., Volume VII, Part I, 257–320.

Davis (1974). David Brion Davis, "Slavery and the Post-World War II Historians" *Daedalus* 103: 1–16.

Davis (1984). David Brion Davis, *Slavery and Human Progress* (New York).

Debevoise (1938). Neilson C. Debevoise, *A Political History of Parthia* (Chicago).

Degler (1971). Carl N. Degler, *Neither Black Nor White: Slavery and Race Relations in Brazil and the United States* (New York).

Degrassi (1954). Atilius Degrassi, *Fasti Capitolini* (Turin).

De Laet (1949). Siegfried J. De Laet, *Portorium: Etude sur l'organisation douanière chez les romains* (Brugge).

Deman and Raepsaet-Charlier (1981–1982). Albert Deman and Marie-Thérèse Raepsaet-Charlier, "Notes sur la guerre de Spartacus" *Acta Classica Universitatis Scientiarum Debreceniensis* 17–18: 83–97.

De Martino (1974). Francesco De Martino, "Intorno all'origine della schiavitù a Roma" *Labeo* 20: 163–93.

De Martino (1979). Francesco De Martino, *Storia economica di Roma antica* (Florence).

den Boer (1972). W. den Boer, *Some Minor Roman Historians* (Leiden).

Dillard (1972). J. L. Dillard, *Black English: Its History and Usage in the United States* (New York).

Doi (1978). Masaoki Doi, "A Historical Meaning of Spartacus' Uprising" *Senshu Jinbunronshu* 20: 23–90.

Doi (1985). Masaoki Doi, "The Present Stage of Studies on Spartacus' Uprising and Its Problems" *Studies in Humanities* 35: 17–45.

Drews (1962). Robert Drews, "Diodorus and His Sources" *American Journal of Philology* 83: 383–92.

Duchêne (1986). Hervé Duchêne, "Sur la stèle d'Aulus Caprilius Timotheos, sômatemporos" *Bulletin de correspondance hellénique* 110: 513–30.

Ducrey (1968). Pierre Ducrey, *Le Traitement des prisonniers de guerre dans la Grèce antique* (Paris).

Dumézil (1980). Georges Dumézil, *Camillus* (Berkeley).

Dumont (1967). J.-C. Dumont, "La Signification de la révolte" *Revue des Etudes Latines* 45: 89–98.

Duncan-Jones (1974). Richard Duncan-Jones, *The Economy of the Roman Empire: Quantitative Studies* (Cambridge).

Ebel (1976). Charles Ebel, *Transalpine Gaul: The Emergence of a Roman Province* (Leiden).

Eck (1978). W. Eck, "Zum neuen Fragment des sogenannten Testamentum Dasumii" *Zeitschrift für Papyrologie und Epigraphik* 30: 277–95.

Elkins (1976). Stanley M. Elkins, *Slavery: A Problem in American Institutional and Intellectual Life*, 3d edn. (Chicago).

Erim (1958). Kenan Erim, "Morgantina" *American Journal of Archaeology* 62: 79–90.

Etienne (1981). Robert Etienne, "Les rations alimentaires des esclaves de la 'familia rustica' d'après Caton" *Index* 10: 66–77.

Farrington (1937). Benjamin Farrington, *Diodorus Siculus: Universal Historian* (University of Wales Press Board).

Finley (1969). M. I. Finley, *Aspects of Antiquity: Discoveries and Controversies* (New York).

Finley (1976). M. I. Finley, "Introduction," in M. I. Finley, ed., *Studies in Roman Property* (Cambridge), 1–6.

Finley (1979). M. I. Finley, *Ancient Sicily*, 2d edn. (London).

Finley (1980). M. I. Finley, *Ancient Slavery and Modern Ideology* (New York).

Finley (1983). M. I. Finley, *Economy and Society in Ancient Greece* (New York).

Finley (1986a). M. I. Finley, "Revolution in Antiquity" in Roy Porter and Mikuláš Teich, eds., *Revolution in History* (Cambridge), 47–60.

Finley (1986b). M. I. Finley, *Ancient History: Evidence and Models* (New York).

Flacelière and Chambry (1972). Robert Flacelière and Emile Chambry, *Plutarque: Vies, Tome Vll* (Paris).

Flambard (1983). Jean-Marc Flambard, "Les collèges et les élites locales à l'époque républicaine d'après l'exemple de Capoue," in M. Cébeillac-Gervasoni, ed., *Les "Bourgeoisies" municipales italiennes aux IIᵉ et Iᵉʳ siècles av. J.-C. Colloques internationaux du centre national de la recherche scientifique n.609. Sciences humaines* (Paris), 75–89.

Forrest and Stinton (1962). W. G. Forrest and T. W. C. Stinton, "The First Sicilian Slave War" *Past and Present* no. 22, 87–92.

Frank (1927). Tenney Frank, "The Bacchanalian Cult of 186 B.C." *Classical Quarterly* 21: 128–32.

Frank (1933). Tenney Frank, *An Economic Survey of Ancient Rome*, Volume I, *Rome and Italy of the Republic* (Baltimore).

Frank (1935). Tenney Frank, "On the Migration of Romans to Sicily" *American Journal of Philology* 56: 61–64.

Fraschetti (1981). Augusto Fraschetti, "Per una prosopografia dello sfruttamento: Romani e Italici in Sicilia (212–44 A.C.)" *SRPS* I, 51–77.

Frayn (1984). Joan M. Frayn, *Sheep-Rearing and the Wool Trade in Italy during the Roman Period* (Liverpool).

Frederiksen (1984). Martin Frederiksen, *Campania* (British School at Rome).

Friedländer (1908–1913). Ludwig Friedländer, *Roman Life and Manners under the Early Empire* (London).

Frier (1977). Bruce Woodward Frier, "The Rental Market in Early Imperial Rome" *Journal of Roman Studies* 67: 27–37.

Frier (1985). Bruce W. Frier, *The Rise of the Roman Jurists: Studies in Cicero's pro Caecina* (Princeton).

Fuks (1968). Alexander Fuks, "Slave War and Slave Troubles in Chios in the Third Century B.C." *Athenaeum* 46: 102–11.

Gabba (1956). Emilio Gabba, *Appiano e la storia delle guerre civili* (Florence).

Gabba (1967). Emilio Gabba, *Appiani Bellorum Civilium Liber Primus* (Florence).

Gabba (1976). Emilio Gabba, *Republican Rome, The Army and the Allies* (Berkeley).

Garlan (1984). Yvon Garlan, "War and Siegecraft" *CAH*, 2d edn., Volume VII, Part I, 353–62.

Garlan (1987). Yvon Garlan, "War, Piracy and Slavery in the Greek World" *Slavery and Abolition* 8: 7–21 = M. I. Finley, ed., *Classical Slavery* (London), 7–21.

Garnsey (1988). Peter Garnsey, *Famine and Food Supply in the Graeco-Roman World* (Cambridge).

Garnsey and Rathbone (1985). Peter Garnsey and Dominic Rathbone, "The Background to the Grain Law of Gaius Gracchus" *Journal of Roman Studies* 75: 20–25.

Gaspar (1985). David Barry Gaspar, *Bondmen and Rebels: A Study of Master-Slave Relations in Antigua* (Baltimore).

Geggus (1982). David Patrick Geggus, *Slavery, War and Revolution: The British Occupation of Saint Domingue, 1793–1798* (Oxford).

Genovese (1972). Eugene D. Genovese, *Roll, Jordan, Roll: The World the Slaves Made* (New York).

Genovese (1979). Eugene D. Genovese, *From Rebellion to Revolution: Afro-American Slave Revolts in the Making of the Modern World* (Baton Rouge).

Glueck (1965). N. Glueck, *Divinities and Dolphins* (London).

Gordon (1924). M. L. Gordon, "The Nationality of Slaves under the Early Roman Empire" *Journal of Roman Studies* 14: 93–111.

Green (1961). Peter Green, "The First Sicilian Slave War" *Past and Present* no. 20, 10–29.

Griffin (1976). Miriam T. Griffin, *Seneca: A Philosopher in Politics* (Oxford).

Griffiths (1970). J. Gwyn Griffiths, *Plutarch's De Iside et Osiride* (University of Wales Press Board).

Gruen (1968). Erich S. Gruen, *Roman Politics and the Criminal Courts, 149–78 B.C.* (Cambridge, Mass.).

Gruen (1974). Erich S. Gruen, *The Last Generation of the Roman Republic* (Berkeley).

Gruen (1984). Erich S. Gruen, *The Hellenistic World and the Coming of Rome* (Berkeley).

Guarino (1979). Antonio Guarino, *Spartaco: Analisi di un mito* (Naples).

Guarino (1980). Antonio Guarino, "Spartaco professore?" *Labeo* 26: 325–27.

Guido (1977). Margaret Guido, *Sicily: An Archaeological Guide* (London).

Hamilton (1969). J. R. Hamilton, *Plutarch, Alexander: A Commentary* (Oxford).

Harmand (1967). Jacques Harmand, *L'armée et le soldat à Rome de 107 à 50 avant notre ère* (Paris).

Harris (1971). William V. Harris, *Rome in Etruria and Umbria* (Oxford).

Harris (1979). William V. Harris, *War and Imperialism in Republican Rome 327–70 B.C.* (Oxford).

Harris (1980). William V. Harris, "Towards a Study of the Roman Slave Trade" *Memoirs of the American Academy in Rome* 36: 117–40.

Hassall, Crawford and Reynolds (1974). Mark Hassall, Michael Crawford and Joyce Reynolds, "Rome and the Eastern Provinces at the End of the Second Century B.C." *Journal of Roman Studies* 64: 195–220.

Herman (1980–1981). G. Herman, "The 'Friends' of the Early Hellenistic Rulers: Servants or Officials?" *Talanta* 12/13: 103–49.

Higman (1984). B. W. Higman, *Slave Populations of the British Caribbean, 1807–1834* (Baltimore).

Hopkins (1978). Keith Hopkins, *Conquerors and Slaves: Sociological Studies in Roman History, Volume 1* (Cambridge).

Hopkins (1983). Keith Hopkins, *Death and Renewal: Sociological Studies in Roman History, Volume 2* (Cambridge).

Hornblower (1981). Jane Hornblower, *Hieronymus of Cardia* (Oxford).

Jal (1963). Paul Jal, *La guerre civile à Rome* (Paris).

James (1963). C. L. R. James, *The Black Jacobins: Toussaint L'Ouverture and the San Domingo Revolution* (New York).

Jones (1971). C. P. Jones, *Plutarch and Rome* (Oxford).

Jonkers (1933). E. J. Jonkers, *Economische en sociale toestanden in het romeinsche rijk, blijkende uit het corpus iuris* (Wageningen).

Kamienik (1970). Roman Kamienik, "Die Zahlenangaben über den Spartakus—Aufstand und ihre Glaubwürdigkeit" *Das Altertum* 16: 96–105.

Kamienik (1972). Roman Kamienik, "Spartakus' Rückzug nach der Schlacht bei Mutina und die misslungene Überfahrt nach Sizilien" *Das Altertum* 18: 235–43.

Kamienik (1976). Roman Kamienik, "Gladiatorial Games during the Funeral of Crixus: Contribution to the Revolt of Spartacus" *Eos* 64: 83–90.

Keaveney and Madden (1982). Arthur Keaveney and John A. Madden, "Phthiriasis and Its Victims" *Symbolae Osloenses* 57: 87–99.

Kee (1983). Howard Clark Kee, *Miracle in the Early Christian World: A Study in Socio-Historical Method* (New Haven).

Kent (1969–1970). R. K. Kent, "African Revolt in Bahia: 24–25 January 1835" *Journal of Social History* 3: 334–56.

Kent (1979). R. K. Kent, "Palmares: An African State in Brazil," in Price (1979a), 170–90.

Keppie (1984). Lawrence Keppie, *The Making of the Roman Army: From Republic to Empire* (Totowa, N.J.).

Kilson (1964). Marion D. de B. Kilson, "Towards Freedom: An Analysis of Slave Revolts in the United States" *Phylon* 25: 175–87.

Klein (1978). Herbert S. Klein, *The Middle Passage* (Princeton).

Klein (1986). Herbert S. Klein, *African Slavery in Latin America and the Caribbean* (New York).

Knight (1970). Franklin W. Knight, *Slave Society in Cuba during the Nineteenth Century* (Madison).

Kolchin (1986). Peter Kolchin, "Some Recent Works on Slavery outside the United States: An American Perspective" *Comparative Studies in Society and History* 28: 767–77.

Kolendo (1978). Jerzy Kolendo, "Les esclaves dans l'art antique: La stèle funéraire d'un marchand d'esclaves thrace découverte à Amphipolis" *Archeologia* 29: 24–34.

Kolendo (1981). Jerzy Kolendo, "L'esclavage et la vie sexuelle des hommes libres à Rome" *Index* 10: 288–97.

Kopytoff (1976a). Barbara Klamon Kopytoff, "Jamaican Maroon Political Organization: The Effects of the Treaties" *Social and Economic Studies* 25: 87–105.

Kopytoff (1976b). Barbara Klamon Kopytoff, "The Development of Jamaican Maroon Ethnicity" *Caribbean Quarterly* 22: 33–50.

Kopytoff (1978). Barbara Klamon Kopytoff, "The Early Political Development of Jamaican Maroon Societies" *William and Mary
Quarterly* 35: 287–307.

Kopytoff (1987). Barbara K. Kopytoff, "Religious Change among the Jamaican Maroons: The Ascendance of the Christian God
within a Traditional Cosmology" *Journal of Social History* 20: 463–84.

Kühne (1962). H. Kühne, "Zur Teilnahme von Sklaven und Freigelas-
senen an den Bürgerkriegen der Freien im 1. Jahrhundert
v. u. Z. in Rom" *Studii Clasice* 4: 189–209.

Latte (1970). K. Latte, *Römische Religionsgeschichte* (Munich).

Le Bonniec (1958). Henri Le Bonniec, *Le culte de Cérès à Rome, des origines
à la fin de la République* (Paris).

Lévêque (1968). Pierre Lévêque, "La guerre à l'époque hellénistique," in
Jean-Pierre Vernant, ed., *Problèmes de la guerre en Grèce
ancienne* (Paris), 261–87.

Levi (1972a). Mario Attilio Levi, "Schiavitù e rivoluzione nella Repub-
blica romana" *Index* 3: 168–74.

Levi (1972b). Mario Attilio Levi, "La tradizione sul Bellum Servile di
Spartaco" *Actes du Colloque 1971 sur l'esclavage* (Paris),
171–74.

Levick (1983). Barbara Levick, "The *Senatus Consultum* from Larinum"
Journal of Roman Studies 73: 97–115.

Liebeschuetz (1979). J. H. W. G. Liebeschuetz, *Continuity and Change in Roman Religion* (Oxford).

Lintott (1968). A. W. Lintott, *Violence in Republican Rome* (Oxford).

Lowe (1985). J. C. B. Lowe, "Cooks in Plautus" *Classical Antiquity* 4:
72–102.

MacMullen (1967). Ramsay MacMullen, *Enemies of the Roman Order: Trea-
son, Unrest, and Alienation in the Empire* (Cambridge,
Mass.).

Magie (1950). David Magie, *Roman Rule in Asia Minor to the End of
the Third Century after Christ* (Princeton).

Malitz (1983). Jurgen Malitz, *Die Historien des Poseidonios* (Munich).

Manganaro (1964). Giacomo Manganaro, "Città di Sicilia e santuari panel-
lenici nel III e II sec. a.C." *Historia* 13: 414–39.

Manganaro (1967). Giacomo Manganaro, "Über die zwei Sklavenaufstände
in Sizilien" *Helikon* 7: 205–22.

Manganaro (1972). Giacomo Manganaro, "Per una storia della Sicilia romana" *ANRW* I, 1: 442–61.

Manganaro (1980). Giacomo Manganaro, "La provincia romana," in Emilio
Gabba and Georges Vallet, eds., *La Sicilia antica* (Naples),
II, part 2, 411–61.

Manganaro (1982). Giacomo Manganaro, "Monete e ghiande inscritte degli
schiavi ribelli in Sicilia" *Chiron* 12: 237–44.

Manganaro (1983). Giacomo Manganaro, "Ancora sulle rivolte 'servili' in Sicilia" *Chiron* 13: 405–409.

Manni (1981). Eugenio Manni, *Geografia fisica e politica della Sicilia
antica* (Rome).

Maróti (1976). Egon Maróti, "The *Vilicus* and the Villa-System in Ancient Italy" *Oikumene* 1: 109–24.

Marshall (1972). Bruce A. Marshall, "Crassus' Ovation in 71 B.C." *Historia*
21: 669–73.

178   Bibliography

Marshall (1973).   B. A. Marshall, "Crassus and the Command against Spar-
                     tacus" *Athenaeum* 51: 109–21.
Martorana (1982–   Giuseppe Martorana, "Kore e il prato sempre fiorito di
    1983a).   Enna" *Kokalos* 28–29: 113–22.
Martorana (1982–   Giuseppe Martorana, "Il riso di Demetra in Sicilia" *Ko-
    1983b).   kalos* 28–29: 105–12.
Mason (1974).   Hugh J. Mason, *Greek Terms for Roman Institutions: A
                     Lexicon and Analysis* (Toronto).
Mattingly (1986).   Harold B. Mattingly, "Scipio Aemilianus' Eastern Em-
                     bassy" *Classical Quarterly* 36: 491–95.
Mau (1907).   August Mau, *Pompeii: Its Life and Art* (New York).
Maxey (1938).   Mima Maxey, *Occupations of the Lower Classes in Ro-
                     man Society* (Chicago).
Mazza (1981).   Mario Mazza, "Terra e lavoratori nella Sicilia tardorepub-
                     blicana" *SRPS* I, 19–49.
Meiggs (1982).   Russell Meiggs, *Trees and Timber in the Ancient Medi-
                     terranean World* (Oxford).
Middleton (1983).   Paul Middleton, "The Roman Army and Long-Distance
                     Trade," in Peter Garnsey and C. R. Whittaker, eds., *Trade
                     and Famine in Classical Antiquity* (Cambridge), 75–83.
Millar (1984).   Fergus Millar, "The Political Character of the Classical
                     Roman Republic" *Journal of Roman Studies* 74: 1–19.
Millar (1986).   Fergus Millar, "Politics, Persuasion and the People" *Jour-
                     nal of Roman Studies* 76: 1–11.
Mullin (1972).   Gerald W. Mullin, *Flight and Rebellion: Slave Resistance
                     in Eighteenth-Century Virginia* (New York).
Nagle (1976).   D. Brendan Nagle, "The Etruscan Journey of Tiberius
                     Gracchus" *Historia* 25: 487–89.
Nicolet (1974).   Claude Nicolet, *L'ordre équestre à l'époque républicaine
                     (312–43 av. J.-C.)*, Tome I: *Définitions juridiques et struc-
                     tures sociales* (Paris).
Nicolet (1977).   Claude Nicolet, *Rome et la conquête du monde médi-
                     terranéan, 246–27 avant J.-C.*, Tome premier, *Les struc-
                     tures de l'Italie romaine* (Paris).
Nicolet (1978).   Claude Nicolet, *Rome et la conquête de monde médi-
                     terranéan, 246–27 avant J.-C.*, Tome second, *Genèse d'un
                     empire* (Paris).
Nippel (1984).   Wilfried Nippel, "Policing Rome" *Journal of Roman Stud-
                     ies* 74: 20–29.
Nock (1933).   Arthur Darby Nock, "Paul and the Magus," in F. J. Foakes-
                     Jackson and K. Lake, eds., *The Beginnings of Christianity*
                     (London), V, 164–88.
Nock (1959).   Arthur Darby Nock, "Posidonius" *Journal of Roman
                     Studies* 49: 1–15.
Oates (1934).   Whitney J. Oates, "A Note on Cato, *De Agri Cultura*, LVI"
                     American Journal of Philology 55: 67–70.
Ogilvie (1965).   R. M. Ogilvie, *A Commentary on Livy, Books 1–5* (Ox-
                     ford).
Oliva (1965).   Pavel Oliva, "Die charakteristischen Züge der grossen
                     Sklavenaufstände zur Zeit der römischen Republik," in
                     Elisabeth Charlotte Welskopf, ed., *Neue Beiträge zur Ge-
                     schichte der alten Welt* (Berlin), II, 75–88.

Ormerod (1924). Henry A. Ormerod, *Piracy in the Ancient World* (Liverpool).

Pareti (1927). Luigi Pareti, "I supposti 'sdoppiamenti' delle guerre servili in Sicilia" *Rivista di filologia e di istruzione classica* 5: 44–67.

Patterson (1967). Orlando Patterson, *The Sociology of Slavery: An Analysis of the Origins, Development and Structure of Negro Slave Society in Jamaica* (London).

Patterson (1979). Orlando Patterson, "Slavery and Slave Revolts: A Sociohistorical Analysis of the First Maroon War, 1665–1740," in Price (1979a), 246–92.

Patterson (1982). Orlando Patterson, *Slavery and Social Death* (Cambridge, Mass.).

Pelham (1911). H. F. Pelham, "Pascua," in F. Haverfield, ed., *Essays by Henry Francis Pelham* (Oxford), 300–311.

Pelling (1979). C. B. R. Pelling, "Plutarch's Method of Work in the Roman Lives" *Journal of Hellenic Studies* 99: 74–96.

Pelling (1980). C. B. R. Pelling, "Plutarch's Adaptation of His Source-Material" *Journal of Hellenic Studies* 100: 127–40.

Phillips (1985). William B. Phillips, Jr., *Slavery from Roman Times to the Early Transatlantic Trade* (Minneapolis).

Potter (1979). T. W. Potter, *The Changing Landscape of South Etruria* (London).

Potter (1987). T. W. Potter, *Roman Italy* (Berkeley).

Préaux (1978). Claire Préaux, *Le monde hellénistique: La Grèce et l' Orient de la mort d'Alexandre à la conquête romaine de la Grèce (323–146 av. J.-C.)*, Tome premier (Paris).

Price (1976). Richard Price, *The Guiana Maroons: A Historical and Bibliographical Introduction* (Baltimore and London).

Price (1979a). Richard Price, ed., *Maroon Societies: Rebel Slave Communities in the Americas*, 2d edn. (Baltimore).

Price (1979b). Richard Price, "Kwasimukamba's Gambit" *Bijdragen tot de Taal-, Land- en Volkenkunde* 135: 151–69.

Price (1983a). Richard Price, *To Slay the Hydra: Dutch Colonial Perspectives on the Saramaka Wars* (Ann Arbor).

Price (1983b). Richard Price, *First-Time: The Historical Vision of an Afro-American People* (Baltimore).

Ramin and Veyne (1981). Jacques Ramin and Paul Veyne, "Droit romain et société: les hommes libres qui passent pour esclaves et l'esclavage volontaire" *Historia* 30: 472–97.

Rathbone (1981). D. W. Rathbone, "The Development of Agriculture in the 'Ager Cosanus' during the Roman Republic: Problems of Evidence and Interpretation" *Journal of Roman Studies* 71: 10–23.

Rathbone (1983). D. W. Rathbone, "The Slave Mode of Production in Italy" *Journal of Roman Studies* 73: 160–68.

Rawson (1986). Beryl Rawson, "Children in the Roman *Familia*," in Beryl Rawson, ed., *The Family in Ancient Rome: New Perspectives* (London), 170–200.

Rawson (1971). Elizabeth Rawson, "The Literary Sources for the Pre-Marian Army" *Papers of the British School at Rome* 39: 13–31.

Rawson (1975). Elizabeth Rawson, "Caesar's Heritage: Hellenistic Kings and Their Roman Equals" *Journal of Roman Studies* 65: 148–59.

Reekmans (1981). Tony Reekmans, "Les esclaves et leurs maîtres dans les oeuvres en prose de Sénèque le philosophe" *Index* 10: 237–59.

Reinhold (1970). Meyer Reinhold, *History of Purple as a Status Symbol in Antiquity* (Brussels).

Reynolds (1983). L. D. Reynolds, ed., *Texts and Transmissions* (Oxford).

Rich (1983). J. W. Rich, "The Supposed Roman Manpower Shortage of the Later Second Century B.C." *Historia* 32: 287–331.

Richmond and Stevens (1942). I. A. Richmond and C. E. Stevens, "The Land-Register of Arausio" *Journal of Roman Studies* 32: 65–77.

Rickman (1980). Geoffrey Rickman, *The Corn Supply of Ancient Rome* (Oxford).

Rizzo (1976). Francesco Paolo Rizzo, "Posidonio nei frammenti diodorei sulla prima guerra servile di Sicilia," in *Studi di storia antica offerti dagli allievi a Eugenio Manni* (Rome), 259–293.

Robertson (1987). Noel Robertson, "The Nones of July and Roman Weather Magic" *Museum Helveticum* 44: 8–41.

Robinson (1920). E. S. G. Robinson, "Antiochus, King of the Slaves" *Numismatic Chronicle* 20: 175–76.

Robinson (1981). Olivia Robinson, "Slaves and the Criminal Law" *Zeitschrift der Savigny-Stiftung für Rechtsgeschichte, Romanistische Abteilung* 98: 213–54.

Roes and Vollgraf (1952). Anne Roes and W. Vollgraf, "Le canthare de Stevensweert" *Monuments et mémoires publiés par l'Académie des Inscriptions et Belles-Lettres* (Fondation Eugène Piot) 46: 39–67.

Rose (1982). Willie Lee Rose, *Slavery and Freedom* (New York).

Rossiter (1978). J. J. Rossiter, *Roman Farm Buildings in Italy* (Oxford).

Rouland (1977). N. Rouland, *Les esclaves romains en temps de guerre* (Brussels).

Rowland (1970). Robert J. Rowland, Jr., "Grain for Slaves: A Note on Cato, *De Agricultura*" *Classical World* 63: 229.

Rubinsohn (1971). Zeev Wolfgang Rubinsohn, "Was the Bellum Spartacium a Servile Insurrection?" *Rivista di Filologia* 99: 290–99.

Rubinsohn (1982). Zeev Wolfgang Rubinsohn, "Some Remarks on the Causes and Repercussions of the So-Called 'Second Slave Revolt' in Sicily" *Athenaeum* 60: 436–51.

Runciman (1983). W. G. Runciman, "Capitalism without Classes: The Case of Classical Rome" *British Journal of Sociology* 34: 157–81.

Russell (1973). D. A. Russell, *Plutarch* (London).

Russell-Wood (1982). A. J. R. Russell-Wood, *The Black Man in Slavery and Freedom in Colonial Brazil* (London).

Sabbatini Tumolesi (1980). Patrizia Sabbatini Tumolesi, *Gladiatorum Paria: Annunci di spettacoli gladiatorii a Pompeii* (Rome).

Saint-Denis (1980). E. de Saint-Denis, "Eloge du chou" *Latomus* 39: 838–49.

Salmon (1982). E. T. Salmon, *The Making of Roman Italy* (Ithaca).

Scardigli (1979). Barbara Scardigli, *Die Römerbiographien Plutarchs: Ein Forschungsbericht* (Munich).

Schwartz (1979).   Stuart B. Schwartz, "The *Mocambo*: Slave Resistance in
                      Colonial Bahia," in Price (1979a), 202–26.
Schwartz (1985).   Stuart B. Schwartz, *Sugar Plantations in the Formation
                      of Brazilian Society: Bahia, 1550–1835* (Cambridge).
Scobie (1986).   Alex Scobie, "Slums, Sanitation, and Mortality in the Ro-
                      man World" *Klio* 68: 399–433.
Scramuzza (1937).   V. M. Scramuzza, *Roman Sicily*, in Tenney Frank, ed., *An
                      Economic Survey of Ancient Rome*, Volume III (Balti-
                      more).
Scullard (1981).   H. H. Scullard, *Festivals and Ceremonies of the Roman
                      Republic* (Ithaca).
Sfameni Gasparro   Giulia Sfameni Gasparro, *I culti orientali in Sicilia* (Lei-
      (1973).   den).
Shapiro (1984).   Herbert Shapiro, "The Impact of the Aptheker Thesis: A
                      Retrospective View of *American Negro Slave Revolts*"
                      Science and Society 48: 52–73.
Shatzman (1968).   Israel Shatzman, "Four Notes on Roman Magistrates"
                      Athenaeum 46: 345–54.
Sherk (1984).   Robert K. Sherk, ed., *Rome and the Greek East to the
                      Death of Augustus* (Cambridge).
Sherwin-White   A. N. Sherwin-White, *The Roman Citizenship*, 2d edn.
      (1973).   (Oxford).
Sherwin-White   A. N. Sherwin-White, "Rome, Pamphylia and Cilicia"
      (1976).   *Journal of Roman Studies* 66: 1–14.
Sherwin-White   A. N. Sherwin-White, *Roman Foreign Policy in the East,
      (1983).   168 B.C. to A.D. 1* (London).
Sicard (1957).   G. Sicard, "Caton et les fonctions des esclaves" *Revue
                      historique de droit français et étranger* 37: 177–195.
Skocpol and Somers   Theda Skocpol and Margaret Somers, "The Uses of Com-
      (1980).   parative History in Macrosocial Inquiry" *Comparative
                      Studies in Society and History* 22: 174–97.
Smith (1978).   Morton Smith, *Jesus the Magician* (New York).
Spranger (1960).   Peter P. Spranger, *Historische Untersuchungen zu den
                      Sklavenfiguren des Plautus und Terenz* (Wiesbaden).
Staerman (1969).   E. M. Staerman, *Die Blütezeit der Sklavenwirtschaft in
                      der römischen Republik* (Wiesbaden).
Stampacchia (1976).   Giulia Stampacchia, *La tradizione della guerra di Spar-
                      taco da Sallustio a Orosio* (Pisa).
Stampacchia (1980).   Giulia Stampacchia, "La rivolta di Spartaco come rivolta
                      contadina" *Index* 9: 99–111.
Stampp (1956).   Kenneth M. Stampp, *The Peculiar Institution: Slavery in
                      the Ante-Bellum South* (New York).
Stampp (1980).   Kenneth M. Stampp, *The Imperiled Union: Essays on the
                      Background of the Civil War* (New York).
Ste. Croix (1981).   G. E. M. de Ste. Croix, *The Class Struggle in the Ancient
                      Greek World* (Ithaca).
Ste. Croix (1984).   Geoffrey de Ste. Croix, "Class in Marx's Conception of
                      History, Ancient and Modern" *New Left Review* 146: 94–
                      111.
Stockton (1971).   David Stockton, *Cicero: A Political Biography* (Oxford).
Strasburger (1965).   Hermann Strasburger, "Poseidonios on Problems of the
                      Roman Empire" *Journal of Roman Studies* 55: 40–53.
Syme (1964).   Ronald Syme, *Sallust* (Berkeley).

Syme (1978).   Ronald Syme, "Mendacity in Velleius" *American Journal of Philology* 99: 45–63.

Syme (1985).   Ronald Syme, "The Testamentum Dasumii: Some Novelties" *Chiron* 15: 41–63.

Talbert (1984).   Richard J. A. Talbert, *The Senate of Imperial Rome* (Princeton).

Tchernia (1983). André Tchernia, "Italian Wine in Gaul at the End of the Republic," in Peter Garnsey, Keith Hopkins, and C. R. Whittaker, eds., *Trade in the Ancient Economy* (London), 87–104.

Thomsen (1980).   Rudi Thomsen, *King Servius Tullius: A Historical Synthesis* (Copenhagen).

Tomulescu (1979). C. St. Tomulescu, "Quelques petites études de droit romain" *Bullettino dell'istituto di diritto romano* 21: 95–117.

Toynbee (1965).   Arnold J. Toynbee, *Hannibal's Legacy* (London).

Treadgold (1980). Warren T. Treadgold, *The Nature of the Bibliotheca of Photius* (Washington, D.C.).

Treggiari (1969). Susan M. Treggiari, *Roman Freedmen during the Late Republic* (Oxford).

Treggiari (1975). Susan M. Treggiari, "Jobs in the Household of Livia" *Papers of the British School at Rome* 43: 48–77.

Treggiari (1976). Susan M. Treggiari, "Jobs for Women" *American Journal of Ancient History* 1: 76–104.

Verbrugghe (1972). Gerald P. Verbrugghe, "Sicily 210–70 B.C.: Livy, Cicero and Diodorus" *Transactions of the American Philological Association* 103: 535–59.

Verbrugghe (1973). Gerald P. Verbrugghe, "The 'Elogium' from Polla and the First Slave War" *Classical Philology* 68: 25–35.

Verbrugghe (1974). Gerald P. Verbrugghe, "Slave Rebellion or Sicily in Revolt?" *Kokalos* 20: 46–60.

Verbrugghe (1975). Gerald P. Verbrugghe, "Narrative Patterns in Posidonius' History" *Historia* 24: 189–204.

Veyne (1976).   Paul Veyne, *Le pain et le cirque: Sociologie historique d'un pluralisme politique* (Paris).

Ville (1981).   Georges Ville, *La gladiature en occident des origines à la mort de Domitien* (Paris).

Vogt (1973).   Joseph Vogt, "Zum Experiment des Drimakos: Sklavenhaltung und Räuberstand" *Saeculum* 24: 213–19.

Vogt (1975).   Joseph Vogt, *Ancient Slavery and the Ideal of Man* (Cambridge, Mass.).

Vogt and Brockmeyer (1971). Joseph Vogt and Norbert Brockmeyer, *Bibliographie zur antiken Sklaverei* (Bochum).

Volkmann (1961). H. Volkmann, *Die Massenversklavungen der Einwohner eroberter Städte in der hellenistisch-römischen Zeit* (Wiesbaden).

Walbank (1957).   F. W. Walbank, *A Historical Commentary on Polybius*, Volume I (Oxford).

Walbank (1967a). F. W. Walbank, *A Historical Commentary on Polybius*, Volume II (Oxford).

Walbank (1967b). F. W. Walbank, "The Scipionic Legend" *Proceedings of the Cambridge Philological Society* 13: 54–69.

Walbank (1972).   F. W. Walbank, *Polybius* (Berkeley).

Walbank (1979).   F. W. Walbank, *A Historical Commentary on Polybius*, Volume III (Oxford).

Walbank (1981).   F. W. Walbank, "Prelude to Spartacus: The Romans in Southern Thrace, 150–70 B.C.," in Chr. M. Danov and Al. Fol, eds., *Spartacus: Symposium Rebus Spartaci Gestis Dedicatum 2050A*. (Sofia), 14–27.

Walbank (1984).   F. W. Walbank, "Monarchies and Monarchic Ideas" *CAH*, 2d edn., Volume VII, Part I, 62–100.

Wardman (1974).   Alan Wardman, *Plutarch's Lives* (Berkeley).

Watson (1987).   Alan Watson, *Roman Slave Law* (Baltimore).

Welwei (1981).   Karl-Wilhelm Welwei, "Das Sklavenproblem als politischer Faktor in der Krise der römischen Republik," in Hans Mommsen and Winfried Schulze, eds., *Vom Elend der Handarbeit* (Stuttgart), 50–69.

Westermann (1943).   W. L. Westermann, "Athenaeus and the Slaves of Athens" *Harvard Studies in Classical Philology*, Supplementary Volume 1, 451–70.

Westermann (1945).   William Linn Westermann, "Slave Maintenance and Slave Revolts" *Classical Philology* 40: 1–10.

Westermann (1955).   William L. Westermann, *The Slave Systems of Greek and Roman Antiquity* (Philadelphia).

White (1964).   Donald White, "Demeter's Sicilian Cult as a Political Instrument" *Greek, Roman and Byzantine Studies* 5: 261–279.

White (1970).   K. D. White, *Roman Farming* (London).

Whittaker (1987).   C. R. Whittaker, "Circe's Pigs: From Slavery to Serfdom in the Later Roman World" *Slavery and Abolition* 8: 88–122 = M. I. Finley, ed., *Classical Slavery* (London), 88–122.

Wiedemann (1981).   Thomas Wiedemann, *Greek and Roman Slavery* (Baltimore).

Wiedemann (1987).   T. E. J. Wiedemann, *Slavery: Greece & Rome: New Surveys in the Classics, No. 19* (Oxford).

Wilkes (1969).   J. J. Wilkes, *Dalmatia* (London).

Wilson (1966).   A. J. N. Wilson, *Emigration from Italy in the Republican Age of Rome* (Manchester).

Wilson (1983).   N. G. Wilson, *Scholars of Byzantium* (London).

Wirszubski (1950).   Ch. Wirszubski, *Libertas as a Political Idea at Rome during the Late Republic and Early Principate* (Cambridge).

Wiseman (1964).   T. P. Wiseman, *"Viae Anniae" Papers of the British School at Rome* 33: 21–37.

Wiseman (1971).   T. P. Wiseman, *New Men in the Roman Senate, 139 B.C.–A.D. 14* (Oxford).

Wiseman (1985).   T. P. Wiseman, *Catullus and His World* (Cambridge).

Yavetz (1983).   Zwi Yavetz, *Julius Caesar and His Public Image* (Ithaca).

Ziegler (1955).   Konrat Ziegler, "Die Herkunft des Spartacus" *Hermes* 83: 248–50.

Ziolkowski (1986).   Adam Ziolkowski, "The Plundering of Epirus" *Papers of the British School at Rome* 54: 69–80.

Index

.

Full nomenclature is normally used for Roman citizens, except for authors (e.g., Suetonius) and emperors (e.g., Nero). The following abbreviations are used: cos. = consul; pr. = praetor; tr. pl. = tribune of the *plebs* (*tribunus plebis*); q. = quaestor; cens. = censor. All dates are B.C.